ADVANCED

EXPERT

STUDENT'S RESOURCE BOOK with key

Jan Bell and Nick Kenny

Contents

Contents

Vocabulary development 1

> CB p. 10

Collocations: adjectives + nouns

1 Complete each sentence with an adjective from A and a noun from B.

A

| high impressive long main strong wide |

B

| CV hours preference priority salary variety |

1 I don't really have a(n) _____ for the kind of job I'm looking for when I graduate.
2 Graduates can't really expect to be earning a(n) *high salary* to start with.
3 I suppose my *main priority* is to just get a foot on the career ladder.
4 It would also be very useful to be given a(n) *wide variety* of experience.
5 Preferably, this would be done without having to work very *long hours*.
6 However, first I need to write a really *impressive* in order to get an interview. *CV*

Collocations: verbs + nouns

2 Choose the correct answers.

Ever since I **(1)** *put* / *set* my heart on becoming an architect at the age of six, I have **(2)** *taken* / *done* it very seriously and **(3)** *made* / *put* a lot of effort into following my dreams. I have had to **(4)** *overcome* / *win* a lot of setbacks along the way in order to **(5)** *take* / *gain* expertise in my field. If I'm going to **(6)** *reach* / *achieve* my aims, I will have to **(7)** *seize* / *catch* every opportunity that comes up and **(8)** *make* / *do* as many useful contacts as I possibly can.

strong preference

Phrasal verbs and expressions with *take*

3 Complete each sentence with a word from A and a preposition from B. The prepositions may be used more than once.

A

| aback advantage exception notice pity pleasure pride stride |

B

| by in of on to |

1 I've always enjoyed sport and my whole family takes a lot of _____ watching football.
2 He was freezing, so I eventually took _____ him and lent him my coat.
3 The teacher was taken _____ the strength of the boy's feelings. She had no idea he was so upset.
4 I took _____ the tone in which she spoke to me and replied angrily.
5 Although her child was crying, the woman took no _____ her and went on chatting.
6 He works extremely hard and takes _____ doing his homework perfectly.
7 We took _____ a break in the rain to run home.
8 My father is very calm and takes everything _____ his _____ .

Word formation: adjectives and nouns

4 Complete the sentences with words formed from the words in brackets.

1 A _____ (success) _____ (apply) will be one who is _____ (confidence).
2 Good _____ (qualify) are not enough; there must be some _____ (evident) that you are genuinely _____ (interest) in the job.
3 To avoid _____ (disappoint), you need to remain _____ (optimism) and be very _____ (determination).
4 For me, the most important thing is _____ (reliable). I'm also looking for someone who is an excellent _____ (communicate) and is prepared to show _____ (flexible) in their approach to their work.

Use of English (Paper 1 Part 1)

Multiple-choice cloze

1 Read the whole text quickly to get the general meaning.

2 Read the text again carefully and think about the type of word that will fit in each gap. Can you predict the answer without looking at the options?

3 Do the task.

4 Read through the text again, with your answers in place. Does it make complete sense?

EXPERT STRATEGY

For this task, you need a good knowledge of fixed expressions, phrasal verbs and collocations. Add any new ones you come across to your vocabulary notebook and remember to review them regularly.

HELP
➤ Q4 Only one of these words can be followed by *to*.
➤ Q5 Only one of these words can be followed by *of*.
➤ Q7 The word you need begins with a negative prefix.

EXPERT LANGUAGE

Which question tests your knowledge of verb + noun collocations?

*For questions **1–8**, read the text below and decide which answer (**A, B, C** or **D**) best fits each gap. There is an example at the beginning (**0**).*

Work placements

Work placements give students the chance to (**0**) _A_ hands-on experience of the workplace before they embark on their chosen career. As well as enhancing students' knowledge of the particular industry, placements also provide an opportunity for them to (**1**) _____ to grips with managing a workload, (**2**) _____ deadlines and being part of a team.

On some UK degree courses, year-long work placements are a compulsory course (**3**) _____ . These are often (**4**) _____ to as 'sandwich placements' because they take place between the second and final years of study. On other courses, students can opt to do a placement (**5**) _____ of a taught module if they wish. Even where this isn't the (**6**) _____ , students often arrange placements for themselves in the summer holidays.

Applying for a work placement can be as competitive as applying for a permanent job and many UK companies now hold formal interviews. (**7**) _____ paid employment, however, work placements aren't covered by employment legislation, so students should always ensure that the (**8**) _____ and conditions are agreed in writing beforehand.

0	A gain	B earn	C grow	D form
1	A make	B get	C find	D have
2	A reaching	B succeeding	C arriving	D meeting
3	A item	B matter	C element	D issue
4	A referred	B considered	C regarded	D mentioned
5	A instead	B alternative	C rather	D substitute
6	A truth	B way	C fact	D case
7	A Opposite	B Dissimilar	C Unlike	D Contrary
8	A rules	B terms	C laws	D codes

Language development 1

➤ **CB** p. 13, **EG** p. 173

Perfect and simple forms

1 Choose the correct answers.

1 I *gained* / *'ve gained* a considerable amount of expertise since starting up my company.

2 She was relieved to hear that she *was* / *had been* on the shortlist for the job she wanted.

3 Although the company *made* / *has made* very little profit so far this year, it shows potential.

4 I *never had* / *had never had* an interview before, so I felt very nervous.

5 He *didn't work* / *hasn't worked* at all since he handed in his notice.

6 I *finished* / *had finished* the report as soon as the meeting was over.

7 At the interview, I was asked why I *decided* / *had decided* to take a gap year after university.

8 Julian suddenly realised where he *met* / *had met* his boss before.

Perfect, simple and continuous forms

2 Complete the sentences with the correct form of the verbs in the box. Use the same verb for each pair of sentences.

eat   leave   read   stay   travel

1 a This time last year I _____ around Colombia.
  b When I visited South America, I _____ to Colombia, Brazil and Chile.

2 a I _____ all day and there are still 50 pages to go.
  b I _____ the whole book yesterday in one sitting.

3 a Keith usually _____ with me when he's in Rome.
  b Keith _____ with me at the moment while his parents are away.

4 a She _____ so many snacks by the time she left Tim's house that she couldn't face any dinner that evening.
  b She _____ all day and was so full that she could hardly move.

5 a We _____ (probably) at the usual time if you need a lift.
  b I _____ the key under the mat, shall I?

Mixed verb forms

3 Complete the texts with the correct form of the verbs in brackets. More than one answer may be possible.

Two young people talk about doing work placements

Stella

I **(1)** _____ (work) unpaid for a well-known magazine at the moment , where I **(2)** _____ (write) short articles for the last three months. The boss usually **(3)** _____ (give) me ridiculously tight deadlines, so I **(4)** _____ (be) under pressure the whole time. Quite often, I **(5)** _____ (feel) I can't go on any longer at this pace, especially since I **(6)** _____ (not get) any money for what I do. I **(7)** _____ (realise), though, that the experience of the last few months **(8)** _____ (be) very good for me in terms of the skills I **(9)** _____ (acquire). However, I **(10)** _____ (still/think) that employers should not be allowed to take advantage of new graduates in this way.

Luke

When I **(11)** _____ (leave) university ten months ago, I **(12)** _____ (have) absolutely no idea of what I was going to do next. I **(13)** _____ (work) far too hard for my final exams to give it a moment's thought! A month or so after leaving, I **(14)** _____ (apply) for work experience with a small marketing firm, mainly because lots of people **(15)** _____ (tell) me that this was the way to improve my CV. At the interview, they **(16)** _____ (promise) to pay me travel expenses, but after a few weeks I still **(17)** _____ (not see) any sign of any money and I **(18)** _____ (spend) a fortune on train fares, which made me a bit irritated. On the positive side, a short while later I **(19)** _____ (land) a really interesting job at another firm, mainly because of all the experience I **(20)** _____ (gain) during my work placement. So it was worth it after all!

Use of English (Paper 1 Part 2)

Open cloze

1 Read the whole text quickly to get the general meaning.

2 Read the text again carefully and think about the type of word that will fit in each gap.

3 Do the task.

4 Read through the text again, with your answers in place. Does it make complete sense?

*For questions **1–8**, read the text below and think of the word which best fits each gap. Use only **one** word in each gap. There is an example at the beginning (0).*

My dream career

When it **(0)** *comes* to choosing a career, some people know from an early age exactly what they want to do. For Christel Kayibi, **(1)** _____ is studying law at King's College, London, it was the film *Legally Blonde*, featuring a lawyer with a heart of gold, that switched her **(2)** _____ to the legal profession – even **(3)** _____ Christel is nothing like the film's ditzy heroine. What the film did was to **(4)** _____ Christel aware that she possessed the analytical skills required of a lawyer. As she says, 'I like figuring **(5)** _____ problems and the film made me realise that was **(6)** _____ lawyers did.'

As a teenager, Christel believed the law was an elite profession and that her ambition was little **(7)** _____ than a pipe dream. A combination of hard work and family support have made her dream come true, however. 'My dad was always big on education. We had a study hour each evening. When you finished your homework **(8)** _____ that hour was up, you were expected to pick up a book.'

Listening (Paper 3 Part 1)

Multiple choice

1 Read the instructions and the context sentences in the task and answer the questions.

1 How many extracts are you going to hear?
2 What is each extract about?

2 Now read the context sentence and questions for Extract One. How much do you find out about the topic and the speakers?

3 🎧 02 Do the task.

You will hear three different extracts. For questions **1–6**, choose the answer (**A**, **B** or **C**) which fits best according to what you hear. There are two questions for each extract.

Extract One

You hear two law graduates talking about their education and choice of career.

1 What surprised the man about his university?
 A the attitude of some of the students
 B the emphasis on vocational education
 C the broad range of subjects being taught

2 What aspect of studying law do both speakers appreciate?
 A the wide variety of jobs it prepares you for
 B the way it gives you clear targets to aim for
 C the fact that you are committed to your career path

Extract Two

You hear part of an interview with a recent graduate.

3 Immediately after his degree course finished, he felt
 A in need of a break before embarking on a career.
 B relieved that he had some time to think about his future.
 C sorry that he hadn't applied to a graduate recruitment scheme.

4 How did he approach finding his first job as a graduate?
 A He targeted the sector he hoped to work in.
 B He prioritised posts that would give him useful skills.
 C He made random applications in order to gain experience.

Extract Three

You hear part of a discussion programme about career choices.

5 What did the man learn from his initial mistake?
 A Job satisfaction should be a top priority.
 B A well mapped-out career plan is essential.
 C It's wrong to rush into important decisions.

6 How does the woman feel about her current career?
 A She always knew that it was the right thing for her.
 B She accepts that she was quite lucky to find it.
 C She regrets not having aimed for it earlier.

Vocabulary development 2

> **CB** p. 16

Feelings

1a Replace the words in bold with a word from the box. Add a preposition if necessary.

*apprehensive   daunted   distracted   frustrated
intimidated   motivated   overwhelmed   tense*

1 I was a bit **nervous and unable to relax** when I was learning to ride. I felt **worried and not confident because of** the instructor and in the end, I dropped out of the class.
2 He was a responsible, **hard-working and enthusiastic** student but he would sometimes be **unable to concentrate** during the lessons. He found it hard to take in all the new information at first.
3 She was a bit **worried** that she wouldn't do well when she first joined the class because she'd never done anything like it before. She refused to be **discouraged**, though, and against the odds, she managed to keep up with the rest of the students.
4 My first week doing computer studies made me feel **upset because I didn't do well** and totally **unable to cope with** the amount of new information. It put me off completely.

b Find phrasal verbs in Exercise 1a that match these meanings.

1 stay at the same level as others
2 understand and remember; absorb
3 made me not want to do something
4 stopped going

Teaching and learning

2 Complete the definitions with words from the box.

*coaches   instructors   lecturers   professors
teachers   trainers   tutors*

1 _____ are teachers of the highest rank in a British university.
2 _____ give lessons to just one student or to small groups.
3 _____ help people learn a sport or a practical skill.
4 _____ usually work in a school.
5 _____ teach in a British university.
6 _____ help a person or team to improve in a sport.
7 _____ teach people the skills they need for a job.

Collocations

3 Choose the correct answers.

1 I was hopeless *in / at* everything I did to begin with and continually *on / by* edge.
2 I tried to learn vocabulary *at / by* heart but I was incapable *of / for* remembering anything the next day.
3 I used to get impatient *to / with* myself. It was different *from / by* anything else I'd done.
4 Because it wasn't at all similar *to / as* the way I learnt as a child, I felt *on / under* pressure.
5 At first I felt depressed *for / by* my lack of progress *in / on* the subject.
6 I was a bit half-hearted *about / of* going to class and not at all inspired *with / by* the teacher.

4 Complete the text with words from the box.

*clear   investment   key   outcomes   pay   status
top   value*

What makes a good school?

A recent report on the best global education systems concluded that in **(1)** _____-ranking countries such as Finland and South Korea, there is no **(2)** _____ correlation between good **(3)** _____ for teachers and better educational performance. However, it was noted that in these countries, teachers tend to have a high **(4)** _____ in society. In addition, the most successful countries educationally fund each community equally, whether they are poor or affluent. There is also heavy **(5)** _____ in teacher education and a high **(6)** _____ is placed on learning by both society and parents. The aim of the study was to help policy makers and school leaders identify the **(7)** _____ issues leading to successful educational **(8)** _____ .

Reading (Paper 1 Part 8)

Multiple matching

1 Read the title of the text and the introductory sentence. What do you think *subjects* means in the title?

2 Read the task and mark the key words in each question.

3 Read the text quickly to get an idea of how it is structured and what issues are discussed in each section. What is the main focus of each section?

4 Look at question 1 and find the sections of the text that talk about the students' families. Look for words and expressions that describe family relationships. Write the question number next to these sections so you can find them again quickly. Then read these sections carefully and decide which section matches the exact wording of question 1.

5 Repeat the procedure for the other questions.

HELP

➤ Q2 Which section begins with the writer indicating that she is giving a personal opinion?
➤ Q3 Look for when the tests were first introduced.
➤ Q10 Look for a word that means the same as *reflect*.

EXPERT STRATEGY

Don't try to read the text in detail before you've read the questions and know what you're looking for.

EXPERT LANGUAGE

Look back at the text. Find the names of subjects studied in US schools.

EXPERT WORD CHECK

civic identity   decried   embedded
far-minded   frazzled   heated debate
social anthropology   stirred up
threefold   trumpeting

You are going to read an article about some tests taken by high school students in the USA. For questions 1–10, choose from the sections (A–D). The sections may be chosen more than once.

In which section does the writer mention:

students' families may be influencing their choice of certain subjects? `1`

personal experience that supports the idea that certain subjects should be more widely studied? `2`

the original aim of the AP tests? `3`

how the tests are unlike others in the US system? `4`

an underlying attitude that may account for the unpopularity of certain subjects? `5`

the reason that students feel under pressure to take the tests? `6`

historical reasons for the emphasis placed on certain school subjects? `7`

different views as to the educational value of the tests? `8`

lack of information regarding the effects of choices made in these tests? `9`

a trend in society which isn't reflected in these tests? `10`

Vocabulary

6 Find words in the text that mean:

1 tired and anxious (section A) _____
2 extra or additional (section A) _____
3 caused (section A) _____
4 a state of constant change (section B) _____
5 make use of something in a way that will bring good results (section B) _____
6 talking about something proudly (section B) _____
7 improve (section C) _____
8 directed/guided to (section C) _____
9 stopped studying a subject (section D) _____
10 encourage something to develop (section D) _____

SUBJECTS OF DESIRE

Does the USA need more computer scientists and engineers? Or does it actually require people who understand political history and prose?

A

Each summer, thousands of frazzled families in the USA endure high school exam season. For many teenagers, the toughest challenge revolves around the so-called Advanced Placement, or AP, tests. In theory, these are voluntary, supplementary exams,
5   which were devised six decades ago to let talented teenagers experience introductory college work. In practice, however, the fight to get into American colleges is now so competitive that more and more kids are being pushed into taking these exams. In 2012, more than two million students took 3.7 million AP tests,
10 more than double the number a decade earlier, and five times the number two decades before. Unsurprisingly, this explosion has stirred up heated debate. John Tierney, a politics professor and Boston high school teacher, decried the exams as a waste of valuable teaching resources, something which the AP organisers
15 don't accept.

B

What is most interesting of all about these exams is the question of what those kids are choosing to study. If you look at the US high school education system overall, it's admirably broad in scope. Indeed, the AP is one of the few places where specialism
20 rules: teenagers typically choose to sit exams in just one or two subjects from 39 different courses. Now, you might think that in this era of economic flux, technological innovation and globalisation, students and schools would opt for subjects that tap into this reality. Policy makers today are trumpeting so-called
25 STEM subjects (science, technology, engineering and maths) and parents know that these subjects tend to produce jobs. But the AP exams don't mirror that at all. In 2013, for example, according to the AP website, the most popular exam to take, by a long margin, was English literature and composition: 824,000 kids sat those
30 tests, a threefold increase on the decade. In second place was American history, which attracted 428,000 students, twice the number of a decade before. In third place, with 360,000 students, was one STEM subject: calculus. After that came US politics and government, psychology and world history. Biology ranked below
35 that, while chemistry and computing science were further down the list. And physics was so unpopular that seven times more students sat the English exams than physics.

C

The AP website itself doesn't comment on the pattern, and it's unclear whether the AP subject choice influences students'
40 degree subject. Some of those opting for AP poetry, in other words, may still become engineers. Indeed, it would be nice to think – or dream – that some far-minded teenagers are deliberately using the AP exam to enhance their communication skills or civic knowledge of the American constitution before
45 they become scientists. In truth, though, I suspect that most students are picking English and history because it seems an easy thing to do, given the slant of their prior education (or the education of the parents who are helping them study). I would also bet that very few humanities students are being steered
50 towards calculus and physics 'just for fun': in high school, as in western society more broadly, science has an aura of exclusivity and inaccessibility; mental barriers are erected at an early age. But frankly, that is a tragedy.

D

Speaking for myself, I've spent my life embedded in the
55 humanities: after doing English, French, maths and art at school, I did degrees in social anthropology before becoming a journalist. But in spite of that background – or rather, because of it – I'm keenly aware of the value of STEM subjects. Indeed, I wish I hadn't dropped science at such a young age. That doesn't
60 mean, let me stress, that literature and history aren't extremely valuable subjects – they are. After all, studying these subjects in high school has helped to foster a common civic identity in America, particularly given its immigrant roots. Indeed, many of those arriving in the country didn't initially come from English-
65 speaking cultures, which is one explanation for these subjects being taught so heavily. But a seven-to-one ratio between prose and physics seems a strange one for modern America – most of all at a time of economic challenge and technological change.

Language development 2

> **CB** p. 18, **EG** p. 174

The passive: tenses

1 Complete the text with the correct form of the verb *be*. More than one answer may be possible.

A bid to improve
educational performance

Much to the delight of high school students, it is likely that the beginning of the school day **(1)** _____ delayed at some point in the future in order that teenagers can get more sleep.

After studies **(2)** _____ carried out in the United States over three years with 90,000 students across three states, it **(3)** _____ shown that educational performance increased dramatically when students got more sleep. There were also far fewer car accidents! Currently, this experiment **(4)** _____ rolled out across a wider range of schools with very positive results. Obviously, much more research **(5)** _____ needed, but there are hopes that there will be similar results when a pilot study **(6)** _____ trialled in the UK later this year.

2 Complete the sentences with the correct passive form of the verbs in brackets.

1 The university campus _____ (locate) just outside the city.
2 Subjects _____ (always/teach) by lecturers at the forefront of their specialism.
3 The university _____ (originally/open) in 1928.
4 In recent years more and more teaching facilities _____ (develop).
5 Next year, all first year students who require it _____ (guarantee) accommodation on campus.
6 A vast amount of money _____ (continually/ invest) in state-of-the-art technology.

Modal passives

3 Rewrite the sentences in the passive.

1 I think a reputable driving instructor, rather than your parents, should teach you.
   _____
2 You can't use some models of vehicle for the test.
   _____
3 They might cancel your test if you don't have the right documents.
   _____
4 The instructor should have taken me on the big roundabout before I took the test.
   _____
5 The instructor may shout at you sometimes.
   _____
6 You have to show your provisional licence to the instructor on your first lesson.
   _____

Passive -*ing* forms and infinitives

4 Find and correct the mistakes in the sentences.

1 The government is being criticise for their new inspection policy.
2 You should be prepared to be asking some questions by the interview panel.
3 We insisted on being tell what had happened.
4 Older students really resent be made to wear a uniform.
5 I want to be keep informed about what happens next.
6 He is expecting to be pick up at midday.

Impersonal passive structures

5 Rewrite the sentences beginning with the words in brackets.

1 Everyone says he was a truly inspirational teacher. (he)
   _____
2 We expect them to be arriving at around six o'clock. (they)
   _____
3 The situation is now known to be far worse than had been first thought. (it)
   _____
4 The Education Secretary is believed to be handing in his resignation later today. (it)
   _____
5 It is understood that there is very little chance of a peace agreement at this stage. (there)
   _____
6 They are hoping to have more news before the end of the evening. (it)
   _____

Use of English   (Paper 1 Part 4)

Key word transformations

1 Read the instructions for the task and look at the example. Think about how the two sentences are different and notice how the meaning hasn't changed.

2 Do the task.

For questions **1–10**, complete the second sentence so that it has a similar meaning to the first sentence, using the word given. **Do not change the word given.** You must use between **three** and **six** words, including the word given. Here is an example (**0**).

0 Brad would only play football if he could be the goalkeeper.
ON
Brad _insisted on being_ the goalkeeper when he played football.

1 Jason was very surprised to be offered the first job he had applied for.
CAME
It _____ Jason when he was offered the first job he had applied for.

2 Delia found the application form very hard to fill in.
DIFFICULTY
Delia _____ filling in the application form.

3 Brian was just about to accept a job in a local bank when he was invited to an interview in the USA.
POINT
Brian _____ a job in a local bank when he was invited to an interview in the USA.

4 Even if she works really hard, Yana won't get promotion in that company.
HOW
No _____ , Yana won't get promotion in that company.

5 Fiona's parents did not approve of her choice of career.
MEET
Fiona's choice of career _____ approval.

6 Jamal was disappointed with his performance in the maths test.
SOURCE
Jamal's performance in the maths test _____ him.

7 Students are strictly forbidden to use the staff car park.
NO
Under _____ use the staff car park.

8 The course on statistics was even better than Gina had expected.
LIVED
The course on statistics more than _____ expectations.

9 Simon was really very serious about his studies.
TOOK
Simon _____ indeed.

10 The most important thing for many graduates is repaying their student loans.
PRIORITY
For many graduates, the main _____ of their student loans.

Writing (Paper 2 Part 2: Letter/Email)

➤ **CB** pp. 20–21, **EW** p. 194

> **EXPERT STRATEGY**
> - Decide on why you are writing and what you hope to achieve.
> - Underline the points in the task which you need to include.
> - Include an interesting opening and closing sentence or short paragraph.

Analysing the task

1   Read the writing task and answer the questions.

1   Who are you writing to?
2   What is the main purpose of the letter?
3   What style of language will you write in?
4   What three pieces of advice must you include in your letter?

> *You have received a letter from your 21-year-old cousin, who is about to leave university.*
>
> …
> I really don't know what to do next. I know the most sensible thing would be to look for a permanent job. But other people have said it's best to get different kinds of work experience – probably unpaid – before I decide what I want to do. And part of me fancies travelling overseas. What do you think about these ideas?
>
> *Write your **letter** in reply, offering advice, in **220–260** words.*

Developing ideas

2   Think about the pros and/or cons of the ideas mentioned in the task and make notes under these headings.

	Pros	Cons
going straight into a permanent job		
doing work experience		
travelling overseas		

3   Read the notes opposite. Which ideas from the task do they refer to? Are they giving advice for or against the ideas? More than one answer may be possible.

1   I'd advise you not to settle down yet – you're still very young.
2   Why don't you see a bit of the world, which will give you the time and space to think about what to do next?
3   I'd be careful if I were you. It can be hard work and you may feel resentful if you're not paid for it.
4   What I've found great about having a 'real' job is earning enough money to be independent.
5   The problem is that you'd need to work in a bar or something first to fund it, and I don't recommend doing that for too long. It can be tedious!
6   It might be good for your CV to try out different jobs.

Using appropriate language

4   Underline the expressions of advice in Exercise 3.

5a   Cross out the linking phrase in each group that is too formal for this context.

1   As well as that, … / In addition, … / On top of that, … / Besides, …
2   Having said that, … / Mind you, … / Even so, … / Nevertheless, …
3   Personally, … / In my view, … / Quite honestly, …
4   … , while … / … , whereas … / In contrast, …

b   Join the pairs of contrasting sentences in Exercise 3 using linking phrases from Exercise 5a.

I'd advise you not to settle down yet – you're still very young. Having said that, what I've found great about …

Opening and closing an informal letter

6   Tick the sentences that are appropriate for opening and closing an informal letter.

Opening
1   Great to hear from you.
2   It was very nice to receive news of you.
3   I was really happy to have information about you.
4   Sorry I haven't been in touch for so long.
5   In reply to your last letter, I am writing to offer some advice.

Closing
1   Good luck with the decisions and your results, and see you soon.
2   I sincerely hope you manage to come to a decision.
3   Hope the next few weeks go well.
4   Take care.
5   Speak to you soon.

Writing task

7   Now do the task in Exercise 1.

Vocabulary development 1

> **CB** p. 26

Compound adjectives: describing characteristics

1 Match the words to make compound adjectives. Which compound adjectives are hyphenated? Which are written as one word?

1	laid	a	forward
2	level	b	witted
3	straight	c	spirited
4	out	d	contained
5	absent	e	back
6	high	f	minded
7	self	g	spoken
8	quick	h	headed

2 Replace the words in bold with a compound adjective from Exercise 1. Make any changes necessary.

MY FAMILY

My older sister Emma is always **(1) very relaxed**. She is also **(2) sensible** and has a tendency to **(3) keep herself to herself**. Jan, my younger sister, **(4) always thinks of clever or funny things to say without thinking for a long time**. She's also extremely **(5) lively and good fun** but can rub people up the wrong way because she's so **(6) blunt**. As for my parents, my mum is lovely and **(7) honest and open**, and my dad is kind but very **(8) forgetful** at times**.**

Using affixes to form opposites

3 Replace the words in bold with their opposites. Form them using the affixes in the box.

dis- im- in- -less un-

1 Alice is **tactful** and **sensitive**.

2 Jessie's incredibly **sociable** and very **considerate** towards other people.

3 Tom is **practical** and very **organised**.

4 Kate is very **patient** and **loyal**.

5 James is **selfish** but **sincere**.

Phrasal verbs

4 Choose the correct answers.

1 I felt that the school had let me *down / off* when it expelled me.
2 At first, the teachers looked *down / over* on the students who they thought were lazy.
3 I hope that issues in technology sort themselves *up / out* very soon.
4 It took me ages to cotton *up / on* to what is happening.
5 I'll be fine once the shock has worn *out / off*.
6 It never occurred to me to turn *down / up* his proposal.
7 Everyone says I take *over / after* my father in personality.
8 Technology has a way of taking *on / over* your life if you allow it to.

Word formation: attitudes

5 Complete the forum posts with words formed from the words in brackets.

My inspiration!

💬 **Colum:** When I decided to change my course, my tutor was incredibly **(1)** _____ (support) even though he didn't want me to change. He's really **(2)** _____ (passion) about his subject.

💬 **Molly:** My best friend Sophia has always been there for me through thick and thin. At one time I went through quite an **(3)** _____ (aggression) phase but she was never **(4)** _____ (criticise) of me.

💬 **Helen:** I've always been really **(5)** _____ (ambition) and you would expect that there would be a fair amount of **(6)** _____ (hostile) from my brothers, but they've been great.

Expressions with *change*

6 Complete each sentence with one word.

1 Well that makes _____ change!
2 Have you got £5 _____ change?
3 Give me five minutes to _____ changed.
4 Can I change these dollars _____ pesos?
5 I think I might change the furniture _____ this summer.
6 Why don't you wash up _____ a change?

Use of English   (Paper 1 Part 1)

Multiple-choice cloze

1   Read the title of the text. Who might have a secret menu?

2   Read the whole text quickly to get the general meaning.

3   Do the task.

4   Read through the text again, with your answers in place. Does it make complete sense?

HELP
➤ Q1   Which verb completes this fixed expression with *aback*?
➤ Q3   Which of the words means the same as *obviously*?
➤ Q6   Only one of the words can be followed by *as*.

EXPERT STRATEGY

Don't forget that the four words have a similar meaning but only one will fit the gap perfectly.

EXPERT LANGUAGE

Find three examples of the past perfect in the text.

For questions **1–8***, read the text below and decide which answer (***A, B, C*** or* **D***) best fits each gap. There is an example at the beginning (***0***).*

The secret menu

Coffee isn't generally **(0)** __A__ to be a teenage drink, so I was somewhat **(1)** _____ aback when my 12-year-old daughter suggested going for one. What had aroused her interest, however, wasn't so much the coffee but **(2)** _____ the fact that a major chain of coffee shops was selling a 'secret menu', not listed in public. Stories about this had gone viral amongst teenagers on social media. **(3)** _____ , the idea of ordering drinks their parents have never heard of appealed to them. No doubt the chain itself had placed those links on social media – a **(4)** _____ of genius as a marketing strategy but also a striking **(5)** _____ of our age. Until the mid-twentieth century, people were **(6)** _____ as either adults or children. The concept of the teenager only **(7)** _____ to life as consumer companies discovered a new market for their goods. They realised that by making teen brands **(8)** _____ from parental brands, and just a little subversive, they could create demand for their products. Coffee is just the latest example of this.

0	A thought	B defined	C classified	D referred
1	A sent	B taken	C given	D put
2	A greater	B sooner	C rather	D further
3	A Clearly	B Eventually	C Accordingly	D Effectively
4	A smack	B swipe	C shot	D stroke
5	A symbol	B badge	C figure	D logo
6	A supposed	B regarded	C believed	D judged
7	A emerged	B grew	C sprang	D rose
8	A diverse	B unique	C opposite	D distinct

Language development 1

> **CB** p. 29, **EG** p. 174

Review of relative clauses

1 Complete the text with relative pronouns. Add commas where necessary.

An inspiration to us all

Simon Revell **(1)** _____ has just received an award for creativity by the Heart Foundation is a heart attack survivor himself.

After suffering a major cardiac arrest two years ago, he was rushed to hospital **(2)** _____ he received life-saving treatment. Sadly, this left him paralysed down one side. Says Simon, 'The things **(3)** _____ I valued most in life, playing the guitar and painting, seemed to be at an end **(4)** _____ was terrifying.'

Simon needed an outlet for his creativity. The answer came when he was given a laptop. Using his left hand, he began to write stories and songs telling the story of his remarkable recovery and the challenges **(5)** _____ he's had to overcome.

Simon **(6)** _____ stories have been turned into a book gives a powerful insight into what life is like for people **(7)** _____ are recovering from a heart attack.

2 Join the sentences using relative clauses. Use the sentence in brackets in the relative clause. Add commas where necessary and leave out the relative pronouns if possible.

1 The woman inspired me to go into publishing. (I met her at your party.)

   _____

2 That singer was fantastic. (I can never remember her name.)

   _____

3 I got the idea from my brother. (He went there last year.)

   _____

4 The concert is on 10 March. (I'm supposed to be going to the dentist's on that day.)

   _____

5 We're going to Andorra for a couple of days. (It should be very interesting.)

   _____

6 It was after midnight. (I finally got to bed.)

   _____

7 We went to a restaurant. (I'd never been there before.)

   _____

8 Fred is hoping to be an actor. (He lives over the road.)

   _____

3 Tick (✓) the correct sentences. Correct the mistakes in the wrong ones.

1 Lucy is volunteering with a charity, who aim is to help young people.
2 The main aim of the project is to prevent bullying, that is so common amongst groups of teenagers.
3 It is a complex problem, which it needs to be fought on many fronts.
4 It appears that those who bully have often been victims themselves.
5 The strategy will focus on encouraging the young people that go to the meetings to think about their behaviour.
6 The group leader, who admits she was once a bully herself, has spoken out about her own behaviour.
7 A famous singer, who's son was bullied at school, is helping to fund the project.
8 The project, which it's said to be one of the most successful around at the moment, welcomes new volunteers.

Relative pronouns with prepositions

4 Choose the correct answers.

1 Saturday is the day *on which / on when / on that* I tend to visit my aunt.
2 I've seen two gigs recently, *of both which / both of which / which both of* were very original.
3 The person *with who I went / I went with / whom with I went* got ill on the first day.
4 Do you know the girl *to who Jo's talking / to Jo's talking / Jo's talking to*?
5 The job *for that Mark applied / Mark applied for / which Mark applied for it* is well-paid.
6 This is the film for *where / that / which* she is known best.

Use of English (Paper 1 Part 2)

Open cloze

1 Read the title of the text. What do you think the text will be about?

2 Read the whole text quickly to get the general meaning.

3 Read the text again carefully and think about the type of word that will fit in each gap.

4 Do the task.

5 Read through the text again, with your answers in place. Does it make complete sense?

HELP

➤ Q2 You need a word with a negative meaning here.
➤ Q6 Which verb collocates with *initiative*?
➤ Q8 You need an object pronoun here.

EXPERT STRATEGY

Remember that you can only write one word in each gap. Don't use contractions — they count as two words.

EXPERT LANGUAGE

Find two phrasal verbs in the text.

*For questions **1–8**, read the text below and think of the word which best fits each gap. Use only **one** word in each gap. There is an example at the beginning **(0)**.*

Facebook friends: the art of deletion

Like a lot of people, **(0)** _when_ I first signed up for Facebook, I accepted and issued far **(1)** _____ many friend requests, including people I **(2)** _____ knew at all. Later, it struck me that I really didn't want all these casual acquaintances to have a window onto my private life. I had a choice: either do less on Facebook **(3)** _____ restrict access. But **(4)** _____ do you cut back on your friends list without upsetting people?

Some users ask you to tick a box if you want to remain on their friends list. **(5)** _____ polite, this is also risky. You may find all your friends desert you or, worse still, that nobody responds. A much better idea is to **(6)** _____ the initiative and 'unfriend' people. But it's hard.

(7) _____ adults, we allow friendships to grow or wane gradually because to cut **(8)** _____ short abruptly is to risk giving offence. Eventually, I decided to delete anyone I hadn't actually seen or contacted for three years. Fortunately, nobody seemed to mind.

Listening   (Paper 3 Part 4)

Multiple matching

1   Read the instructions for the tasks. How many extracts are you going to hear?

2a   Look at Task One. What are you listening for? Mark the key words in the options.

b   Now look at Task Two. What are you listening for? Mark the key words in the options.

3   🎧 03   Do the tasks. Remember that you must choose one option from each task for each speaker.

You will hear five short extracts in which university students are talking about someone they regard as a role model.

TASK ONE	TASK TWO

*For questions **1–5**, choose from the list (**A–H**) what first impressed each speaker about their role model.* | *For questions **6–10**, choose from the list (**A–H**) how each speaker feels about their role model now.*

While you listen you must complete both tasks.

TASK ONE		TASK TWO	
A his modesty		A surprised by his level of commitment	
B his generosity			
C his attention to detail	Speaker 1 [1]	B concerned for his welfare	Speaker 1 [6]
D his determination	Speaker 2 [2]	C proud of his achievements	Speaker 2 [7]
E his patience with others	Speaker 3 [3]	D forgiving of his weaknesses	Speaker 3 [8]
F his willingness to admit mistakes	Speaker 4 [4]	E excited by his latest projects	Speaker 4 [9]
	Speaker 5 [5]	F amused by his reputation	Speaker 5 [10]
G his loyalty to friends		G understanding of his difficulties	
H his professional integrity		H admiring of his courage	

HELP

➤ **Q1** Listen for what is said about the teacher's maps and diagrams.

➤ **Q5** Which option matches the spirit of the sportsman's charity work?

➤ **Q6** Listen to what the speaker says about the person's faults.

➤ **Q10** Listen for the word *amazed*. What is the speaker referring to?

EXPERT STRATEGY

Remember, you won't hear the exact wording of the options on the recording. Listen for the gist of what the speakers are saying; the options summarise their ideas.

EXPERT LANGUAGE

Find examples of different noun suffixes in the tasks.

EXPERT WORD CHECK

an independent spirit   baggy   cartography   emulate exacting standards   extrovert   learning difficulties   skinny to go pear-shaped

Reading   (Paper 1 Part 6)

Cross-text multiple matching

1   Read the title of the text. What do you think a 'fly-on-the-wall documentary' is?

2   Read the task and mark which reviewer is being referred to in each question. Then mark the key words in each question.

3   Read all the reviews quickly to understand what the reviewers are saying about the programme.

4   Look at question 1 and find Reviewer A's opinion in the text. Then read the other texts and find the sections where each reviewer talks about the head teacher's decision. Decide which other reviewer shares the same opinion as A.

5   Repeat the procedure for questions 2 and 3. For question 4, you need to read all the texts to see what each of the reviewers says about this.

HELP

➤ Q2   Reviewer B has a positive opinion – only one of the others is positive on this issue.

➤ Q3   Look at the beginning of review C for the opinion.

➤ Q4   Look for the word *profession* in all four texts and read that section carefully.

EXPERT STRATEGY

Always read the questions first in this task. Use the information and vocabulary in the questions to help you find the relevant piece of text in each extract.

EXPERT LANGUAGE

Find a determiner in review D.

EXPERT WORD CHECK

audience ratings   combative compelling viewing   doddle exploding the myth   give the go-ahead glimpse   oblivious   shed light stereotype   vindicate

---

You are going to read four reviews of a 'fly-on-the-wall' television documentary, which followed the daily life of staff and students in a large inner-city secondary school. For questions 1–4, choose from the reviews A–D. The reviews may be chosen more than once.

Which reviewer:

has a different opinion to Reviewer A about how wise the head teacher was to allow the programme to be made?   ☐ 1

shares Reviewer B's opinion about the value of this particular programme?   ☐ 2

expresses a similar view to Reviewer C on how objective the film-makers managed to be?   ☐ 3

has a different attitude to the others towards the teaching profession in general?   ☐ 4

Vocabulary

6a   Match the verbs (1–6) with the words and phrases (a–f) to make common expressions. Then find the expressions in the text.

1 go	a	light on something
2 shed	b	something into the public eye
3 have	c	a long way towards (doing) something
4 restore	d	the go-ahead
5 bring	e	a knock-on effect
6 give	f	someone's confidence in something

b   Match the expressions in Exercise 6a with their meanings.

1 make something known to many people   _____
2 provide information that makes something easier to understand   _____
3 help a lot to make something happen   _____
4 make someone believe in something again   _____
5 cause other events or situations but not directly   _____
6 give someone permission to do something   _____

TVcameras
in the Classroom:
a fly-on-the-wall documentary

A When the idea of this fly-on-the-wall documentary was originally suggested to the school's head teacher, he was justifiably concerned that it wouldn't present a balanced picture of life in his school and could lead to unfair criticisms of his staff. Exposing teachers and
5 pupils to such scrutiny was a risk, yet the finished programme vindicates his decision to go ahead. It shows us the everyday reality of life in the classroom but doesn't appear to have an agenda. What it reveals is that complex issues, often hidden from the rest of adult society, are part and parcel of life for teachers. The programme goes
10 a long way towards exploding the common myth that teaching is a doddle, comprising short working days and extended holidays. These people deserve our respect. By showing challenging moments in classes of difficult students, some with behavioural problems, the documentary raises relevant issues for debate and airs complex issues.
15 It makes for compelling viewing.

B This programme sheds welcome light on the world of secondary education in the UK. Originally planned as an exposé of the problems facing teachers in inner-city schools, it has actually managed to break through the stereotypes to show us what lies beneath. It was a
20 brave move to allow cameras into the school but it does seem to have had some positive knock-on effects. In last night's programme, one teacher claimed he was now regarded with more respect by a class with whom he had previously had a very combative relationship. The risks of misrepresentation in any such programme are high.
25 The temptation to edit out those sequences that do not provide entertaining viewing can lead to a biased picture emerging. But the film-makers seem to have avoided those particular pitfalls. If this programme has gone some way towards enhancing the reputation of teaching and enticing a new generation into the profession, then it
30 was worth making for that reason alone.

C The editors of the programme inevitably focus on moments
35 they think will engage the audience – that's their brief, after all. They're in the business of audience ratings and their inclination is to concentrate on moments of conflict and drama. For me, this is exploitation as I'm sure that some of the disruption is occurring solely for the benefit of the camera. Whatever was the
40 head teacher thinking of in agreeing to this intrusion? Although the teachers are shown in a good light, one wonders why they had allowed these conflicts to arise in the first place. They did nothing to restore my confidence in the profession. Quite what this programme has added to the debate about education in this
45 country remains unclear to me.

D I felt very enthusiastic about the concept of this programme: a documentary that would bring the teaching profession into the public eye and show not only the problems but also the good that teachers do. I can see why the head teacher gave the idea
50 the go-ahead. However, as I watched last night's programme, I had mixed feelings. Why didn't we see the studious children being asked about their feelings? It's depressing to watch learning being disrupted by students who clearly have little interest in being there and deeply worrying to see teachers
55 apparently oblivious to the needs of the majority. Just occasionally, we get glimpses of something more reassuring. On exam results day students were shown crying, either from delight or disappointment, emotions evidently shared by their teachers.

Vocabulary development 2

Words often confused

1 Choose the correct answers.

1 There is a slight *opportunity / possibility* that the plane may be delayed.
2 I hope I'll get the *occasion / chance* to travel before I settle down.
3 There should be equal *opportunities / possibilities* for everyone to do well.
4 There is no *chance / occasion* of me ever buying a car like that.
5 I think the party is going to be a really special *opportunity / occasion*.
6 Are you Mr Smith, by any *chance / possibility*?
7 There's a strong *possibility / opportunity* that he might go back to the US soon.
8 Now is the perfect *occasion / opportunity* to have a quick break.

Word formation: nouns

2 Complete the text with nouns formed from the verbs in brackets.

Failure breeds success!

- Walt Disney was once fired by a newspaper (1) _____ (edit) because he 'lacked (2) _____ (imagine) and had no good ideas'. His businesses ended up bankrupt until he found a recipe for (3) _____ (succeed).

- Stephen King received 30 (4) _____ (reject) for his first book. He finally gave up and it was his wife's (5) _____ (encourage) that made him try again. He is now one of the world's best-selling authors.

- Steve Jobs, a college dropout, was fired from Apple, the company he founded. Later he said this was the best thing that could have happened to him because starting again sparked his (6) _____ (create). He then went on to invent (7) _____ (produce) such as the iPod, iPhone and iPad.

- Michael Jordan is possibly the best basketball (8) _____ (play) of all time. Yet he wasn't included in his school team and has often experienced (9) _____ (fail). 'On 26 occasions I have been entrusted to take the game's winning (10) _____ (shoot) and I missed. I have failed over and over and over again in my life. And that is why I succeed.'

Phrasal verbs

3 Replace the words in bold with the correct form of the phrasal verbs in the box. Make any changes necessary.

> break out (of somewhere) catch (someone) out
> get away with (something) get over (something)
> give (yourself) up let (someone) off

1 The criminal finally went to the police station and **confessed what he had done**.
2 The police **allowed** the young offender **to escape punishment** on that occasion.
3 He broke into the house but nobody caught him, so he **wasn't punished**.
4 When she'd **recovered from** her addictions, she led a crime-free life.
5 They **escaped from** prison at least three times.
6 The police finally **made** the offender **say something which proved he'd been lying**.

Law and crime

4 Complete the text with the correct form of the words in the box.

> arrest bars charge commit release sentence
> serve trouble

Famous ex-criminals who made it good

- TV star Martha Stewart was once (1) _____ with conspiracy and making false statements and found guilty. She was (2) _____ to a few months in prison but after her (3) _____ she launched her comeback on TV.

- After actor Christian Slater was (4) _____ for assault, he attended a rehabilitation facility before (5) _____ a term in jail. He then managed to turn his life around.

- Actor Danny Trejo has been the 'tough guy' in over 200 films but earlier in his life he was often in (6) _____ with the law and spent some time behind (7) _____ for robbery. When a Hollywood director asked if he would be able to play someone who'd (8) _____ a robbery, he replied, 'I've done a few of those!'

Language development 2

➤ **CB** p. 34, **EG** p. 175

Use of articles

1 Complete the text with *a*, *the* or Ø (no article).

There have always been **(1)** _____ disagreements over how to treat our prisoners. Should they be given **(2)** _____ same luxuries that we take for granted or left in **(3)** _____ cold cell 24/7? Should **(4)** _____ punishment be **(5)** _____ goal? Or should **(6)** _____ rehabilitation into (7) _____ society be our main aim?

Although **(8)** _____ UK spends a higher amount of money on **(9)** _____ public order than **(10)** _____ US or any EU country, our jails are highly ineffective and extremely overcrowded. If lowering **(11)** _____ number of criminals is **(12)** _____ motivation for **(13)** _____ imprisonment, we are failing; most under-18s are reconvicted within **(14)** _____ year of their release.

So it would appear that (15) _____ justice systems are not only expensive but fail to rehabilitate or improve behaviour. This is clearly (16) _____ very important issue which needs to be discussed further.

Singular/Plural nouns and verb agreement

2 Complete the sentences with the present or present perfect form of the verbs in brackets.

1 I don't think the news _____ (be) particularly interesting.
2 The police _____ (try) to come down really hard on drink-driving at the moment.
3 Everyone I talk to _____ (seem) to be in favour of appointing a new director.
4 My family _____ (have) a tough time so far this year.
5 I agree that £20 _____ (be) too much money to give a five-year-old.
6 The majority of people I've spoken to _____ (not like) the idea of a change in the law.
7 Statistics _____ (show) that far fewer people smoke these days.
8 A number of people still _____ (want) to leave the union.

Determiners and pronouns

3 Find and correct the mistakes in some of the sentences. Tick (✓) the correct sentences.

1 I've already read the two books you lent me and all of them were fantastic.
2 Unfortunately, we haven't got neither of those in stock at the moment.
3 Each person has to register before being allowed to enter.
4 We spent whole day shopping.
5 None wants to come with me.
6 I remember hardly any of the maths I studied.
7 A great deal of prisoners go on to reoffend.
8 I have very little patience for such a ridiculous argument.

4 Choose the correct answers.

Dancing
their sentence away

(1) *A / The* recent YouTube clip which has attracted much attention shows hundreds of prisoners from Cebu Rehabilitation Centre in **(2)** *Philippines / the Philippines* dancing to Michael Jackson's song *Thriller*. Since it was posted, **(3)** *a / the* clip of the prisoners in their orange uniforms has been watched more than 1.3 million times and a new world record has been set for the greatest **(4)** *amount / number* of inmates dancing simultaneously in the same place.

Byron Garcia, security consultant for the Cebu provincial government, says the dance routine has helped to dramatically improve the behaviour of the **(5)** *majority / whole* of the inmates. Those serving sentences or awaiting trial have got **(6)** *the whole / all of* day to practise their routines. It takes their mind off revenge or planning an escape. **(7)** *A few / Plenty* former inmates have even become dancers. Participation is voluntary but **(8)** *few / several* of them choose to do it. **(9)** *Everyone / All* seems totally absorbed in the performance.

Mr Garcia has been taken aback by **(10)** *how many / how much* people have seen the video, which he originally posted in order to share his work with other members of the penal community. The viewings have become a source of great pride to the inmates.

Use of English (Paper 1 Part 3)

Word formation

1 Read the title of the text. Why do you think the bakery has this name?

2 Read the whole text quickly to get the general meaning.

3 Read the text again carefully and think about the form of the word needed to fit in each gap.

4 Do the task.

5 Read through the text again, with your answers in place. Does it make complete sense?

HELP

➤ Q1 Add a suffix to create the general word for the hotel and restaurant trade.

➤ Q3 You need to make a noun from this verb.

➤ Q8 Add a prefix that means 'again' to the verb. What tense will the new verb be in?

EXPERT STRATEGY

For this task, you need a good knowledge of prefixes, suffixes and spelling rules. When learning new vocabulary, make a note of other words that can be formed from the word you are learning (e.g. a noun formed from a verb, the negative form of an adjective). Also make a note of the spelling rules that apply when the form of a word changes.

EXPERT LANGUAGE

Find two linkers of contrast in the text.

*For questions 1–8, read the text below. Use the word given in capitals at the end of some of the lines to form a word that fits in the gap **in the same line**. There is an example at the beginning (0).*

Bad Boys' Bakery

In (0) _response_ to the UK government's wish to encourage the rehabilitation of offenders, Brixton prison in London has set up its own craft bakery. Founded by the celebrity chef Gordon Ramsay, the Bad Boys' Bakery is a fully-stocked professional kitchen that supplies local (1) _____ establishments. The inmates learn traditional bakery skills rather than a mechanised method because what's called 'artisan bakery' is becoming (2) _____ popular. In this way, prisoners have the chance to go for jobs in what is a (3) _____ sector of the economy after their release. Despite the successes, there are obvious (4) _____ in trying to operate a commercial kitchen in a prison because it is a(n) (5) _____ place. For example, security concerns or (6) _____ of prison staff can lead to last-minute lockdowns. Such unavoidable (7) _____ in production make it hard to guarantee a reliable supply to all customers. Nonetheless, there are already signs that the bakery is having a positive effect. So far, only three percent of those who have undergone training in the kitchen have (8) _____ , compared to around 45 percent overall.

RESPOND	
CATER	
INCREASE	
GROW	
DRAW	
PREDICT	
SHORT	
INTERRUPT	
OFFEND	

Writing (Paper 2 Part 2: Report)

➤ **CB** pp. 36–37, **EW** p. 193

Analysing the task

1 Read the task and answer the questions.
1 Who are you writing the report for?
2 What style of language will you use?
3 What three things do you have to include?

> You are a student representative on your school council. The council has been asked to get the views of other students at the school on the current policy of permanent exclusion from school for students who continually break school rules. You have been asked to write a report for the principal, outlining the benefits and drawbacks of exclusion from school. Give the school council's views on what should be done.

*Write your **report** in **220–260** words.*

Developing ideas

2 Look at some students' comments on exclusion and decide whether they are in favour of (✓) or against (✗) exclusion.
1 Why should another school have to deal with the problem?
2 Excluding students makes things worse for them.
3 It gives other students the opportunity to work without being disturbed.
4 It's less stressful for teachers if they don't have to focus on discipline.
5 It means the school has given up on these students.
6 There are usually good reasons for misbehaviour. Can't they see a psychologist?
7 It shows that bad behaviour won't be tolerated.

Organising your report

3 What order (1–6) will these points be in in your report? More than one answer may be possible.
a recommendations
b summary of feedback
c (reporting views on) the benefits of exclusion
d how you got the information
e the aims of the report
f (reporting views on) the drawbacks of exclusion

4 Choose one of these paragraph plans and plan your report. Decide on the headings and whether/ where you will include bullet points or numbers.

A

1 introduction (aims of the report)
2 how you got the information
3 reporting views on exclusion (for and against)
4 summary of feedback
5 recommendations

B

1 introduction (aims of the report, how you got the information)
2 reporting views in favour of exclusion
3 reporting views against exclusion
4 conclusion (summary and recommendations)

Using appropriate language

5a Match these groups of sentence openings with the headings in Exercise 3. One of the groups goes with two headings.
1 _____
i We think that on balance, it's probably best to …
ii Taking everything into account, the best option …
iii If you want my opinion, …
2 _____
i Students were given a questionnaire in which …
ii We chatted to people about the issue …
iii Students were asked to attend a meeting …
3 _____
i To sum up, …
ii OK, so the general feeling was …
iii In conclusion, …
4 _____
i The arguments in favour of excluding troublesome students were …
ii There were loads of pros and cons, including …
iii In the main, students were of the opinion that …
iv According to most students, …
v It was felt by the majority of those we spoke to …
vi The main things that cropped up …
vii A high proportion of those interviewed expressed the view that …
5 _____
i The aim/main purpose of this report is to …
ii What I'm hoping to try and do in this report is …
iii The report discusses/outlines/describes …

b Which of the sentence openings in Exercise 5a are too informal for a report?

Writing task

6 Now do the task in Exercise 1.

Vocabulary development 1

> CB p. 42

Word formation

1   Complete the text with words formed from the words in brackets.

How to be creative: tips from a young writer

- Learn to work wherever and whenever and be (1) _____ (adapt). I now come up with more ideas when I'm surrounded by noise.
- Don't be too hard on yourself. The need for (2) _____ (perfect) can block you. And even if you get stuck, you'll break through sooner or later.
- When I'm setting up a plot, it's very time-consuming. Creativity develops over a period of time and you need to be (3) _____ (persist).
- Experiment! And don't be too (4) _____ (fuss) about the first draft – just get something down on paper and move on. You can always come back to it later.

Phrasal verbs

2   Find phrasal verbs in Exercise 1 that mean:

    1 organising; putting into place   _____
    2 return   _____
    3 start doing something new or different   _____
    4 write   _____
    5 manage to do something successfully   _____
    6 think of   _____

Verbs to describe movement

3a   Put the verbs in the box under one of the headings.

    crawl   creep   dash   dawdle   drift   nip
    plod   plunge   pop   race   saunter   shoot
    sidle   sneak   soar   tear   wander

    1 move fast
    2 go somewhere quickly for a short time
    3 move slowly/aimlessly
    4 move quietly in order not to be noticed

b   Match the sentence halves.

    1 She popped   _____
    2 Flora shot   _____
    3 He spent a year drifting   _____
    4 The dog sidled   _____
    5 He plunged   _____
    6 Tom plodded   _____

    a along, head down, trying to ignore the rain.
    b around Europe, staying a few days here and there.
    c past me, obviously late, hardly pausing to say hello.
    d past, hoping I wouldn't notice what was in his mouth.
    e in for a quick coffee on the way back from the dentist's.
    f into the pool with a shout of delight.

4   Complete the sentences with the past form of verbs from Exercise 3a, used in a metaphorical sense.

    1 My spirits _____ as I realised I'd won the race.
    2 I _____ on with the book, not enjoying it at all.
    3 We _____ along the motorway at 10 mph because of the traffic.
    4 It was such a boring talk that my mind _____ and I couldn't concentrate.
    5 She _____ off while he was watching TV.

Film

5   Complete the text with the words in the box.

    budget   deal   debut   motion   realise   released
    shoot   soundtrack

Aardman

Aardman is a company which was founded by Peter Lord and David Sproxton in 1972 as a way of trying to (1) _____ their ambition to produce an innovative (2) _____ film. The project had a very tight (3) _____ and was their first attempt to (4) _____ an animated film for adults using real-life conversations as the (5) _____ for the film.

Lord and Sproxton became successful enough to hire more animators, three of whom were about to make their (6) _____ as directors. One of these was Nick Park, who later developed the clay models that featured the adventures of Wallace and Gromit. Two of these films, *A Grand Day Out* and *The Wrong Trousers*, went on to win Academy Awards.

Aardman later worked with Dreamworks to make *Chicken Run*, which was (7) _____ in 2000, to great success. They signed a (8) _____ to make four more films but later decided to terminate the agreement.

Use of English   (Paper 1 Part 1)

Multiple-choice cloze

1 Read the whole text quickly to get the general meaning.

2 Read the text again carefully and think about the type of word that will fit in each gap. Can you predict the answer without looking at the options?

3 Do the task.

4 Read through the text again, with your answers in place. Does it make complete sense?

HELP

➤ Q3 You need the word that means 'although'.

➤ Q4 Only one of the words collocates with *part*.

➤ Q8 Followed by *in*, the correct option means 'take part in'.

EXPERT STRATEGY

Think carefully about the exact meaning of each option before making a decision about which one fits the context.

EXPERT LANGUAGE

Find three examples of the present perfect passive in the text.

*For questions **1–8**, read the text below and decide which answer (**A, B, C** or **D**) best fits each gap. There is an example at the beginning (0).*

One brick at a time

The Lego story **(0)** _A_ back to 1958, the year in which its creator, Gotfred Kirk Christiansen, filed a patent for the distinctive plastic brick. Since then, production has been going ahead at full **(1)** _____ , with millions of pieces being made every year – more than 80 bricks for every person on Earth! It is thought that over four million Lego men have been constructed since 1974, so it may not be long before they **(2)** _____ the real thing. What's more, Lego is believed to be the world's largest producer of tyres, **(3)** _____ very small ones, as these are an **(4)** _____ part of the kits from which Lego vehicles are constructed.

The appeal of Lego **(5)** _____ in the fact that it offers a blank canvas in 3D. Kids might be **(6)** _____ into two camps – instinctive builders and followers of plans – but young and old **(7)** _____ can build anything with the stuff, and generally do. Since the late 1990s, the brand has also been heavily **(8)** _____ in the videogame industry, with their iconic mini-figures starring in high-profile games.

0 A dates	B begins	C takes	D comes
1 A pace	B rush	C snap	D steam
2 A surpass	B exceed	C outnumber	D override
3 A albeit	B however	C indeed	D otherwise
4 A inward	B integral	C intact	D inborn
5 A lies	B shows	C stays	D lives
6 A joined	B divided	C shared	D allotted
7 A akin	B similarly	C identically	D alike
8 A included	B implied	C involved	D implicated

Language development 1

> **CB** p. 45, **EG** p. 177

Review of future forms

1 Choose the correct answer (A, B or C).

1 Don't forget that French film _____ next month.
   A will be shown
   B is being shown
   C is shown

2 Afterwards, the director _____ about the process of adapting books to the screen.
   A will be talking
   B talks
   C will have talked

3 I'd love to hear him speak but _____ for the US by then.
   A we'll be leaving
   B we'll have left
   C we'll have been leaving

4 Tickets _____ on sale as from next Tuesday.
   A are being
   B will have been
   C will be

5 We've decided that _____ other speakers later in the year.
   A we're inviting
   B we're going to invite
   C we invite

6 I'll let you know as soon as the programme _____ .
   A comes out
   B is coming out
   C will have come out

7 I'm sure _____ it very interesting.
   A you'll find
   B you're finding
   C you'll have found

8 Anyway, I must go. The last train _____ in half an hour.
   A will have left
   B will leave
   C leaves

Expressions with future meaning

2 Choose the correct expression in brackets and use it to rewrite the underlined parts of the sentences.

1 The train will arrive in approximately 20 minutes on Platform 6. (*be due to / be on the verge of*)

2 I'm going out any minute. Can you be quick? (*be likely to / be about to*)

3 You can ask her if you like, but I'm sure she'll refuse. (*expect to / be bound to*)

4 I'm going to give up with this homework. I can't understand a word! (*be to / be on the point of*)

5 The talks will break down very soon. (*be on the verge of / be due to*)

6 There are rumours that Beyoncé will be headlining next year's festival. (*be likely to / be bound to*)

Future in the past

3 Complete the email extract with the correct form of the phrases in the box.

be about to/sign up   be due to/hand in
be going to/join   be going to/offer   will not/be
will not/take

I know I said last year that I **(1)** _____ a drama group in the new year but life has just got in the way, as usual! I had assumed that the work I'd been given **(2)** _____ too much time but it turned out to be quite tough and I had to work really hard to get it done. I **(3)** _____ the work two weeks ago but that didn't happen, so I missed the deadline. But I've just finished now, thank goodness!

Then, just as I **(4)** _____ for the new play which takes place in April, I realised that there **(5)** _____ any good parts left in the production by that time and they **(6)** _____ me a non-speaking part. So anyway, I've now decided that I'm going to take up ballroom dancing instead.

4 Choose the correct answers.

1 We were *on the verge of / due to* having a breakthrough when the funding was cut.

2 I knew the news *was about to / would* be bad, so I wasn't surprised.

3 I thought the government *were bound to / would have* raised taxes, so I was pleasantly surprised when they didn't.

4 The football club *was to / would* transfer at least two players but decided against it at the last minute.

5 We were *on the point of phoning / to have phoned* you when you arrived.

6 He was just *about to /due to* leave the house when he saw her text.

Use of English (Paper 1 Part 3)

Word formation

1 Read the title of the text. What is a trophy generally used for?

2 Read the whole text quickly to get the general meaning.

3 Read the text again carefully and think about the form of the word needed to fit in each gap.

4 Do the task.

5 Read through the text again, with your answers in place. Does it make complete sense?

HELP

➤ Q1 Add both a prefix and suffix to create a word that means 'exceptional'.

➤ Q3 Add a suffix and remember to double the final consonant.

➤ Q6 You need to add two suffixes to this word. Check the spelling carefully.

EXPERT STRATEGY

Remember that your answers must be spelled correctly. Some letters may be lost or changed in base words when you add a suffix, so check carefully.

EXPERT LANGUAGE

Find a phrasal verb made up of three words in the text.

*For questions **1–8**, read the text below. Use the word given in capitals at the end of some of the lines to form a word that fits in the gap **in the same line**. There is an example at the beginning (0).*

A fitting trophy

The Brit Award for Music is a(n) (0) __highly__ coveted prize awarded annually to a performer who has made a(n) (1) _____ contribution to British popular music. The prize celebrates the creativity of the UK music scene and is awarded at a(n) (2) _____ televised ceremony. In 2012, the job of designing a new trophy to be presented to the (3) _____ fell to Sir Peter Blake, one of the country's most (4) _____ artists. Sir Peter has long been interested in the (5) _____ of art into the world of popular culture and music, and he came up with an elegant trophy which was typical of his work. Coloured red, white and blue, it (6) _____ incorporates some of the classic motifs of the pop art movement, capturing the (7) _____ and fun of the music scene and of the event itself. To celebrate the completion of the trophy, a fine art print was produced in a limited edition of 150, which went on sale with a letter of (8) _____ . This print has now become a collector's item in its own right.

HIGH

STAND

PRESTIGE

WIN
INFLUENCE

INTEGRATE

SUCCESS

VITAL

AUTHENTIC

Listening (Paper 3 Part 2)

Sentence completion

1 Read the instructions for the task. Who is going to be speaking? What will that person be speaking about?

2 Read the sentences in the task. How much do you find out about the topic?

3 Try to predict the type of information that you need to listen for in each gap.

4 🎧 04 Do the task.

HELP
> Q1 You are listening for an expression made up of two words.
> Q2 Three personal qualities are mentioned – listen for which one is most important.
> Q3 Listen to what Aaron says about risks – the answer comes soon afterwards.

EXPERT STRATEGY

Remember that you have time to read through the sentences before you listen. Use this time to think about the topic and make predictions about the missing words.

EXPERT LANGUAGE

Find two adjective + preposition collocations in the task.

EXPERT WORD CHECK

backgammon   calculated risks
copywriter   employability
key indicator   outline   perseverance
push boundaries   recruiter   tenacity

You will hear a student called Aaron Cole giving a presentation about how leisure activities can influence a person's job prospects. For questions 1–8, complete the sentences with a word or short phrase.

How leisure interests can influence job prospects

Aaron says that the term (1) _____ is used to describe what employers are aiming for when they take job candidates' leisure interests into consideration.

Aaron identifies (2) _____ as the key personal quality associated with participation in endurance sports.

Aaron says that an enjoyment of adventure sports might suggest a suitability for jobs requiring (3) _____ skills.

Aaron says that only those job applicants with experience in the role of (4) _____ should mention playing team sports.

Aaron was surprised to learn that jobs in (5) _____ are seen as suitable for more creative people.

Where employers are developing their (6) _____ presence, candidates with good written communication skills are in great demand.

Aaron gives the example of policy development as an area where (7) _____ -minded people are likely to do well.

Aaron warns against listing what recruiters refer to as (8) _____ on a job application.

Vocabulary development 2

➤ CB p. 48

Entertainment

1 Choose the correct answers.

A

A: I know you loved the book *War Horse*. Have you seen the film **(1)** *version / edition*?

B: I have but I actually preferred it **(2)** *on /at* stage.

A: Yes, the puppets were amazing and it was such a **(3)** *powerful / strong* cast, wasn't it?

B: Yes. The stage show was **(4)** *broadcast / streamed* in cinemas all over the country, so I saw it twice.

A: I tried to get tickets when it first **(5)** *began / opened* but ended up queuing for **(6)** *returns / cancellations*.

B

A: I'm not usually that keen on opera but the woman in the **(7)** *main / major* role was fantastic, wasn't she?

B: I thought so too. Really **(8)** *convincing / likely*. She deserved her standing **(9)** *applause / ovation*.

A: And it's received **(10)** *wild / rave* reviews.

B: I might go again when it comes here **(11)** *in / on* tour.

C

A: Where was the film **(12)** *located / set*?

B: In Italy, in the 16th century. But the **(13)** *plot / theme* was really far-fetched.

A: Who played the **(14)** *person / part* of Ludovico?

B: Someone I'd never heard of. But I suspect he'll **(15)** *receive / make* a name for himself soon. He **(16)** *gave / did* an astonishing performance.

A: Apparently, that actor's been **(17)** *proposed / nominated* for lots of awards.

B: I'm not surprised. He **(18)** *placed / put* a lot into it.

Near synonyms

2 Replace the words in bold with words and phrases from Exercise 1.

1 Have you seen the modern **remake** of that 60s film?

_____

2 The football will be **transmitted** live on TV.

_____

3 I found his performance really **persuasive**.

_____

4 The critics gave the gig an **enthusiastic reception**.

_____

5 The drama **took place** in medieval times.

_____

6 He is on the verge of **becoming famous**.

_____

7 The **story line** was a bit weak.

_____

8 He **invested** a lot **in** the part.

_____

Phrasal verbs

3 Complete the phrasal verbs in the sentences with the particles in the box.

forward   in   into   off (x2)   on (x2)   out

1 The film came _____ last year.
2 It took _____ straightaway.
3 It's based _____ a best-selling book.
4 The film company put a lot of money _____ the production.
5 However, the film adaptation has come _____ for criticism from some people.
6 The leading actor has been put _____ for an Oscar.
7 He pulled _____ a remarkable performance, despite the weak script.
8 The rest of the cast also put _____ fantastic performances.

Useful language: exchanging ideas

4 Match the sentence halves.

1 I'm not into ballet myself. Having said that, _____
2 I know what you mean about musicals _____
3 Right, anyway, let's move on _____
4 It's a tricky one, but let's go for _____
5 Actually, _____
6 That's a difficult one _____

a I have to admit that I find circuses really boring but I'm obviously in the minority here.
b but they can be really good fun as well.
c because I haven't thought about it much up to now.
d and talk about stand-up comedy next.
e films, shall we, since we all like those?
f I haven't actually seen one performed live.

Reading (Paper 1 Part 7)

Gapped text

1 Read the title of the text and the introductory sentence. What do you think the text will be about?

2 Read the main text quickly and answer the questions.
  1 What does Martin do?
  2 What different things does Martin collect?
  3 Which of his collections is most important?
  4 What has he written?

3a Read the task and the paragraph before gap 1. What type of photography is it talking about? Which of the options is about this type of photography?

  b Now read the paragraph after gap 1. What do you think *here* in line 8 refers to?
  Which option introduces this idea?

4 Do the rest of the task.

HELP

➤ **Q2** The text before the gap is describing movement. Which option picks up on this?

➤ **Q3** Look at the pronoun *their* after the gap (line 24). Who might this be referring to?

➤ **Q5** The text before the gap ends with a question. Which option picks up on this?

EXPERT STRATEGY

Read the text before and after each gap, marking key words and checking all reference words. Do the same in the options A–G.

EXPERT LANGUAGE

Look back at the main text. Find examples of compound nouns and adjectives, where two words are joined by a hyphen.

EXPERT WORD CHECK

*bull market   candid   enduring legacy
insider market   kudos   maverick
overspill   provenance   public domain
research tool   tea caddies*

You are going to read a magazine article. Six paragraphs have been removed from the article. Choose from the paragraphs A–G the one which fits each gap (1–6). There is one extra paragraph which you do not need to use.

A Having said that, he is the first to admit that his collection is not comprehensive. 'I get sent a lot of books. I get sent a lot of bad books,' he says. 'If I don't want a book, I'll give it away. But occasionally, something really fantastic turns up.'

B He doesn't deny this but reminds me that he's looking for things before anyone else is looking for them. 'That's what's happened in China. When people see what we've come across in China, they are absolutely bog-eyed.'

C He's been adding to it ever since his first acquisitions as a student in Manchester but only became really hooked once he'd started earning. 'You probably have to be an obsessive person to collect, if you're going to do it seriously and thoroughly, which I attempt to do.'

D Since then, the selective listings have encouraged an insider market to emerge amongst collectors, publishers and photographers. Inclusion brings kudos to both the publisher and to a photographer's reputation, and almost guarantees an eventual rise in the resale value.

E To find an example of this groundbreaking work, we need look no further than the Japanese photobook. Until the 1980s, this was a specialist area, reserved for a few maverick enthusiasts, historians and collectors.

F Using something a little more sophisticated, I'm trying to capture my own image of the man at his home in Bristol, surrounded by his book collection. Surprisingly, he's not an easy subject; partly because he looks so sceptical; partly because he keeps opening books up on the floor to show me things and so I have to keep asking him to stand up.

G We eventually arrive in a small room stacked with boxes and lined with shelves of books. 'China and Latin America are down here,' he says, 'Well, some of China … and Latin America overspill.' It's too tight for two, so we go next door, where a cabinet holds some of his novelty watch collection – another of his passions.

From *selfie* to photographic *art*

I meet the British photographer on a mission to revise the history of photography.

Martin Parr is one of the best-known photographers in the UK. His reputation derives from his candid pictures of others, but he is also a dedicated exponent of the selfie – he may even have invented the term. His series
5 of self-portraits, taken in photo booths all around the world, began long before the mobile phone camera was invented.

> **1**

We are here to talk about his books but Parr collects pretty much everything, from Chinese tea caddies to
10 miniature televisions, commemorative plates to cigarette cases decorated with Russian space-dogs: 'Yes, Laika, Strelka and Belka, they're the three most famous.' That's before you get to his photographic prints, some of which I pause to admire on the walls of the stairwell as he leads
15 the way to the basement.

> **2**

Parr is in his early 60s and, alongside his reputation as a photographer, his most enduring legacy is likely to be the 12,000 photography books he has collected over the past 35 years. What began as a hobby has
20 developed into a mission to change the way the history of photography is defined and understood. As a collector, he has discovered, documented and promoted previously unknown areas of photographic bookmaking.

> **3**

Parr is quick to acknowledge their contribution but once
25 he discovered what was there, it was his own enthusiasm that brought those books to the fore. 'The main thing I've learnt,' he says, 'is how lazy and narrow-minded our histories of photography have been and how, with some investment and some application, there is so much
30 to discover.' When I ask if he has estimated the value of the collection, he says, 'I haven't. But I know it would be substantial.'

> **4**

His critics are quick to point out, however, that in being one of its generators, he has also been one of the chief
35 beneficiaries of the growing interest in photography books and the steep rise in prices. Isn't he now competing in a bull market he has helped to create?

> **5**

In 2004, Parr published the first volume of The Photobook: A History, an edited selection of his
40 collection, illustrated with layouts from each volume, written by his friend and collaborator, the photo-historian Gerry Badger. Initially pored over solely by photography fans, dealers and collectors, the work quickly became indispensable for auction
45 houses, which often had little else to quote by way of provenance for a photographer's work.

> **6**

So what would he like to see happen to this valuable collection? 'Eventually, I want it to go into a public collection, to be looked after and be used as a research
50 tool,' he replies. 'That's the whole point, really. There is no particularly good photographic book collection in the public domain in the UK. The Tate Museum in London is my preferred venue. I'm in discussion with them but nothing has been determined.'

Language development 2

> **CB** p. 50, **EG** p. 178

Modals and semi-modals (Part 1)

Obligation and necessity

1 Choose the correct answers.

1 These days, people *mustn't usually / don't usually have to* dress up to go to the theatre.
2 You *must / don't have to* remind me to switch off my phone during the performance. I always forget!
3 I made a mistake with the time, so we *didn't need / needn't have* rushed. It starts at 2.30, not 2.00!
4 We *had to / needed* get there a bit earlier so that I could allow time to collect the tickets from the box office.
5 I *must / have to* remember to pay you for the tickets later.
6 You *needn't wait / needn't have waited*. I'll catch you up in a minute.

Advice, recommendation, criticism, permission

2 Complete the sentences with the correct form of *should*, *ought to*, *had better*, *must* or *can*. More than one answer may be possible.

1 It's a brilliant adaptation. You really _____ go and see it!
2 Do you think we _____ get the tube if there's going to be a lot of traffic?
3 Sorry, but you _____ take that glass into the auditorium. Plastic ones are available at the bar.
4 You _____ told me you were going to see it. I've always wanted to go.
5 You _____ get upset. It does get happier.
6 When I was your age, we _____ get part-time jobs because our parents wouldn't let us.

Ability

3 Tick (✓) the correct sentences. Correct the mistakes in the wrong ones.

1 I could finally borrow the car and drive up and visit my parents last week.
2 He could have come with us to the gig but the tickets were sold out.
3 I could sing quite well but was too shy to perform in public.
4 I could pass my violin exam in the end but only after a lot of extra work.
5 Unfortunately, they couldn't come with us after all.
6 Next year we will can apply for an audition.

Possibility/Probability, deduction

4 Cross out the one incorrect answer in each sentence.

1 They're not answering the phone. They _____ have shut down for the day.
   A might
   B could
   C should
2 He _____ have seen our text by now. I sent it ages ago.
   A must
   B might
   C should
3 She caught the last train, so she _____ be home before midnight.
   A can
   B should
   C may
4 They _____ be nearly here by now, I'm sure. It's six o'clock.
   A must
   B could
   C should
5 It _____ have broken already. I only bought it yesterday.
   A can't
   B may
   C couldn't

Mixed modals

5 Choose the correct modal verb. Then complete the sentences with the correct form of the verbs in brackets.

1 You *can't / mustn't* _____ (see) Jim yesterday. He's still in Brazil.
2 I wonder who it was. It *could / should* _____ (be) his brother, perhaps. They are quite similar.
3 You *must / should* _____ (tell) me yesterday that you would need money. I've run out!
4 You know you *needn't / mustn't* _____ (wear) jewellery in school. Take it off.
5 I *can't / needn't* _____ (worry). Everything was absolutely fine.
6 I *didn't need / mustn't* _____ (explain) as she already knew the situation.

Use of English (Paper 1 Part 4)

Key word transformations

1 Read the instructions for the task and look at the example. Think about how the two sentences are different and notice how the meaning hasn't changed.

2 Do the task.

HELP
➤ **Q1** You need to make a sentence with *used to*.
➤ **Q2** You need to use the word *expected* in your answer.
➤ **Q6** You need a modal verb in your answer.

EXPERT STRATEGY
There are two marks available for each question. To get both marks, your answer has to be completely accurate. Check your answers carefully to make sure they are completely accurate.

EXPERT LANGUAGE
Find five examples of the passive in your answers.

*For questions **1–10**, complete the second sentence so that it has a similar meaning to the first sentence, using the word given. **Do not change the word given.** You must use between **three** and **six** words, including the word given. Here is an example (**0**).*

0 She didn't call me, even though she said she would.
SUPPOSED
She <u>was supposed to call me</u> but she didn't.

1 When he was a student, Dan went running every day.
USED
Dan _____ daily basis as a student.

2 Everyone expects that Ronan will win the award.
WIDELY
Ronan _____ win the award.

3 Fiona hasn't seen her brother for over a year.
LAST
It's more _____ saw her brother.

4 We were late arriving at the conference and so we missed the opening ceremony.
BY
The opening ceremony _____ we arrived at the conference.

5 People think that the ring may be more than 1,000 years old.
OVER
The ring _____ 1,000 years old.

6 I'm sure Maurice broke the vase because he looked so guilty.
HAVE
Maurice _____ because he looked so guilty.

7 You have to press the button first, then you can insert coins in the slot.
BEFORE
The button _____ can be inserted in the slot.

8 It's a long time since anyone came to service the photocopier.
NOT
The photocopier _____ ages.

9 Diana was completely taken aback to see her daughter on television.
CAME
It _____ Diana to see her daughter on television.

10 The committee will reach its decision after considering all the facts.
TAKEN
All the facts _____ the committee reaches its decision.

Writing (Paper 2 Part 1: Essay)

➤ CB pp. 52–53, EW p. 191–192

> **EXPERT STRATEGY**
> • Read the task carefully and underline the main points.
> • Read the opinions; they will give you ideas.
> • Make sure you discuss two of the points but decide on the one you think is best.

Analysing the task

1   Read the task and tick (✓) the correct information.
    You have to:
    1 write about all three notes.
    2 use the opinions given.
    3 use the same wording as in the task.
    4 justify your opinions.
    5 come to a conclusion.

> *Your class has attended a talk on how the government could encourage creativity at school. You have made the notes below.*
>
> **Methods by which the government could encourage creativity at school**
> • create more career opportunities
> • make creative subjects compulsory
> • improve teacher training
>
> **Some opinions expressed in the discussion:**
> 'Unless more jobs become available, people won't be motivated to study creative subjects.'
>
> 'You can't force students to be creative.'
>
> 'Teachers should to inspire students.'
>
> *Write an essay for your tutor discussing **two** of the methods in the notes. You should **explain which method you think is more important** for governments to consider and **provide reasons** in support of your answer. You may, if you wish, make use of the opinions expressed in the discussion, but you should use your own words as far as possible.*
> *Write your **essay** in 220–260 words.*

Structuring your essay

2a Put the paragraphs of a student's essay in a logical order: introduction, main body and conclusion.

 b Answer the questions.
    1 Which two notes has the student written about?
    2 Has the student used any of the opinions? If so, have they agreed or disagreed with them?
    3 What is the main point made about each of the two notes?
    4 What are the supporting ideas/examples?

A

Many young people are reluctant to take up anything creative such as drama, music, dance or art because they worry that they might fail at it. If they were obliged to try them out rather than just having them as extra-curricular options, people may discover talents that they were unaware they possessed. A wider range of subjects, to include entrepreneurship, for example, would be more appealing as not everyone is a performance artist.

B

In conclusion, it would appear to me that young people need to be offered every opportunity to engage in creative activities which they might otherwise not consider trying or be unable to do. It would be wonderful if this could be carried over into their working lives, but in my view it is still worthwhile, even if it is kept as a personal interest.

C

It is generally accepted that being creative is as vital for one's personal happiness as much as it benefits society. At one time, young people would turn to writing or drawing when they were bored, whereas now the screen tends to serve this purpose. So how could young people be encouraged to be more inventive and use their imagination?

D

At the moment, many young people feel that there is more chance of obtaining a job if they study something academic. Were more jobs requiring creativity available, it would motivate people to study these subjects instead. At the moment, many are discouraged by feeling that 'creative jobs' are only available for the outstandingly talented.

Using appropriate language: introduction and conclusion

3   Which of these phrases would be useful for a) the introduction b) the conclusion?
    1 In summary, …
    2 It has been claimed that …
    3 To my mind, …
    4 It is common knowledge that …
    5 Overall/On the whole/On balance/Everything considered, …
    6 It is probably true to say that …

Writing task

4   Now do the task in Exercise 1. Remember to make your main points and supporting evidence clear for each of the notes you choose.

4 The global village

4A A small world?

Vocabulary development 1

> CB p. 58

Collocations with *sleep*

1 Complete each sentence with the correct form of a verb from box A and a preposition from box B.

A

get   lose   put   rough   send   sleep (x3)

B

in   on   over (x2)   through   to (x3)

1 I was _____ sleep _____ that issue, so I'm glad it's been sorted out.
2 Our cat was very old and frail. In the end, the vet advised us to have her _____ sleep.
3 We shouldn't underestimate how many homeless people are sleeping _____ the streets.
4 I dozed a lot but didn't _____ sleep until after 3 a.m.
5 The film was so tedious that it _____ us both _____ sleep.
6 I _____ most of the play. I was really tired and the play wasn't very gripping at all.
7 I didn't set the alarm, which meant that I _____ and was late for work.
8 Emilia is _____ at a friend's house tonight, so we can lock up.

Expressions with *fall*

2 Match the sentence halves.

1 I fell fast   _____
2 The toy fell   _____
3 The joke fell   _____
4 The interest rate fell   _____
5 The stress falls   _____
6 She fell desperately   _____

a steeply and we decided not to invest.
b flat and nobody laughed.
c in love and neglected her work.
d asleep as soon as my head touched the pillow.
e to pieces as soon as we tried to use it.
f on the second syllable.

Phrasal verbs with *fall*

3 Use the correct form of *fall* and the particles in the box to make phrasal verbs to replace the phrases in bold.

back   behind   in   out   over   through

1 Although the contract was ready for signing, the deal **wasn't completed** for reasons we never knew.
2 It rained so hard that the shed roof **collapsed**.
3 Laura has **stopped making progress** with her work.
4 Her two boys are so near in age they **quarrel** a lot.
5 Having lost so much money during the recession, Tim had to **rely** on his savings to live on.
6 She tripped and **went down on the ground**.

Idioms: word pairs

4 Complete the sentences with the words in the box.

go   large   miss   parcel   thin   when

1 I go shopping as and _____ I can – I'm so busy.
2 My best friend and I have been through thick and _____ together.
3 Injury is part and _____ of a dancer's life.
4 By and _____ , we get on very well.
5 It's a bit hit and _____ as to whether they will carry out the investigation.
6 I'm not sure if I'll pass my driving test. It's touch and _____ .

Cultural experiences

5 Complete the text with the words in the box.

bear   brought   extensively   invaluable   on   onset
put   rituals

Jacqui has been living abroad off and **(1)** _____ for many years, usually disappearing at the **(2)** _____ of every winter. People initially tried to **(3)** _____ her off the idea of going by herself because they said it might be dangerous. However, she has found it a(n) **(4)** _____ experience because she's learnt so much about different cultures and their various **(5)** _____ , some of which **(6)** _____ little resemblance to her own country's traditions. She has travelled **(7)** _____ for many years now and it has really **(8)** _____ it home to her how much of the world there is still to see.

Use of English   (Paper 1 Part 1)

Multiple-choice cloze

1   Read the whole text quickly to get the general meaning.

2   Read the text again carefully and think about the type of word that will fit in each gap. Can you predict the answer without looking at the options?

3   Do the task.

4   Read through the text again, with your answers in place. Does it make complete sense?

EXPERT STRATEGY

If you are not sure about an answer, you can start by crossing out the options that you are sure are *not* correct.

HELP

➤ Q1 This is a similar expression to *in practice*.
➤ Q3 The word you need means 'it doesn't matter which'.
➤ Q8 Only one of these verbs is a reflexive verb (used with *myself, yourself*, etc.).

EXPERT LANGUAGE

Find examples of linking words and expressions at the beginning of sentences in the text.

For questions 1–8, read the text below and decide which answer (A, B, C or D) best fits each gap. There is an example at the beginning (0).

The dangers of miscommunication

As the world becomes more global, it is easy to **(0)** _A_ prey to the illusion that you can communicate easily across cultures simply by using the English language. In **(1)** _____, miscommunications abound, especially in a business context. **(2)** _____ the English expression *with all due respect*, for example. If you're British, this is a polite way of signalling that you're about to disagree with somebody, but this signal could easily be missed or misinterpreted in an international business meeting. What's more, cultural conventions tend to persist **(3)** _____ language is being spoken. For example, in the USA it is important to finish a meeting by **(4)** _____ up the key points, whereas in Europe meetings often end **(5)** _____ without this level of clarification. In some cultures, managers giving negative feedback to staff will come straight to the **(6)** _____ , but use reassuring language; in others it may be impolite to **(7)** _____ such a direct approach. Clearly, the best way to avoid such breakdowns in communication is to keep **(8)** _____ ourselves that these differences exist.

0	A fall	B get	C come	D have
1	A honesty	B reality	C actuality	D validity
2	A Give	B Regard	C Take	D View
3	A regardless	B nonetheless	C irrespective	D whatever
4	A ending	B totalling	C finalising	D summing
5	A abruptly	B shortly	C roughly	D sharply
6	A issue	B fact	C point	D truth
7	A adopt	B resume	C deliver	D enact
8	A remembering	B recalling	C reminding	D reviewing

Language development 1

➤ CB p. 61

Word families: verb, noun and adjective suffixes

1a Complete the table.

Verb	Noun	Adjective
hesitate	(1) _____	(2) _____
–	happiness	(3) _____
(4) _____	(5) _____	pleasant
persist	(6) _____	(7) _____
(8) _____	defence	(9) _____
(10) _____	(11) _____	hopeful/hopeless
specify	(12) _____	(13) _____
(14) _____	critic	(15) _____
appear	(16) _____	(17) _____
(18) _____	(19) _____	wide
(20) _____	danger	(21) _____
enjoy	(22) _____	(23) _____

1b Look at the words in Exercise 1a and write the suffixes in the correct group.

1 Noun suffixes: _-ion,_ _____
2 Adjective suffixes: _____
3 Verb suffixes: _____

2a Complete the text with nouns or adjectives formed from the words in brackets.

2b Look at your answers to Exercise 2a and add the suffixes from Exercise 1b to your list.

Word families: prefixes to change meaning

3a Replace the phrases in bold by adding the correct prefixes from the box to the adjectives or verbs. Make any changes necessary.

| dis- | en- | im- | in- | mis- | over- | pre- | re- |
| un- | under- | | | | | | |

1 She **isn't very patient** with her brother. _____
2 Marc is a bit **too emotional**. _____
3 She **isn't willing** to help us. _____
4 How can I **make** this picture **larger**? _____
5 I think she has every reason **not** to **trust** him. _____
6 I always **pronounce** that word **wrongly**. _____
7 Do we need to **book** tickets **in advance**? _____
8 The work is **not yet complete**. _____
9 I was **charged too little**. _____
10 You can **use** that plastic bag **again** – don't throw it away. _____

3b Use prefixes from the box in Exercise 3a to change these words. More than one answer may be possible.

1 decorate _____
2 rated _____
3 worked _____
4 probable _____
5 edible _____
6 loyal _____
7 wrap _____
8 understand _____
9 danger _____
10 place _____

CULTURE shock

The idea of living in a new culture for any length of time is often regarded as very **(1)** _____ (romance) but it is not without its problems. It is one thing to be a **(2)** _____ (travel), moving on when you have had enough; it is another to make the **(3)** _____ (decide) to live there for a year or so, perhaps for study or work.

Although living abroad provides a unique opportunity to get to know another society and **(4)** _____ (broad) your horizons, it also requires people to adapt their **(5)** _____ (behave) to the customs of the new culture. It is vital to become aware of the **(6)** _____ (similar) and **(7)** _____ (differ) and to learn rather than judge. If you are **(8)** _____ (patience), this can be the most **(9)** _____ (reward) experience of all. Culture shock occurs when the **(10)** _____ (excite) of adapting to the new environment wears off and there is an **(11)** _____ (aware) that the prevailing **(12)** _____ (culture) attitudes are a world apart from one's own. People go through a stage of feeling **(13)** _____ (confuse) and need time to adjust to their new **(14)** _____ (surround).

Some tips

There are **(15)** _____ (vary) things you can do to prepare yourself before setting off.

• It is **(16)** _____ (use) to read up as much as you can about the culture before your **(17)** _____ (depart). Take an interest in local issues and be open to the new culture.
• Break out of your **(18)** _____ (comfort) cocoon when you get there and play an **(19)** _____ (act) role.
• Be **(20)** _____ (tolerate) and **(21)** _____ (flexibility).

Remember: it all takes time, and culture shock is all part and parcel of living abroad!

Use of English   (Paper 1 Part 3)

Word formation

1   Read the title of the text. What type of research do you think scientists might do on this subject?

2   Read the whole text quickly to get the general meaning.

3   Read the text again carefully and think about how to change the word that will fit in each gap.

4   Do the task.

5   Read through the text again, with your answers in place. Does it make complete sense?

EXPERT STRATEGY

Remember that you may need to make more than one change to some words, e.g. add a prefix *and* a suffix.

HELP

➤ Q3 Look at the beginning of the sentence to see if this word is positive or negative.
➤ Q4 You need to add letters to the beginning of this word.
➤ Q7 You need to add both a prefix and a suffix to this word.

EXPERT LANGUAGE

Find five examples of words with negative prefixes in the text.

*For questions **1–8**, read the text below. Use the word given in capitals at the end of some of the lines to form a word that fits in the gap **in the same line**. There is an example at the beginning (**0**).*

Surrey Sleep Research Centre

Sleep disorders are very (**0**) <u>prevalent</u> in today's world, with up to 20 percent of the European and US population reporting frequent sleep (**1**) _____ . Unfortunately, (**2**) _____ strategies to alleviate sleep complaints and disorders are often (**3**) _____ . That is why the Surrey Sleep Research Centre in the UK is so important. The Centre offers a range of state-of-the-art equipment, (**4**) _____ of recording and analysing both sleep patterns and sleep disorders. The centre is engaged in various types of sleep research, covering fascinating areas, including the regulation of human sleep by our internal body clock and the effects of (**5**) _____ to light on sleep patterns. It is also investigating the causes, consequences and (**6**) _____ of the sleep disorders experienced by shift workers, frequent long-distance air travellers and blind people, as well as the effects of (**7**) _____ sleep on cognition, mood and metabolism. The centre's groundbreaking sleep studies are published in (**8**) _____ respected academic journals and its academics frequently appear on television and feature in the international news media.

PREVAIL

DISRUPT
EFFECT
AVAILABILITY

ABLE

EXPOSE

TREAT

SUFFICE

HIGH

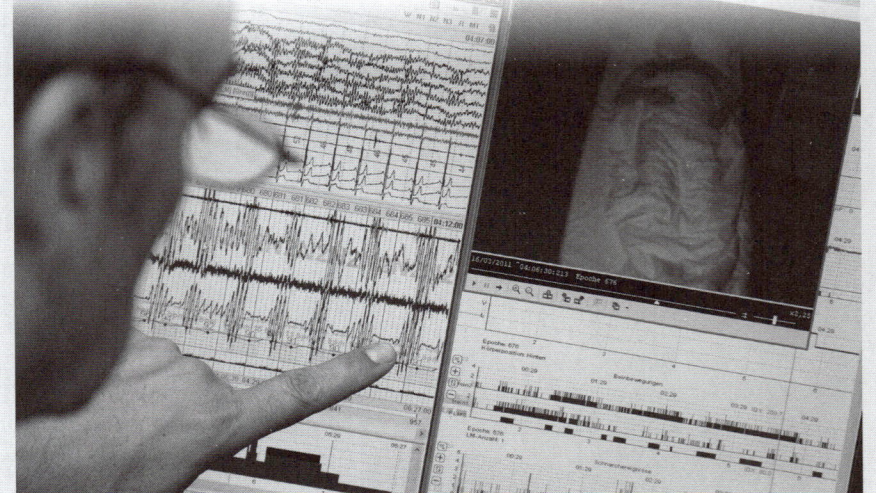

Listening (Paper 3 Part 4)

Multiple matching

1 Read the instructions for the tasks. Will there be a separate listening for each task or do you need to complete them both at the same time?

2a Look at Task One. What are you listening for? Mark the key words in the options.

b Now look at Task Two. What are you listening for? Mark the key words in the options.

3 🎧 05 Do the tasks. Remember that you must choose one option from each task for each speaker.

You will hear five short extracts in which university students are talking about campaign groups they have joined.

TASK ONE	TASK TWO
*For questions **1–5**, choose from the list (**A–H**) each speaker's main reason for joining the group.*	*For questions **6–10**, choose from the list (**A–H**) what each speaker has gained most from being part of the group.*

While you listen you must complete both tasks.

A a wish to keep up a family tradition	A greater self-knowledge
B a need to gain debating experience	B improved communication skills
C a friend's request	C better job prospects
D a speaker's persuasive arguments	D a clearer idea of career options
E a long-standing commitment to a cause	E a stronger sense of purpose
F a chance to influence a decision	F a wider social circle
G a desire to put a principle into practice	G a deeper understanding of society
H an unexpected invitation	H increased awareness of certain issues

Speaker 1 [1]
Speaker 2 [2]
Speaker 3 [3]
Speaker 4 [4]
Speaker 5 [5]

Speaker 1 [6]
Speaker 2 [7]
Speaker 3 [8]
Speaker 4 [9]
Speaker 5 [10]

HELP

➤ Q1 Listen for what happened at the meeting she attended.
➤ Q5 Listen for the phrase *out of the blue* – it relates to the answer.
➤ Q6 Be careful: she talks about her career, but option D is *not* the correct answer.
➤ Q10 Listen for what the job is teaching her.

EXPERT STRATEGY

Read the instructions and options in both tasks before you listen, and mark the key words.

EXPERT LANGUAGE

Find examples of comparative adjectives in the options.

EXPERT WORD CHECK

*affinity   calculating   childcare   cut and thrust
cut out for   doing wonders   hustings   plight
principled stand   tagged along*

Reading   (Paper 1 Part 5)

Multiple choice

1   Read the title of the text and the introductory sentence. What do you think the text will be about? Can you predict the writer's attitude to the topic?

2   Read the text quickly to see if you were right.

3   Read question 1 and mark the key words. Then read the text carefully to find the section which contains the answer.

4   Choose the option that best answers the question according to the text.

5   Repeat the procedure for the other questions.

HELP
> Q1   Read what the writer says about fundraising. Which option does it match?
> Q3   Look at the sentences before *that proposition* to find the answer.
> Q4   Look at the two questions the writer asks in the paragraph.

EXPERT STRATEGY

Mark the words in the question stem that will help you locate the relevant piece of text (e.g. names and main ideas). Sometimes the question tells you which paragraph to look at. In that case, don't let information and ideas from other paragraphs influence your answer.

EXPERT LANGUAGE

Find examples of different adjective suffixes in the first paragraph of the text.

EXPERT WORD CHECK

anti-malarial bednets   catchier
chuckle   door-to-door   drenched
flyer   gathers momentum
parasitic worms   philanthropic
succumbed

You are going to read an article about charity fundraising. For questions 1–6, choose the answer (A, B, C or D) which you think fits best according to the text.

1   What view of the ice bucket challenge is expressed in the first paragraph?
    A   It was a very clever way of generating charitable donations.
    B   It unfairly targeted certain people in the public eye.
    C   It used social pressure in an undesirable way.
    D   Its success took everyone by surprise.

2   What do the two research studies mentioned in the second paragraph suggest?
    A   The most generous people prefer to donate discreetly.
    B   Aggressive forms of fundraising can be counterproductive.
    C   Some people may only donate to charity to keep up appearances.
    D   Targeting certain households can make charity fundraising more effective.

3   The phrase *that proposition* in line 38 refers to
    A   a question posed by the writer himself.
    B   a theory which is popular amongst economists.
    C   a claim made by critics of the ice bucket challenge.
    D   an amount of money raised for one particular charity.

4   In the fourth paragraph, the writer is questioning whether
    A   the challenge was a fair way to raise money.
    B   people taking part in the challenge were really sincere.
    C   those receiving funds from the challenge were in genuine need.
    D   other charities are likely to find success with similar challenges.

5   According to the writer, the main aim of the GiveWell organisation is to
    A   promote the cause of less well-known charities.
    B   give guidance to those intending to make charitable donations.
    C   encourage charities to provide useful equipment rather than money.
    D   ensure that funds raised by charities reach their intended beneficiaries.

6   In the final paragraph, we learn that the writer
    A   now regrets taking part in the ice bucket challenge.
    B   has decided to initiate a charitable challenge of his own.
    C   resents having been put under pressure to give money to charity.
    D   prefers to make a principled choice when donating money to charity.

The ICE BUCKET challenge

What are the pros and cons when a charity fundraising initiative goes viral?

I finally succumbed to social pressure and invited some colleagues to film me having a bucket of iced water tipped over my head. This is the ice bucket challenge. The deal is that people film themselves being drenched, donate money to
5 their local Motor Neurone Disease charity, and then nominate three further people for the same treatment. It is fundraising genius and it went viral at some point. Lady Gaga did it; Mark Zuckerberg did it. By the time you read this, I imagine every celebrity on the planet will have done it. Social pressure
10 is a powerful thing and it's refreshing to see it being used to spread smiles and encourage a generous spirit. This isn't new, of course. Charities have long sought celebrity endorsements and getting famous people to make fools of themselves is part of that venerable tradition.

15 Peer pressure can also produce reluctant givers. Adriaan Soetevent, an economist at the University of Groningen, studied charitable collections in an open basket versus a closed collection bag. The open basket elicited larger donations. And in another clever field experiment run by
20 three economists, Stefano DellaVigna, John List and Ulrike Malmendier, fundraisers went door-to-door raising money. Some households, chosen randomly, had received a flyer warning them exactly when the fundraisers would be around: this warning dramatically increased the chance that the door
25 wouldn't be opened. Not all of us welcome the opportunity to give money to randomly selected charities, it seems.

In this case, however, the social element seemed to be a source of joy, and surely, the ice bucket challenge was a good thing, raising money for a worthy cause while giving
30 us a good chuckle into the bargain. But any good economist has to ask – and I do apologise about this: a good thing compared to what? Some critics of the challenge suggested that it might represent a 'zero-sum game' – in other words,

that more money for Motor Neurone Disease meant less for
35 other charities. The evidence for that proposition is thin, as it happens, but even if the many tens of millions raised by the ice bucket challenge were brand-new charitable giving, we could still ask where that money would best be spent.

The strength of a viral giving campaign, however, is also its
40 weakness: people join in for a laugh because their friends have put them up to it rather than because of a logical analysis of the most worthy cause. Motor Neurone Disease is a truly dreadful condition but so is cancer, ebola or simple starvation. In a world of limited generosity and finite
45 resources, who is to say which cause should be at the head of the queue? The fact that ice bucketeers were donating to a Motor Neurone Disease charity feels entirely arbitrary. If another charity had happened to be the beneficiary instead, very little else about the viral campaign would have
50 changed. Would that have been a better situation?

GiveWell is an organisation which seems well placed to answer such questions: it sets out to give donors the information they need to make the most effective donations. It sounds like an impossible job. GiveWell's approach is
55 to find cost-effective, evidence-based approaches such as distributing anti-malarial bednets and then search for transparent, efficient charities pursuing that approach. One of their top recommendations, for example, is the Schistosomiasis Control Initiative – incidentally, a charity
60 that would benefit from a catchier name. It organises treatment for parasitic worms, a very unappealing cause indeed. But the worms can do a lot of harm and are absurdly inexpensive to treat, hence the finding that the SCI offers value for your donated money.

65 In the end, I sent a few pounds of my ice bucket donation to the Motor Neurone Disease Association. It would have felt wrong, somehow, to do otherwise. I sent a more substantial
70 donation to SCI, surely one of the least media-friendly charities on the planet. All lives are equally valuable but some
75 lives may be saved far more cheaply than others. It seems strange not to respond to a philanthropic bargain.
80 No doubt, some will find this line of reasoning colder than a bucket full of iced water. But the truth is that whenever we give money to one cause rather than another,
85 we're making a decision about how deserving that cause is. When a social media campaign gathers momentum, it is human nature to make that decision spontaneously and without a moment's reflection. It feels good. But feeling good and doing good aren't the
90 same thing.

Vocabulary development 2

> CB p. 64

Issues and opinions: idioms

1 Replace the phrases in bold with an idiom from the box. Put the verbs in the correct form and make any other changes necessary.

agree to differ   dig your heels in
give you the benefit of the doubt   go round in circles
meet somebody halfway   sit on the fence

1 She is **refusing to give in** on this issue.
2 Let's **give up trying to have the same opinion** on this particular issue.
3 We had to **agree to some of the things they wanted** in order to reach a final agreement.
4 She **won't commit herself either way on what she thinks** about this problem.
5 We keep **talking about the same thing without making any progress** – we need to make a decision!
6 I'm not convinced but I'll **accept what you say because I can't prove that you're wrong**.

Issues and opinions: verb + noun collocations

2 Complete the sentences with the correct form of *have*, *take*, *make* or *put*.

1 It's important that we all _____ a say on local issues.
2 The aim is to _____ pressure on the council to find a solution.
3 If we don't _____ a stand now, it'll be too late.
4 We must act together if we want to _____ an influence on decisions made in our name.
5 There is unanimous agreement that we should _____ immediate action.
6 You can help by _____ forward your view on what should happen next.
7 Signing the petition has already _____ a huge difference to the potential outcome.
8 It shows that we are _____ matters very seriously indeed and will not give in.

3 Complete the phrases with verbs from the box.

accept   be   change   come   settle   work

1 _____ to a compromise
2 _____ towards an agreement
3 _____ another point of view
4 _____ strongly opposed to something
5 _____ for a compromise
6 _____ your mind about an issue

Issues and protests

4 Complete the minutes of an informal neighbourhood meeting with words from the box.

basis   consultation   high   opposed   petition
publicity   put   raised   reach   unanimous
way   went

At the meeting of local residents on 4th June, the issue of potential traffic lights at the junction of the two main roads was **(1)** _____ yet again. There was **(2)** _____ agreement that plans should not have been put into place before proper **(3)** _____ with people living in the neighbourhood.

At the meeting, feelings ran very **(4)** _____ . Several people **(5)** _____ forward the point that the traffic lights would indeed make it safer for children who have to cross the busy roads, and the vast majority of those present **(6)** _____ along with that view. However, most people were still **(7)** _____ to the plan, on the **(8)** _____ that the build-up of traffic at the lights would inevitably increase pollution.

The rest of the discussion focused on trying to find a(n) **(9)** _____ round the problem and attempting to **(10)** _____ a compromise.

It was finally agreed that more pressure should be put on the council to justify their plans. Local people are to be encouraged to sign the **(11)** _____ and we agreed to try to generate more **(12)** _____ on the issue through the media.

Language development 2

➤ CB p. 66, EG p. 179

that clauses

1 Rewrite the sentences using *that* clauses.

1 There is no evidence of her involvement in the crime.
There _____ .

2 He is very likely to ask us to work late.
There _____ .

3 Pandas may become extinct, which is very sad.
It _____ .

4 During my research, a high number of people were found to be face-blind.
My research _____ .

5 The teacher explained the wide variety of different learning options available to students.
The teacher explained _____ .

6 A lot of young people have joined the programme this year, which is very encouraging.
It _____ .

Clauses beginning with a question word

2 Complete the sentences with question words from the box.

> how   what (x2)   when   where   which
> who (x2)   why (x2)

1 I'm not sure yet _____ to call my story.
2 _____ you choose to invite is up to you.
3 I've no idea at all _____ café she decided to go to.
4 I just don't understand _____ I could have forgotten it.
5 Shall we decide _____ to go out? Is Monday good for you?
6 I couldn't work out _____ you were talking to.
7 _____ she really wants for her birthday is a new laptop.
8 I was talking to him about _____ I'd decided to become a nurse.
9 I have no idea_____ I'm going to put the grand p ano!
10 _____ she always goes to the same place is a mystery to me.

-ing and *to*-infinitive clauses

3 Complete the text with the infinitive or *-ing* form of the verbs in brackets.

A community cinema

The decision **(1)** _____ (set up) a community cinema on the premises of the local high school meant that it was only possible **(2)** _____ (use) it at the weekends and during the holidays. The initial challenge was obviously for residents **(3)** _____ (raise) enough money to fund the project. In addition, the only way of **(4)** _____ (staff) the cinema was **(5)** _____ (rely on) volunteers.
Despite the difficulties, there was a general feeling that **(6)** _____ (provide) an independent community cinema was essential **(7)** _____ (improve) the quality of life in the town. Despite a rather slow start, the cinema is now very popular and residents are delighted **(8)** _____ (be) offered free parking and refreshments, as well as cheap tickets for a wide range of films.
There are now 15 part-time paid workers, as well as more than 100 volunteers **(9)** _____ (work) there. However, it is still difficult **(10)** _____ (persuade) young people to go to films at what they regard as school.

4 Complete the sentences with words from the box. Put the verbs in the correct form.

> have   it   overstate   share   that (x2)   volunteer
> what   who

1 _____ in the community is not something just for retired people.
2 It's impossible _____ the benefits that it can provide at all ages.
3 For example, it's important _____ young people get experience of the working world as early as possible.
4 Paid work often depends on _____ you know rather than _____ you know – skills and qualifications are often less important than your contacts.
5 _____ is also crucial that retired people have the opportunity _____ their skills and expertise with people less experienced than them.
6 They frequently find that their main worry is _____ too much time on their hands.
7 Some kind of structure in their lives helps enormously and evidence suggests _____ working with a new set of people can help to prolong people's lives.

Use of English (Paper 1 Part 4)

Key word transformations

1 Read the instructions for the task and look at the example. Think about how the two sentences are different and notice how the meaning hasn't changed.

2 Do the task.

EXPERT STRATEGY

Remember that the word given must be included in your answer and it cannot be changed in any way.

HELP

➤ Q1 You need to express future time in the new sentence.
➤ Q3 You need to transform the adjective *concerned* into a noun.
➤ Q4 Use the word *us* in your answer.

EXPERT LANGUAGE

Which two questions test phrasal verbs?

*For questions **1–10**, complete the second sentence so that it has a similar meaning to the first sentence, using the word given. **Do not change the word given.** You must use between **three** and **six** words, including the word given. Here is an example (0).*

0 Mark doesn't like it when people tell him what to do.
RESENTS
Mark _resents being told_ what to do.

1 Debbie is very likely to win the charity run fun.
LIKELIHOOD
In _____ win the charity fun run.

2 Julian couldn't wait to begin his voluntary work placement.
FORWARD
Julian _____ his voluntary work placement.

3 Rachel was particularly concerned about the issue of noise pollution.
OF
The issue of noise pollution _____ to Rachel.

4 Because of the heavy traffic, we didn't arrive in time for the meeting.
PREVENTED
The heavy _____ in time for the meeting.

5 You have to be very committed to do this kind of charity work.
CALLS
This kind of charity work _____ deal of commitment.

6 Delia has always been a loyal supporter of local charities.
LENT
Delia has always _____ local charities.

7 Young people in the community would benefit greatly from the project.
HIGHLY
The project _____ to young people in the community.

8 It is uncertain what effect the new proposals will have.
REMAINS
It _____ seen what effect the new proposals will have.

9 In the end, only a very small number of protestors signed the petition.
HARDLY
In the end, _____ signed the petition.

10 The loss of funding was the end of Jane's plan to go to India.
PAID
The loss of funding _____ Jane's plan to go to India.

Writing (Paper 2 Part 2: Proposal)

➤ **CB** pp. 68–69, **EW** p. 196

EXPERT STRATEGY
- State the purpose of the proposal.
- Divide it into different parts with clear headings.
- Make recommendations.

Analysing the task

1 Read the task and answer the questions.

1 What is the purpose of the proposal?
2 Who are you writing it for?
3 What style of language will you use?

You see this notice on the students' noticeboard at the international language college where you are studying.

A recent survey by the council has revealed that local residents have a number of concerns regarding the college, particularly the noise level late at night and the amount of discarded litter. We are looking for suggestions of how to improve community relations. To this end, the college is prepared to fund some kind of social activity. You are invited to submit a proposal to the principal, outlining ideas for this, after which a decision will be made.

*Write your **proposal** in 220–260 words.*

Developing ideas

2a Read these suggestions for the proposal. Tick the ones you like and add any further ideas.

1 We could offer a variety of conversation classes in different languages for a term.
2 We could organise a food festival.
3 We could send the residents a letter of apology.
4 We could give talks about different cultures.

b Read a student's proposal. Which suggestions from Exercise 2a are put forward? Ignore the words in *italics* at this stage.

Using appropriate language

3 Read the proposal again and replace the words and phrases in italics with these more formal alternatives. Make any other changes necessary.

a in the event of	h in close proximity to
b resolved	i reflect well on
c distributed	j is kept to a minimum
d implemented	k in view of
e at present	l concerns raised
f course of action	
g the principal objective of	

4 Which of the following are typical of a proposal? Find examples in the proposal in Exercise 2b.

1 passive forms/an impersonal style
2 phrasal verbs
3 formal vocabulary
4 contracted forms
5 complex sentences
6 persuasive language

Writing task

5 Now do the task in Exercise 1.

Proposal to improve community relations

■ Introduction
(1) *What I want to do in* this proposal is to suggest ways in which good relations with our neighbours can be reestablished **(2)** *given* the **(3)** *problems which came up* in the recent survey. It is obviously extremely important that a good relationship be maintained with the local community and **(4)** *just now*, this is clearly not happening.

■ Current situation
Since the college is located **(5)** *very near* residential family homes, it is clearly vital that **(6)** *we keep the noise down* after a certain hour. It is understood that there has been a tendency for students to shout and laugh very loudly when walking back from town late at night, which disturbs young children sleeping. It has also been noted that the following mornings takeaway wrappers and empty soft drink cans are often found littering the street, which does not **(7)** *make our town look good*.

■ Recommendations
I would suggest the following **(8)** *plan*:
- a letter of apology to be written by a 'task group' and **(9)** *given out* to local residents.
- contact with our neighbours to be initiated, e.g. hosting an 'international evening' on which we serve typical snacks and drinks from our countries.
- a system to be put in place whereby residents can liaise directly with the students **(10)** *if there are* any further problems.

■ Conclusion
Were the short-term recommendation – the letter – to be **(11)** *put into action* relatively soon and followed by a social event within the month, I feel confident that any present tension could quickly be **(12)** *sorted out*.

Vocabulary development 1

> CB p. 74

Word formation

1 Complete the text with words formed from the words in brackets.

Are pets good for us?

In a recent book on (1) _____ (sustain) living, the authors recommended that pet (2) _____ (own) should restrict the number of pets they have and avoid feeding them top-quality food. The authors argue that it is hard to (3) _____ (justice) giving this kind of food to animals when global resources are becoming scarcer. Feeding more basic food would be (4) _____ (ecology) more friendly and would (5) _____ (less) the negative impact of pets on the environment. However, the argument in (6) _____ (defend) of having pets states that the food currently fed to pets is surplus to human (7) _____ (require) and would otherwise end up in landfill (8) _____ (dispose) sites. In addition, pets are known to (9) _____ (rich) our lives and be (10) _____ (benefit) to our health.

Compound nouns with verbs and prepositions

2 Use the words in the box and the prepositions in brackets to form compound nouns and complete the sentences.

break   build   look   set   sight   turn

1 During a financial _____ (down), people tend to have fewer pets.
2 The _____ (out) for our environment gets ever more depressing.
3 One day there may be a _____ (through) and we may find a solution to world poverty.
4 The programme gave a fascinating _____ (in) into the causes of global warming.
5 It was a huge _____ (back) when the main striker got injured.
6 The _____ (up) to the event seemed to go on all day.

Collocations

3 Complete each sentence with a word from A and a word from B.

A

ecological   limited   natural   renewable   toxic

B

energy   fumes   footprint   habitats   resources

1 The search for more sources of _____ such as wind farms is continuing.
2 If fewer people travelled by car, there would be fewer _____ in the atmosphere.
3 In a world of _____ , everyone should recycle.
4 The destruction of the _____ of some animals and plants has resulted in their extinction.
5 People who use fewer resources are said to have a smaller _____ than others.

The environment

4 Choose the answers.

ECOTOURISM

Ecotourism is the fastest growing area in the holiday business, aiming to preserve and sustain the (1) *diversity / difference* of the world's natural and cultural resources. It is intended as a (2) *low-effect / low-impact* alternative to mass conventional tourism. Environmentalists hope it offers tourists an invaluable (3) *understanding / insight* into the impact of humans on the environment. The purpose may be to educate the traveller and provide funds for the (4) *conservation / keeping* of vital resources such as energy and water. It is also of huge (5) *profitable / economic* benefit for the local community. Since preserving resources is a high priority on these holidays, travellers are urged to (6) *recycle / reclaim* wherever possible and take away non-biodegradable (7) *mess / litter* such as tins, plastic bags and empty bottles, cut noise (8) *pollution / impurity* and generally make a positive impression on society, the environment and economy. However, as many of the destinations require people to travel by air, the lack of ecologically-friendly transport is a critical issue as it contributes to greenhouse gas emissions and therefore to (9) *world / global* warming and (10) *weather / climate* change.

Use of English   (Paper 1 Part 1)

Multiple-choice cloze

1   Read the whole text quickly to get the general meaning.

2   Read the text again carefully and think about the type of word that will fit in each gap. Can you predict the answer without looking at the options?

3   Do the task.

4   Read through the text again, with your answers in place. Does it make complete sense?

HELP

➤ Q2   The answer you need means 'comparatively'.
➤ Q3   Read the rest of the paragraph to see which option is correct.
➤ Q4   Only one of these words can be used after *by*.

For questions 1–8, read the text below and decide which answer (A, B, C or D) best fits each gap. There is an example at the beginning (0).

Man's best friend

There are various theories to **(0)** _A_ for the close relationship that exists between people and dogs. Scientists agree that this bond has its origins in prehistory but various explanations have been **(1)** _____ to suggest how it first came about. Until **(2)** _____ recently, the prevailing theory was that primitive people had been the instigators of the process of domestication. **(3)** _____ this view, primitive people realised that not only were some species of wild dogs good hunters, but that they were also fiercely territorial by **(4)** _____ . In order to take **(5)** _____ of these instinctive skills, people captured young animals, trained them and then bred them in captivity. Recent research, however, suggests that it may have been the dogs which made the first **(6)** _____ , attracted to human settlements by the opportunities to scavenge amongst the waste material that **(7)** _____ there. Like domestic cats, dogs **(8)** _____ from their wild cousins in their ability to digest carbohydrates and starch, and it is thought that such digestive changes facilitated the process of domestication.

0 A account	B explain	C describe	D justify
1 A laid down	B set about	C put forward	D made up
2 A closely	B relatively	C approximately	D respectively
3 A As well as	B Apart from	C In addition to	D According to
4 A nature	B character	C habit	D personality
5 A exploitation	B benefit	C advantage	D profit
6 A move	B contact	C touch	D turn
7 A arrived	B deposited	C dumped	D accumulated
8 A change	B differ	C alter	D contrast

Language development 1

➤ CB p. 77, **EG** p. 180

Gradable and ungradable adjectives

1a Match the gradable adjectives (1–8) with the ungradable adjectives (a–h).

1	pleased	a	unforgettable
2	annoyed	b	disastrous
3	interesting	c	spotless
4	bad	d	stunning
5	attractive	e	furious
6	memorable	f	terrified
7	apprehensive	g	fascinating
8	clean	h	thrilled

b Which of the adjectives in the box are ungradable?

different efficient expensive impossible informative outstanding perfect polluted remarkable spectacular welcoming

Modifying adverbs

2a Which of the adverbs in the box make adjectives stronger? Which make them weaker? Write them in the correct column. One adverb can go in both columns.

a bit/little absolutely completely extremely fairly incredibly pretty quite really seriously slightly somewhat utterly very

Stronger	Weaker

b Tick the adverbs in Exercise 2a which can be used only with ungradable adjectives.

3 Choose the correct answers.

1 Unless we tackle the problem of water shortage, it will be *very / completely* disastrous for the planet.
2 Agriculture uses an *extremely / absolutely* large amount of water.
3 I was *a bit / totally* fascinated by the lecture.
4 I was *slightly / utterly* surprised by her reaction.
5 She found the waterfalls *really / fairly* stunning.
6 It's *highly / absolutely* likely that we will run out of oil.
7 The fridge was *extremely / virtually* empty.
8 It was *absolutely / extremely* impossible to work with all that noise.

Collocations: adverbs + adjectives

4 Cross out the one incorrect option in each sentence.

1 I am _____ opposed to the fur trade.
   A bitterly   B perfectly   C totally
2 It's _____ different from what I expected.
   A highly   B somewhat   C completely
3 The situation is _____ disastrous.
   A absolutely   B utterly   C painfully
4 The area is _____ dependent on tourism.
   A bitterly   B heavily   C completely
5 The proposal is _____ controversial.
   A deeply   B highly   C completely
6 To me, it is _____ obvious that something needs to be done.
   A incredibly   B quite   C painfully
7 The amount of litter is _____ unacceptable.
   A totally   B pretty   C completely
8 It is _____ unlikely that the government will back down on this issue.
   A deeply   B extremely   C highly

5 Read the reviews and look at the modifying adverbs in *italics*. Tick (✓) the correct ones and give alternatives for the ones that are used incorrectly. More than one answer may be possible.

The trip was **(1)** *very* outstanding. The guides were **(2)** *really* charming and the beaches were **(3)** *a bit* deserted. I was **(4)** *rather* disappointed by the size of my room, but I'd go back again tomorrow!

Seeing the wildlife was **(5)** *totally* magical and all the people we met were **(6)** *absolutely* welcoming. It was **(7)** *completely* expensive and the journey there was **(8)** *a bit* stressful, but that wasn't the company's fault.

The location was **(9)** *deeply* spectacular. All the people at the hotel were **(10)** *very* nice and I thought it was **(11)** *quite* good value for money. It was **(12)** *bitterly* different from anywhere else I'd been.

Use of English   (Paper 1 Part 2)

Open cloze

1 Read the title of the text and think about what you are going to read.

2 Read the whole text quickly to get the general meaning.

3 Read the text again carefully and think about the type of word that will fit in each gap.

4 Do the task.

5 Read through the text again, with your answers in place. Does it make complete sense?

EXPERT STRATEGY

After deciding what part of speech is needed for a gap, also think about the form of the word, i.e. whether it needs to be positive or negative, singular or plural, active or passive, etc.

HELP

➤ Q3 What noun completes this fixed phrase that expresses purpose?

➤ Q6 You need a relative pronoun here.

➤ Q7 Look before the gap – this word relates to the year.

EXPERT LANGUAGE

Find an example of inversion in the text.

*For questions 1–8, read the text below and think of the word which best fits each gap. Use only **one** word in each space. There is an example at the beginning (0).*

Shark fin soup

Shark meat is rarely eaten. The animal's flesh has an unpleasant smell, which **(0)** _puts_ most people off. Shark fins, on the other **(1)** _____ , are a traditional delicacy, a key ingredient in shark fin soup. Once only enjoyed by a few wealthy people in China, the soup has become a luxury available all around the world and some shark species face extinction **(2)** _____ a result.

In **(3)** _____ to maintain the supply of fins to restaurants, sharks are caught, their fins shaved off and their bodies thrown back **(4)** _____ the water. **(5)** _____ fins to give them orientation and balance, the sharks die. Particularly upsetting for wildlife campaigners is the fact that the fin itself is virtually tasteless, simply providing a gelatinous liquid to **(6)** _____ other flavours are added.

A movement against shark fin soup began in 2006, **(7)** _____ a WildAid campaign was taken up by a group of businesspeople and celebrities. It has since gathered pace, with a recent report suggesting the soup is **(8)** _____ longer the fashionable dish it once was.

Listening (Paper 3 Part 3)

Multiple choice

1 Read the instructions for the task and answer the questions.
   1 How many speakers are you going to hear?
   2 What are they going to talk about?

2 Look at the questions and mark the key words in the stems and options.

3 How much do you find out about the story from the questions?

4 🎧 06 Do the task.

You will hear an interview with a wildlife biologist called Adam Warwick, who once rescued a bear from drowning. For questions 1–6, choose the answer (A, B, C or D) which fits best according to what you hear.

1 When Adam initially heard reports about the bear, he felt
   A intrigued to hear more about it.
   B hopeful that it wouldn't remain in the area.
   C sure it was one that he'd previously studied.
   D concerned about how local people would react to it.

2 In Adam's opinion, the bear went into the water because
   A it was suffering from the effects of the drug.
   B it was unaware that it had been hit by the dart.
   C it was frightened by the attention of onlookers.
   D it was planning to make its escape across the bay.

3 When Adam reached the bear in the water, he realised
   A it was already unconscious.
   B it was trying to save its own life.
   C it was angry at being intercepted.
   D it was about to start attacking him.

4 How did Adam eventually manage to save the bear?
   A By dragging it along in shallow water
   B By swimming with it towards the shore
   C By enlisting the support of people in a boat
   D By holding its head out of the water until help arrived

5 How does Adam respond to being regarded as a hero?
   A He's embarrassed by some of the attention he's received.
   B He admits to having experienced fear during the rescue.
   C He's offended by the gifts of money he's been sent.
   D He's keen to stress that he was only doing his job.

6 What surprises Adam most about the bears in Florida?
   A the delicate movements they are capable of
   B the level of intelligence they demonstrate
   C their particularly evocative smell
   D their great physical strength

Vocabulary development 2

> **CB** pp. 80–81

Security: collocations

1 Complete each sentence with a word from A and a word from B.

A

biometric   code   phone   security   spy   swipe

B

card   checks   guards   number   satellites   tapping

1 Many airports are now using _____ as proof of identity.
2 In some big schools there are now _____ employed to stand at the doors.
3 People working in offices often have to key in a _____ before they can enter the building.
4 To unlock an electronic door, you sometimes need to run a _____ through the slot of a special reader.
5 The press are often criticised for using _____ to find out information.
6 _____ are sometimes used in military operations.

Prepositional phrases

2 The text below is based on the listening text on page 80 of the Coursebook. Complete it with prepositions from the box. The prepositions may be used more than once.

at   for   in   of   on   to

In a radio interview, a journalist talked about her experiences with a person who hacked into her emails. The person had emailed her contacts to say that she had been held up **(1)** _____ gunpoint **(2)** _____ an attempt to get money from them.

(3) _____ the journalist's amazement, the hacker replied when she wrote him an email demanding her contacts back. What worries the journalist is that it's not just hardened criminals who do it; kids obsessed with technology are also hacking **(4)** _____ secret from their bedrooms, perhaps just **(5)** _____ fun. She points out that hacking puts all our lives **(6)** _____ risk and there should be better procedures **(7)** _____ place to prevent it.

A consultant **(8)** _____ the field of information technology was also interviewed **(9)** _____ the subject **(10)** _____ online crime. He agreed that people should be **(11)** _____ their guard at all times, but pointed out that it is important to keep the danger **(12)** _____ perspective.

Phrasal verbs and idiomatic expressions

3a Complete the sentences with the correct form of the words in the box.

catch   come   fall   freak   get   hush   take

1 Experts _____ up with new protection systems to stop people _____ hold of information.
2 There are often attempts to _____ up what hackers are doing.
3 People often _____ for the scams used by hackers.
4 What really _____ the journalist out was feeling that her identity had ben taken hostage.
5 There are more and more clever ways to _____ people unawares.
6 The computer expert agreed to _____ part in an interview.

b Now look at your answers and the words in bold in Exercise 3a. Match the completed expressions with their meanings.

a manage to find something to use _____
b make someone very upset and anxious _____
c prevent people from knowing about something _____
d do something when someone is not expecting it _____
e participate _____
f think of a new idea _____
g be tricked into something _____

Verbs and adverbs for opinions: intensifying expressions

4 Choose the correct answers.

1
A: I *firmly / absolutely* believe the government should cut the number of CCTV cameras. We're becoming a surveillance society.
B: Mm, I must say I *completely / bitterly* resent being spied on all the time unless it's really necessary.

2
A: I think good security software is *totally / vitally* important.
B: I *quite / really* agree.

3
A: I am *highly / seriously* concerned about how newspapers obtain their stories.
B: Yes, I *strongly / distinctly* object to them hacking into celebrities' phones just to get gossip.

4
A: I wish we didn't have so much airport security. It makes me *entirely / deeply* frustrated.
B: Ah, I *vividly / strongly* remember how quick and easy check-in used to be in the old days.

Reading (Paper 1 Part 8)

Multiple matching

1 Read the title of the text and the introductory sentence. What do you think the members of the team will look like?

2 Read the task and mark the key words in each question.

3 Read the text quickly to get an idea of how it is structured and what issues are discussed in each section. What is the main focus of each section?

4 Look at question 1 and find the sections of the text that talk about the 'hiring' of the team members. Look for words and expressions that describe energetic movements. Write the question number next to these sections so you can find them again quickly. Then read these sections carefully and decide which section matches the exact wording of question 1.

5 Repeat the procedure for the other questions.

HELP
➤ Q2 Look at the section which talks about what one team member wears.
➤ Q3 Look again at the sections that talk about recruitment.
➤ Q7 Be careful: the word *talent* is in the text but not in the section with the answer to this question.

EXPERT STRATEGY

If you are unsure of a question, go on to the next one and come back to it. It may be easier to answer once you have answered some of the others.

EXPERT LANGUAGE

Find four examples of compound adjectives in section A of the text.

EXPERT WORD CHECK

battalion   bewilderment
disconcertingly   forensic investigator
geek   hiring spree   pinpointed
prime suspect   replicas
reverse engineering   sleuths
stock-in-trade

You are going to read an article about a team of computer experts who fight cyber crime. For questions 1–10, choose from the sections (A–D). The sections may be chosen more than once.

In which section does the writer mention:

the decision to embark on an intensive recruitment campaign?	1
a stereotypical image not confirmed by the appearance of one team member?	2
a method of assessing the suitability of those wishing to join the team?	3
evidence that suggests the identity of one particular criminal?	4
research that confirms the level of damage inflicted by cyber criminals?	5
one team member's particular area of technical expertise?	6
the personal qualities required of potential team members?	7
the visual representation of an ongoing investigation?	8
increasing levels of concern amongst those targeted by cyber criminals?	9
a natural talent that has been put to good use?	10

Vocabulary

6 Look at these compound words from the text. Decide which should be written as one word and which should be written as two words. Then look back at the text and check your answers.

1 hacker hunters (title) _____
2 head quarters (Section A) _____
3 cyber crime (Section B) _____
4 short hand (Section C) _____
5 rare breed (Section D) _____
6 trust worthy (Section D) _____
7 family farm (Section E) _____
8 soft ware (Section E) _____

The hacker HUNTERS

A team of elite young experts are on the trail of the cyber criminals

A Somewhere deep within the headquarters of a London-based IT company, a projection flickers on the whitewashed wall of a meeting room. Its uniform multi-coloured dots form an image that wouldn't look out of place in a modern art gallery.
5 But this isn't art; it is science. Each lilac and rose-coloured spot represents one step in a hunt for hackers. For the members of the company's newest security team, a pack of cyber sleuths mostly still in their 20s, these bright lights are flares of corporate
10 danger. The team offers its services to a growing number of corporate clients – companies seeking protection against cyber fraud, activism and industrial espionage, perpetrated by unseen
15 enemies who can be thousands of miles away. In response, the IT company has launched a hiring spree over the past two years to create an in-house battalion of more than 80
20 youthful experts from across the UK and abroad.

B Cyber protection has become one of the IT company's fastest-growing departments, fed in no small part by the increasing number of such
25 attacks and deepening sense of bewilderment and fear within private corporations over who is profiting from these secret cyber wars. Hackers want to steal the secrets and money and damage the reputations of the companies they target. Recent studies show that their persistence pays: the UK government
30 estimates that the cost of cyber crime to the country's economy alone reaches £27 billion annually, while a White House white paper on cyber policy estimated that data theft to US businesses costs close to $1 trillion annually.

C Dan Kelly, a 28-year-old former farm boy turned forensic
35 investigator of computer code heads the team, which has pinpointed a one-man hack attack amid a string of dots, numbers and letters. 'This is malware that's been tied to several campaigns, which targeted people in the western and eastern hemispheres,' says Kelly, who left school at 16, having
40 completed all his qualifications early. Malware is shorthand for the malicious software that is the stock-in-trade of hackers worldwide. 'What we've actually managed to do is tie the malware and the campaigns back to an individual.' Kelly, an expert in reverse engineering – taking code apart to deduce
45 its origin and purpose – points out that the image projected on the team's meeting room wall is also telegraphing something personal about his prime suspect. Much like a graffiti artist, the hacker tagged his work, embedding his signature somewhere within the malware.

D Hiring the right talent has been among the IT company's
50 biggest challenges. Cyber experts – some of whom try out for jobs in simulated sessions of 'ethical hacking' or 'penetration testing', where they attempt to hack into replicas of companies' systems to find any vulnerabilities – are
55 something of a rare breed. Stephen Page, who advises the UK government on the digital issues facing companies, offers a job description of what is needed in a tech detective, no matter the age. 'We need people who are not only technically agile
60 but also totally trustworthy.'

E The poster boy of the team's cyber efforts is Kris McConkey, a 31-year-old who has been obsessed with computers since primary
65 school. McConkey, whose just-so hair, designer stubble and sharp shirts dispel any notion of the hoodie-wearing geek, grew up on a family farm in a rural corner of Ireland and bought his
70 first computer at age 13. The first thing he did, somewhat disconcertingly to his parents, was pull it apart. Luckily, the young teenager also figured out how to fit all the pieces back together. Within the year, he was learning how to dissect computer viruses
75 and malware. By the time he left school, he'd set up his own software company. 'I was always trying to work out how stuff worked and take things to bits – whether it was machinery or radios or anything – just to figure it out. I started doing that with computers and with computer programs as well,' he
80 explains. 'I've pretty much done that either as a hobby or as my job for 16 years now; just trying to work out what the bad guys are up to and how to defend against it.'

7 Look at these phrases from the text and add hyphens where necessary. Then look back at the text and check your answers.

1 a London based IT company (Section A)
2 multi coloured dots (Section A)
3 each rcse coloured spot (Section A)
4 an in house battalion (Section A)
5 a 28 year old former farm boy (Section C)
6 a one man hack attack (Section C)
7 the stock in trade of hackers worldwide (Section C)
8 a hoodie wearing geek (Section E)

Language development 2

➤ **CB** p. 82, **EG** p. 181

Review of conditionals

1 Complete the sentences about home and work security with the pairs of verbs from the box in the correct conditional form. More than one answer may be possible.

> be / invest   feel / carry   get / live   install / know
> need / ask   not leave / not be able to   use / be
> want / recommend

1 If you _____ your home to be secure, the police _____ that you install new window and door locks.
2 Personally, I _____ a dog if I _____ in the middle of the country like you.
3 If business _____ good next year, I _____ in some CCTV cameras.
4 If you _____ smoke alarms, you _____ about the fire much earlier than you did.
5 If you _____ to be away for a few weeks, I _____ Mark to put some lights on a timer switch for you, if you like.
6 If I _____ the ladder in the garden that day, the burglar _____ to climb into the top window which was open.
7 When you _____ a swipe card, the risk of non-authorised people entering the premises _____ reduced.
8 I know you'll ignore me, but I _____ much happier if you _____ a personal alarm when you're on your way home late at night.

Alternatives to *if*

2 Choose the correct answers.
1 It's illegal to tap someone else's phone calls *providing / unless* it is done for reasons of national security.
2 Smoke alarms are great inventions *but for / as long as* you don't burn a lot of toast!
3 Calls to businesses may be monitored *suppose / provided* that you are informed.
4 I am going to install a spam filter on the computer *if / whether* you want me to or not!
5 *Should / Were* we have a break-in, I'd get CCTV cameras put in.
6 I would have lost all my data *were it / whether or not* for Dave's help.
7 I don't open messages from unknown senders, *otherwise / supposing* I might have got a virus.
8 I'd feel happier about leaving the house empty *had / suppose* I remembered to ask a neighbour to pop in from time to time.

3 Find and correct the mistakes in some of the sentences. Tick (✓) the ones that are correct.
1 I'll help you providing that I have time.
2 If it were up to me, I had a smaller car.
3 Should you deciding to come, we'd be happy to put you up.
4 We'd be sitting on the beach by now if you were better at reading maps!
5 I'll go instead unless you don't want to.
6 If you can't understand it, I'm sure I won't be able to.
7 I can come as long that you can drive me back before noon.
8 Should you need anything, please don't hesitate to contact me.

Mixed conditionals

4 Rewrite the sentences using mixed conditionals. Begin with *If*.
1 Sam doesn't know how to encrypt the data, so our business information was hacked.
   _____
2 I can't get on with my work because I left my laptop on the train.
   _____
3 Because people are generally very honest, my phone was returned.
   _____
4 I've lost my credit card, so I won't be able to come shopping with you.
   _____
5 There are CCTV cameras outside the station, so they saw the man that stole my bike.
   _____
6 She got away with it because she knows influential people.
   _____
7 I know a computer expert, which is why I was able to sort out the problem.
   _____
8 He isn't aware of how thorough airport security is, so he didn't allow enough time to catch the flight.
   _____

Use of English   (Paper 1 Part 3)

Word formation

1 Read the title of the text. What is internet fraud? What type of advice do you expect to read?

2 Read the whole text quickly to get the general meaning.

3 Read the text again carefully and think about the form of the word needed to fit in each gap.

4 Do the task.

5 Read through the text again, with your answers in place. Does it make complete sense?

*For questions **1–8**, read the text below. Use the word given in capitals at the end of some of the lines to form a word that fits in the gap **in the same line**. There is an example at the beginning (**0**).*

How to avoid internet fraud

Because the internet allows us to make (0) _payments_ online, criminals are always on the lookout for opportunities to cash in. For example, it's by no means (1) _____ for a buyer to provide credit card details to a seller who actually has nothing to sell and whose website (2) _____ overnight. Needless to say, the criminal then makes (3) _____ use of the card details. That's why before buying anything, it is (4) _____ to do a bit of background research to make sure the site is (5) _____ and well-established. It's a good idea to check out any feedback from previous clients and you should only use sites that offer what's called a secure (6) _____ to collect your card details. A padlock symbol somewhere on the browser should help to put your mind at rest. The internet is also full of get-rich-quick schemes. Companies with (7) _____ websites may offer fantastic returns if you invest your money with them. Beware of these and be (8) _____ ; if something sounds too good to be true, then it probably is.

PAY

USUAL

APPEAR
LEGAL

ADVICE
REPUTE

ACTION

IMPRESS

REAL

Writing (Paper 2 Part 1: Essay)

➤ CB pp. 84–85, EW pp. 191–192

EXPERT STRATEGY
· Structure your essay carefully, to include an introduction, two main paragraphs and a conclusion.
· Include evidence to back up your main points.

Analysing the task

1   Read the task and mark the main points. Then read the opinions, which may give you ideas for what you might write in your essay.

> *Your class has attended a lecture on how schools could be more eco-friendly. You have made the notes below.*
>
> Making schools eco-friendly
> · transport to school
> · energy conservation
> · recycling
>
> Some opinions expressed in the discussion:
> 'If more children would walk or cycle to school, it would cut down on air pollution.'
> 'We should not sell any food or drink if the packaging can't be used again.'
> 'Classrooms are usually overheated in the winter.'
>
> *Write an essay for your head teacher discussing **two** of the suggestions in the notes. You should **explain which suggestion is better** and **give reasons** in support of your answer. You may, if you wish, make use of the opinions expressed in the discussion, but you should use your own words as far as possible.*
> *Write your **essay** in 220–260 words.*

Writing an introduction

2   Read two opening paragraphs for the essay. Which one is more appropriate? Think about which one:
   1 uses impersonal language?
   2 is more general?
   3 leads on well to the next paragraph?

A
> There is little doubt that we should be doing everything we can to help our planet survive. And where better to start than in our schools, with the young people who will be living in the environment of the future?

B
> I think that helping to save the environment is one of the most important things we can do. We should all be doing everything we can because if we don't, there will be no planet left for our children in the future. So let's look at some of the things we can do.

Structuring paragraphs

3   Read the main body of a student's essay and answer the questions.
   1 Which two notes has the student chosen to write about?
   2 What is the main point made about each of the notes? What is the supporting evidence?
   3 What drawbacks to these suggestions are mentioned?

> It is undeniable that more could be done to cut down on the amount of energy used during school hours. The heating is turned up far too high and there is no flexibility for it to be switched off or down. There is something seriously wrong when students are in shirtsleeves in mid-winter. In addition, parts of the school not used so often could be heated less, although this is only an issue during winter.
> Even more crucial than this, however, is the need to restrict the amount of cars which currently clog the surrounding area. At the very least, engines could be turned off whilst people are waiting, to avoid toxic emissions. If we had a safe bicycle park, more people might cycle to school. However, many parents are worried about the busy roads. And whilst walking is beneficial for the health as well as for the environment, some people live too far away. Despite this, what they could do is to make every effort to share lifts or get a bus.

Using appropriate language

4   Find examples of the following in the essay.
   1 complex vocabulary
   2 impersonal style
   3 linking words and phrases
   4 complex sentences

Writing a conclusion

5   Read two conclusions for the essay. Which one is more appropriate? Why?

A
> So, as I said before, it's obvious, really, that we need to ban cars and make students walk or bike to school so that we don't destroy the environment.

B
> To sum up, I would argue that pressure needs to be put on students and parents to get to and from school in a more ecologically responsible way. Cutting down on fossil fuels as well as air pollution makes this change the most immediately important.

Writing task

6   Now do the task in Exercise 1.

Vocabulary development 1

> **CB** p. 90

Communicating: phrasal verbs

1 Replace the words in bold with the word(s) in brackets and the correct form of a verb from the box. Make any other changes necessary.

bring   get (x3)   speak   talk (x2)   try

1 I **persuaded Andy not to lend** Lucy his car. (out of)
2 The boss did a good job **communicating** the importance of the changes to the staff. (over)
3 I'm not brilliant at French but I can **manage in most situations**. (by)
4 Let's **discuss** it this evening before making a final decision. (over)
5 When I go to Poland, I enjoy **having a go at using** the phrases I've learnt. (out)
6 I tried to **explain** to her how serious the situation was but didn't seem to be able to make her understand. (through)
7 At the meeting, I **mentioned** the subject of the pay rise. (up)
8 I couldn't hear a word at the back, so I asked Andrea to **raise her voice**. (up)

Expressions with *speak*, *talk* and *say*

2 Choose the correct answers.

1 I really dislike standing around making small *speak / talk* to people at parties.
2 It goes without *saying / speaking* that I will do anything I can to help.
3 Everybody *talks / speaks* very highly of that new teacher.
4 Liz can usually be relied on to *say / speak* her mind.
5 I still haven't finished decorating, needless to *say / talk*.
6 I haven't a clue what she's *speaking / talking* about. Have you?
7 She didn't *talk / say* a word about what had happened.
8 Could you phone Miranda? We're not really on *talking / speaking* terms at the moment.

Informal expressions: speaking and understanding

3 Match the sentence halves.

1 I can't make head   _____
2 I can never get a word   _____
3 I think Becky got the wrong end _____
4 You took the words right   _____
5 My brother and sister are always having a go _____
6 I think you've missed   _____

a at each other about money.
b of the stick about the arrangements because she's not arrived yet.
c or tail of these instructions. Can you?
d the point of why we're going.
e out of my mouth – that's what I was about to suggest.
f in edgeways when Mandy's around.

Communication

4 Complete the text with words from the box.

*achieve   building   effectively   engaged   express
familiar   means   stand*

Types of motivation for language learning

Instrumental motivation

Learning a foreign language is often a **(1)** _____ to an end. People often study a language in order to **(2)** _____ another goal, such as getting into college or getting a better job. They may enjoy the learning process or eventually become **(3)** _____ in the target culture, but their main motivation is *instrumental*: a language can help them to fulfil a college language requirement or **(4)** _____ out in a tough job market.

Integrative motivation

For some learners, the main motivation for studying a language is the desire to understand a culture and society better and **(5)** _____ themselves in the target language. For them, the language is a tool for **(6)** _____ relationships and communicating **(7)** _____ , for example with a friend or family member who speaks the language.

Studies have shown that integratively motivated learners are often more successful and that lack of interest in the target culture may make the learning process more difficult. It is thought that a desire to become **(8)** _____ with the culture and society in which a language is used makes learning it much easier.

Use of English (Paper 1 Part 1)

Multiple-choice cloze

1 Look at the title of the text. What sort of benefits do you expect to read about?

2 Read the text quickly to see if you were correct.

3 Read the text again carefully and think about the type of word that will fit in each gap. Can you predict the answer without looking at the options?

4 Do the task.

5 Read through the text again, with your answers in place. Does it make complete sense?

HELP

➤ **Q2** You need to choose the option that makes a phrasal verb with *for*.
➤ **Q3** You need the word that means 'increases'.
➤ **Q8** Only one of these words can be followed by *at*.

EXPERT LANGUAGE

Find two examples of prefixes that indicate number in the text.

For questions 1–8, read the text below and decide which answer (A, B, C or D) best fits each gap. There is an example at the beginning (0).

The benefits of bilingualism

Physiological studies have found that speaking two or more languages is a **(0)** _A_ asset to the cognitive process. The brains of bilingual people operate differently to those of **(1)** _____ language speakers, and these differences offer several mental benefits.

Speaking a foreign language is thought to improve the functionality of the brain because it **(2)** _____ for both recognition of and communication in different language systems. This then **(3)** _____ an individual's ability to negotiate meaning in other problem-solving tasks as well. Indeed, students who study foreign languages **(4)** _____ a tendency to do better than their monolingual **(5)** _____ in tests of maths too. Rather like a muscle, the brain **(6)** _____ well to being used. Learning a language involves memorising rules and vocabulary and this helps to improve other **(7)** _____ of memory, which explains why multiple language speakers are often better at remembering names or shopping lists. Finally, given that multilingual people are **(8)** _____ at switching between two systems of speech, writing and structure, they also make good multi-taskers in a variety of other contexts.

0	A great	B deep	C wide	D heavy
1	A solitary	B lone	C sole	D single
2	A forces	B calls	C demands	D requires
3	A lifts	B pumps	C boosts	D pushes
4	A have	B bring	C get	D make
5	A equals	B peers	C matches	D fellows
6	A replies	B answers	C responds	D accepts
7	A aspects	B items	C objects	D angles
8	A accustomed	B capable	C adapted	D skilled

Language development 1

➤ **CB** p. 93

Spelling rules

1 Complete the sentences with the correct form of the words in brackets.

1 Jess is quite tidy but her brother is even _____ (tidy).
2 There have been quite a few _____ (crash) on this road recently.
3 Have you _____ (lay) the table for dinner yet?
4 She noticed there were a lot of _____ (mosquito) around.
5 Isn't that the same college your sister once _____ (study) at?
6 He smiled _____ (cheerful) when he saw me.
7 She's a very _____ (rely) worker.
8 The city gets _____ (visit) from all over the world.

Words that are difficult to spell

2 Find and correct 12 spelling mistakes in the email extracts.

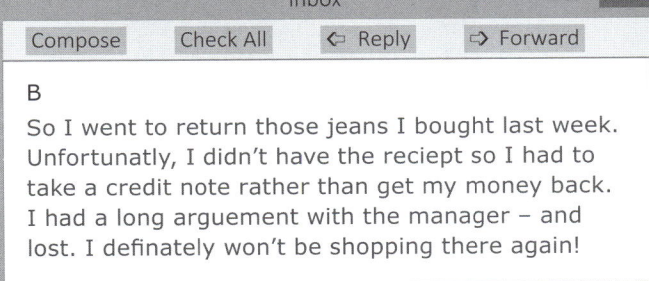

Inbox

Compose | Check All | ⇦ Reply | ⇨ Forward

A

I've finally made the desicion to join the liesure centre and enrol for the gym because I am worried about my lack of fitness. Of course, there is no garantee I'll get healthier but at my age it's neccesary to do something because I love deserts and want to carry on eating them without feeling too guilty!

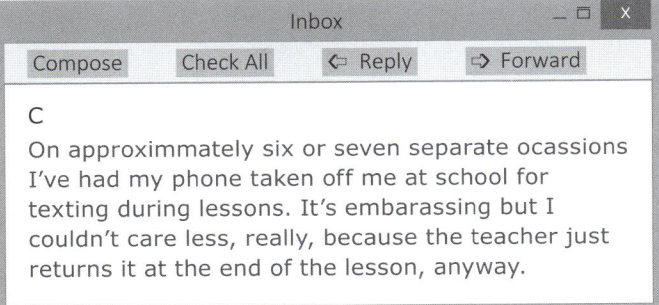

Inbox

Compose | Check All | ⇦ Reply | ⇨ Forward

B

So I went to return those jeans I bought last week. Unfortunatly, I didn't have the reciept so I had to take a credit note rather than get my money back. I had a long arguement with the manager – and lost. I definately won't be shopping there again!

Inbox

Compose | Check All | ⇦ Reply | ⇨ Forward

C

On approximmately six or seven separate ocassions I've had my phone taken off me at school for texting during lessons. It's embarassing but I couldn't care less, really, because the teacher just returns it at the end of the lesson, anyway.

Words that are easily confused

3 Choose the correct answers.

1 I'm positive that my team won't *lose / loose* again this week.
2 I don't think I'll come – I'm *quiet / quite* tired.
3 How does the news *effect / affect* our chances?
4 I think we just have to *except / accept* the decision.
5 I'm sure you'll get better at this – it'll just take a bit more *practise / practice*.
6 Can you *insure / ensure* that the delivery will arrive on time?
7 That was a complete *waste / waist* of time.
8 Are we *aloud / allowed* to cross here?
9 I'm going *weather / whether* you want me to or not.
10 I *past / passed* him on the street.

Hyphens

4 Add hyphens where necessary. Tick (✓) the correct sentences.

1 He had to have a three hour operation the other day.
2 James is quite a thoughtful person at times.
3 His son is brown eyed and dark haired.
4 That's my ex girlfriend over there.
5 He's out of work at the moment.
6 Do you get on well with your coworkers?
7 There are over 400 Indo European languages.
8 I think you should follow up your phone call with an email.
9 Have you been to that new department store?
10 The hotel had a 15 metre pool, a gym and a children's play area.

Use of English   (Paper 1 Part 2)

Open cloze

1 Read the title of the text and think about what you are going to read.

2 Read the whole text quickly to get the general meaning.

3 Read the text again carefully and think about the type of word that will fit in each gap.

4 Do the task.

5 Read through the text again, with your answers in place. Does it make complete sense?

HELP
➤ Q2 You need a relative pronoun here.
➤ Q4 Which preposition indicates change from one thing to another?
➤ Q5 Read ahead in the sentence to find the word this gap connects to.

EXPERT LANGUAGE

Find an example of the future in the past in the text.

*For questions 1–8, read the text below and think of the word which best fits each gap. Use only **one** word in each gap. There is an example at the beginning (0).*

The first emailer

One evening in 1971, **(0)** _when_ Raymond S Tomlinson was working late in a laboratory in Massachusetts, he witnessed a fridge-sized computer receiving a line of text he had typed into a similarly bulky machine positioned a metre away. He can't remember **(1)** _____ the message was, nor the exact date on **(2)** _____ it was sent, but the 29-year-old had just sent the first ever email.

Tomlinson designed his programme **(3)** _____ a tool for users to communicate on Arpanet, the US military network that 20 years later was to evolve **(4)** _____ the internet. The email address he created for himself, *Tomlinson@bbn-tenexa*, incorporated his name, the operating system, his location and the 'at' sign, which was recently deemed **(5)** _____ iconic of the computer age that it was acquired by New York's Museum of Modern Art. **(6)** _____ to Tomlinson, he chose it because it was the only preposition on the keyboard.

What's **(7)** _____ , email wasn't Tomlinson's only contribution to the history of electronic communication. He went **(8)** _____ to help develop global positioning systems, supercomputers and video conferencing software.

Listening (Paper 3 Part 1)

Multiple choice

1 Read the instructions and the context sentences in the task and answer the questions.

1 How many extracts are you going to hear?
2 What is each extract about?

2 Now read the context sentence and questions for Extract One. How much do you find out about the topic and the speakers?

3 🎧 07 Do the task.

EXPERT STRATEGY

Remember that you will often be listening for the opinions of the speakers, not just facts about the topic.

HELP

➤ Q1 Listen to the end of the man's turn to find the answer.
➤ Q2 Listen for what she says about her school.
➤ Q3 Be careful: the answer comes before you hear the word *faculty*.

EXPERT LANGUAGE

Which question is about the opinions of both speakers?

EXPERT WORD CHECK

*best of breed   democratise
demystify   ethos   full immersion
lingua franca   overwhelming   relic
skill set   software applications*

You will hear three different extracts. For questions 1–6, choose the answer (A, B or C) which fits best according to what you hear. There are two questions for each extract.

Extract One

You hear two language teachers talking about language learning.

1 What does the man appreciate most about his current job?
   A He gets the chance to use his full range of languages.
   B He's been able to change the way that languages are taught.
   C He finds the approach to language learning matches his own.

2 What does the woman suggest about her experience of learning English?
   A It made her doubt the wisdom of one particular method.
   B It made her determined to become a linguist.
   C It made her a more independent person.

Extract Two

You hear two academics discussing the issue of university courses in other European countries being taught in English.

3 The woman feels that the demand for courses taught in English
   A is artificially created by the universities.
   B reflects the ambitions of the staff who teach on them.
   C results from a need to attract students from a wide range of countries.

4 How has the man's faculty sought to help international students?
   A by allowing them to make recordings of the teachers
   B by providing language support during tutorials
   C by making lectures available as podcasts

Extract Three

You hear part of a discussion programme about technology in the workplace.

5 What is the man doing?
   A arguing in favour of a rethink in attitudes
   B suggesting that traditional distinctions are becoming irrelevant
   C complaining that the needs of business are not being met by suppliers

6 The speakers agree that the pace of change is being driven by
   A the increasing demands being faced by workers.
   B the activities of certain leading software companies.
   C the development of more integrated operating systems.

Reading (Paper 1 Part 6)

Cross-text multiple matching

1 Read the title of the text, which is a film title. Have you seen the film? What was it about?

2 Read the task and mark which blogger is being referred to in each question. Then mark the key words in each question.

3 Read all the reviews quickly to understand what the bloggers are saying about the film.

4 Do the task.

EXPERT STRATEGY

Use a highlighter to mark up the references in the text relevant to each question. Use a different colour for each question.

HELP

➤ Q1 Look for an expression which means 'makes you think.'
➤ Q2 Find the word *repeatedly* in section B. Look for other ways of expressing this idea.
➤ Q4 Look for different words and expressions that refer to the end of the film.

EXPERT LANGUAGE

Find two examples of adverbs used to make adjectives stronger in review C.

EXPERT WORD CHECK

genre hype imagery instil nuances poignantly scrutiny sentimentality shortcomings

You are going to read four reviews by bloggers of a film called The Sixth Sense. For questions **1–4**, choose from the bloggers **A–D**. The bloggers may be chosen more than once.

Which blogger:

doesn't share Blogger A's view regarding the film's deeper meaning? `1`

expresses a different view to Blogger B regarding how worthwhile it is to watch the film more than once? `2`

shares Blogger C's view regarding the attention to detail in the film's storyline? `3`

has a different view from the others regarding the initial impact of the film's final scene? `4`

Vocabulary

5a Match 1–6 with (a–f) to make common expressions. Then find the expressions in the text.

1 ticks	a the tail
2 get under	b scrutiny
3 twist in	c the point
4 miss	d your skin
5 glued to	e the box
6 stands up to	f your seat

b Match the expressions in Exercise 6a with their meanings.

1 fulfils all the criteria _____
2 is correct in all its details _____
3 fail to recognise what is important _____
4 have an emotional effect on someone _____
5 a surprise ending _____
6 absorbed by a performance _____

The Sixth Sense

A On first seeing *The Sixth Sense* years ago, it exceeded my expectations in almost every respect. I believe that a great movie is one that helps the viewer perceive life and the world differently. *The Sixth Sense* is one of those
5 extraordinary movies which ticks that box for me. The ending came as such a bolt out of the blue on that first viewing that I felt compelled to rewind and watch it all through once more, in an effort to work out why I hadn't seen it coming. During that second viewing, I came
10 to it from a completely different perspective and yet my enjoyment was hardly diminished at all. Like many viewers, coming back to it years later, I've tried to detect shortcomings in the plot but failed to pinpoint any at all. What makes this film so wonderful to watch isn't simply
15 the acting, or the terror it instils, or even the plot itself; it's the way in which the director carefully crafts a tale that completely absorbs the viewer.

B *The Sixth Sense* enjoys being playful with our imagination. Having said that, I don't consider it heavily
20 philosophical or particularly thought-provoking. It's one that I've gone back to repeatedly, though, and it repays the effort because every time I watch it, I pick up on little nuances I haven't spotted before. It is a brilliant film, plain and simple. It is unique in that it relies on imagination and
25 psychology to scare you. The director did a fabulous job constructing the imagery of the film and I genuinely didn't suspect the final plot twist until it was revealed. *The Sixth Sense* goes in my book as the single greatest psychological horror film I've ever seen. It stands up
30 to the closest possible scrutiny. You won't find any inconsistencies in the way the story unfolds, no matter how many times you watch it.

C This is an incredibly powerful film, awash with emotion but never stooping to sentimentality. It really gets under
35 your skin and makes you reconsider your own existence in ways you'd never expect. This is the story of one frightened little boy that you'll never forget. All your worst childhood nightmares are here and then some. Still, to anyone who complains that they figured out the secret
40 halfway through, I have this to say: you may be smarter than me but that doesn't make this a bad movie. Suffice to say that for most of us the twist in the tale is just shockingly delightful. The force of the denouement is very much lost on a second viewing, of course, but it's
45 nonetheless intriguing trying to spot any clues planted along the way. Even if the idea of that doesn't enthral you, I'd say don't miss the chance to see this movie again, simply because it's an almost perfect example of its genre.

D There can be no denying that the unfolding of the plot
50 in *The Sixth Sense* is particularly clever but to my mind, the hype about the surprise ending actually distracts people's attention from the film's finer qualities. I have some sympathy when people say that a plot twist doesn't make a film but surely, they are missing the point about
55 this one. The director's skill here is the way he both keeps you glued to your seat and makes you reflect on some eternal questions. Maybe I read too much into this very wonderful film but few touch on these subjects so poignantly and so well. Coming back to this film after so
60 many years, I can see that it has been widely imitated and that lessens the impact. For that reason alone, you might prefer to resist the temptation to sit through it again.

Module 6
A sixth sense

Vocabulary development 2

➤ **CB** pp. 96–97

Emotional reactions: idiomatic expressions

1 Complete the sentences with prepositions from the box.

down	in (x3)	off	on	out	over

1 When I heard about my son's new job, I was _____ cloud nine.
2 We were _____ two minds about what to do next.
3 It was a beautiful day and we were _____ very high spirits.
4 You seem a little _____ of sorts today – are you OK?
5 He hardly spoke all evening – he was _____ such a rage.
6 My father went _____ the deep end when I told him about the accident.
7 He's always a bit _____ in the dumps on Mondays.
8 She was _____ the moon about the news.

Emotional reactions: collocations and everyday expressions

2 Choose the correct answer (A, B or C).

1 OK, I must try to _____ *my temper* and be polite.

   A keep   B maintain   C hold

2 He needs to _____ *himself together* and stay calm.

   A take   B pull   C throw

3 I'm afraid situations like that _____ *me mad.*

   A drive   B push   C turn

4 When the restaurant got the bill wrong, my mother _____ *a scene*, as usual.

   A did   B had   C made

5 My patience is _____ *thin* with my children at the moment.

   A wearing   B feeling   C going

6 Until my dog eventually turned up, I was _____ *myself with worry.*

   A over   B up   C beside

7 I felt so emotional that I _____ *into tears.*

   A burst   B fell   C spilled

8 I *was thrilled to* _____ with the news.

   A scraps   B bits   C slice

9 I _____ *into a rage* with the manager .

   A ran   B leapt   C flew

10 *It really gets on my* _____ when trains are cancelled for no apparent reason.

   A nerves   B mind   C brains

3 Match the expressions in *italics* in Exercise 2 with their meanings. Write the infinitive of the expressions.

1 cause a fuss   _____
2 make someone very, very angry   _____
3 be unable to control yourself because
  you are very angry, worried, etc.   _____
4 manage to control your anger   _____
5 be very, very excited   _____
6 suddenly become very angry   _____
7 start crying   _____
8 stop being emotional   _____
9 run out   _____
10 annoy someone   _____

4 Choose the correct answers.

1 If you are seething, you are *angry / disappointed.*
2 If something winds you up, it *annoys / worries* you.
3 If you are scared stiff, you are *livid / terrified.*
4 If you couldn't care less about something, you are *distracted / indifferent.*
5 If you well up, it's because you find something *moving / annoying.*
6 If you are sick and tired of something, you feel *ill / bored.*
7 If you are on edge, you are *angry / nervous.*
8 If you snap at someone, you *say / do* something angrily.

5 Complete the conversations with words or phrases from Exercise 4.

1

A: You look rather angry.
B: I'm absolutely (1) _____ with rage, actually.
A: What's (2) _____ you up so much?
B: Oh, I'm just (3) _____ of my boss.
A: Oh dear! I've never seen you so agitated.
B: It's true. I even (4) _____ at one of my colleagues earlier.
A: That's unlike you.

2

A: What's up?
B: I'm a bit on (5) _____ about this presentation I have to do.
A: Really? You said earlier that you couldn't (6) _____ less about it.
B: I think I was trying to convince myself.
A: Look, you're (7) _____ up just talking about it. You poor thing.
B: Yes, I'm actually (8) _____ stiff about it.

Language development 2

➤ **CB** p. 98, **EG** p. 182

Verb + -*ing* or infinitive with *to*?

1 Complete the text with the correct form of the verbs in brackets.

Are you a super-taster?

Do you avoid **(1)** _____ (eat) broccoli and other leafy vegetables because you find them too bitter? Do you struggle **(2)** _____ (finish) rich desserts or dislike **(3)** _____ (drink) coffee because you find it too bland? If so, you may be among the 25 percent of the population who sensory perception scientists refer to as super-tasters.

Superior sensitivity can actually be scientifically proved: the basic laboratory assessment involves **(4)** _____ (taste) a drug commonly known as PROP. If you find it very bitter, it means you're a super-taster. I volunteered **(5)** _____ (do) the test and found the drug very bitter. I also agreed **(6)** _____ (let) researchers **(7)** _____ (try) another test on me, which meant **(8)** _____ (count) the number of fungiform papillae (which house your taste receptors) on your tongue. Over 30 means you're a super-taster, and I got 35.

Many chefs are super-tasters, but if you are considering **(9)** _____ (become) a chef, you're advised **(10)** _____ (not bother). Apparently, being a super-taster is as much a disadvantage as an advantage.

Verb + object + infinitive/-*ing*

2 Complete the sentences using the words in brackets. Add pronouns where necessary.

1 They missed the last bus but their parents arranged for _____ (a taxi / bring / home).
2 My father is ratty with my sister for scratching his car when he told _____ (not / drive).
3 I've been waiting for my friends for ages. I was expecting _____ (arrive / an hour ago).
4 I really wanted to see that band but my parents _____ (not let / go).
5 The sun was really hot – I could feel _____ (burn / the back of my neck).
6 I'm not sure about those chillis. My friends warned _____ (not eat).
7 She didn't want to go hang-gliding but her boyfriend made _____ (do).
8 We looked everywhere for my earring and eventually found _____ (lie / in the long grass).

Verb + -*ing* form/infinitive with a change of meaning

3 Choose the correct answers.

1 I forgot *turning off / to turn off* the oven, so my pizza burned.
2 This time I remembered *to take / taking* my keys with me. Here they are!
3 I'm late home because I stopped *doing / to do* some shopping.
4 I stopped *to run / running* after I twisted my ankle.
5 I'll never forget *to meet / meeting* you all those years ago.
6 She went on *to be / being* the first woman to win the Booker Prize twice in a row.
7 I regret *informing / to inform* you that the train terminates at this stop.
8 I regret *leaving / to leave* school before doing my exams.
9 He went on *spending / to spend* money even when he knew he shouldn't.
10 We've decided to try *to live / living* in Spain for a while – we'll see how it goes.

4 Tick (✓) the correct sentences. Correct the mistakes in the wrong ones.

1 I'd better to get back to work soon or I'll be fired.
2 I meant buying you a present but it went out of my mind.
3 I remember putting the money in that drawer, so where is it?
4 They invited me joining their book group but I didn't fancy it.
5 Do you really think he'll keep to go for another eight kilometres?
6 I had a go at helping Jo doing her maths homework.
7 I tried to stop the protest but just couldn't manage it.
8 I've just noticed Mike do the gardening. That makes a change!

Use of English (Paper 1 Part 3)

Word formation

1 Read the title of the text. What is the sixth sense? Do you believe it exists?

2 Read the whole text quickly to get the general meaning.

3 Read the text again carefully and think about the form of the word needed to fit in each gap.

4 Do the task.

5 Read through the text again, with your answers in place. Does it make complete sense?

HELP

➤ Q2 You need a plural noun here.
➤ Q4 You need to add both a prefix and a suffix to this word.
➤ Q6 Add a suffix to create a word that means 'many more times'.

EXPERT LANGUAGE

Find one example of each of the following in the text:
1 a phrasal verb
2 a verb + preposition collocation

For questions 1–8, read the text below. Use the word given in capitals at the end of some of the lines to form a word that fits in the gap in the same line. There is an example at the beginning (0).

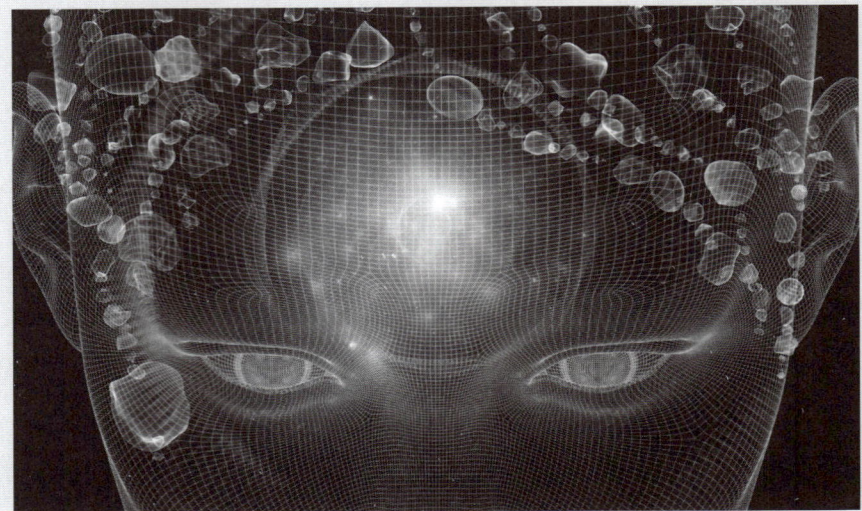

Do you have a sixth sense?

If you've ever felt that someone was watching you, it might not have been just your **(0)** imagination .   IMAGINE
Scientists have found evidence to suggest that people do experience a prickling **(1)** _____ when they are   SENSE
being watched.
A team of **(2)** _____ carried out two experiments   RESEARCH
and believe they have finally proved the **(3)** _____   EXIST
of a sixth sense. In one experiment, a volunteer in
a sealed room concentrated on making a second
volunteer outside the room feel **(4)** _____ or   COMFORT
relaxed, even though he was only visible via CCTV and
the second volunteer was **(5)** _____ of the CCTV   AWARENESS
connection. Electrodes then measured the 'prickle
effect' on the second volunteer's skin. The electronic
monitor proved **(6)** _____ that this 'direct mental   REPEAT
interaction' was possible.
Other scientists remain **(7)** _____ , however.   SCEPTIC
Professor Richard Wiseman of Hertfordshire University
said: 'The number of times you turn around and find
someone not looking at you far **(8)** _____ the   NUMBER
times when you do, but you only remember the times
you turned round to see someone looking.'

Writing (Paper 2 Part 1: Essay)

➤ **CB** p. 100, **EW** pp. 191–192

> **EXPERT STRATEGY**
>
> Make sure:
> - each paragraph develops coherently, using linking words.
> - the language is the appropriate level of formality.

Analysing the task

1   Read the task and mark the following:

    1 who you are writing for
    2 what you need to include.

> *Your class has attended a discussion on the impact of mobile phones on modern society. You have made the notes below.*
>
> **The impact of mobile phones on modern society**
> - communication
> - health and safety
> - language skills
>
> **Some opinions expressed in the discussion:**
>
> 'I think they're responsible for why people don't talk to each other as much as they did once.'
>
> 'It's made a huge difference to many people's lives, who can now get help when they need it.'
>
> 'People don't bother to spell properly any more.'
>
> *Write an essay for your tutor discussing **two** of the points in the notes. You should **explain which point you think is more important**, **giving reasons in support of your answer.** You may, if you wish, make use of the opinions expressed in the discussion, but you should use your own words as far as possible.*
> *Write your **essay** in **220–260** words.*

Structuring paragraphs

2a   Read some topic sentences a student wrote for the main body of their essay. Which of the three notes in the task is each sentence about?

    1 There has been a lot of publicity about how speaking on mobile phones for too long can be bad for you. For me, this argument is outweighed by the huge benefits that the elderly in particular have gained from using them.

    2 It is true that people use special text language, but it's not because they can't write well.

    3 I think that people actually get in touch with each other more than they used to, even if they might not actually speak.

b   Match the sentences in Exercise 2a with the opinions in the task. Does each sentence agree or disagree with the opinion?

c   Match the supporting points and examples (a–g) with the topic sentences (1–3) in Exercise 2a.

    a Keeping in contact is so much more convenient than it once was. _____

    b This is certainly true for the very young or old. _____

    c Many accidents are caused by people using their mobiles when they are driving. _____

    d It could be argued that this is quite a creative use of language. _____

    e It is invaluable for parents checking up on their young people. _____

    f Some linguists think it has helped young people to express themselves better. _____

    g People who are shy find this form of contact much easier. _____

3   Use these linking expressions to connect the topic sentences in Exercise 2a with the supporting points in Exercise 2c. More than one answer may be possible.

- Strangely enough / Surprisingly, …
- The reason for this is that / This is probably because …
- … particularly in the case of …
- In fact / After all, …
- For example, …
- In addition, …
- On the other hand / However / Despite this, …

Using appropriate language

4   Look at some ideas for each paragraph and choose the most appropriate phrase (A or B) from each pair.

Para 1: introduction
A It is often claimed that mobile phones have had a negative effect on …
B Lots of people reckon that mobiles have been a bad thing for …

Para 2
A Something that loads of people complain about is …
B One of the objections to the use of mobile phones is …

Para 3
A On the positive side, they are perceived as being …
B What people say they like about them is that they're …

Para 4: conclusion
A If pushed to make a choice, I'd come down on the side of mobile phones.
B On balance, I believe that the advantages of using mobile phones outweigh the disadvantages.

Writing task

5   Now do the task in Exercise 1.

Vocabulary development 1

> **CB** p. 106

Word formation

1 Complete the text with words formed from the words in brackets.

Some **(1)** _____ (psychology) believe that people's **(2)** _____ (behave) often changes when they return home to visit their parents. They might, for example, have a strong **(3)** _____ (react) to something that their parents say to them, however innocently the comment was intended. As a result, their attitude may be quite **(4)** _____ (defend) or even come across as open **(5)** _____ (defy). This can seem a rather **(6)** _____ (character) way for the person to behave and friends and relatives may be very surprised by the strength of their response. It often happens without any conscious **(7)** _____ (aware) on the person's part and in most cases the feelings they have are totally **(8)** _____ (relevance) to the present time. However, since the feelings probably link back to childhood **(9)** _____ (occur), knowing what triggers them may be able to free people from the **(10)** _____ (limit) imposed by the past.

Home and family: expressions and idioms

2 Complete the sentences with the correct form of the phrases in the box.

at home (x2)   come home (x2)   hit home
home from home   home in   out of house and home

1 When my friend made that comment about me, it really _____ because I knew it was true.
2 As soon as I'd unpacked all my belongings, I immediately felt _____ there.
3 The interviewer _____ on the fact that I'd left my previous job after only a few months.
4 I go on about switching lights off until the cows _____ but nobody takes any notice whatsoever.
5 I love having visitors but I spend my life refilling the fridge; they're eating me _____ .
6 They lost, although they were playing _____ .
7 When is it going to _____ to you that this relationship is over?
8 The hotel was a real _____ – we couldn't have felt more comfortable and relaxed.

Words that are easily confused

3 Choose the correct answers.

1 There are only a *restricted / limited* amount of tickets available for sale on the day.
2 After months of *intensive / intense* fighting, the two sides agreed to have talks.
3 Our opinions *differ / differentiate* in so many ways.
4 I'm amused by her *childlike / childish* enthusiasm.
5 There was a very strange *occurrence / incident* on the road on the way here.
6 The information is *offered / provided* in the brochure.
7 I agree with the *principal / principle* of wearing a uniform while on duty.
8 I think I'm going to *lay / lie* down before we go out.

Living at home

4 Complete the text with the correct form of the words and phrases in the box.

deposit   do your own thing   downside   likelihood
outbursts   pointless   regard   spark off   stone's throw
take for granted

The new family

Official figures show that the number of young adults living with their parents has risen by 25 percent in the last 20 years, mainly because of growing unemployment and rising house prices. So what are the pros and cons?

Tom, 22
'I did rent a flat for a bit, but you soon miss all the things you **(1)** _____ such as finding milk in the fridge and hot water for the showers. On the **(2)** _____ , though, it's quite hard to just **(3)** _____ as you can when you're independent. My parents get ratty when I leave lights on and so on – that usually **(4)** _____ a row.'

Tom's mother
'In many ways, it's lovely having him back. And it's a bit **(5)** _____ him paying a lot of money to rent a flat when we live only a **(6)** _____ away, and he could be saving up for a **(7)** _____ on a flat to buy. However, I do admit to having **(8)** _____ from time to time with him, mainly about things like using up all the hot water or not keeping the house tidy. I think he **(9)** _____ the place as his student house rather than our home. Although in all **(10)** _____ he'll be here for some time unless the economy picks up.'

Use of English (Paper 1 Part 1)

Multiple-choice cloze

1 Read the whole text quickly to get the general meaning.

2 Read the text again carefully and think about the type of word that will fit in each gap. Can you predict the answer without looking at the options?

3 Do the task.

4 Read through the text again, with your answers in place. Does it make complete sense?

HELP

➤ Q5 You need a word that means 'chance'.
➤ Q7 Read ahead in the sentence – you need to choose the option that makes the contrast.
➤ Q8 Only one of these verbs can be followed by the preposition *up*.

EXPERT LANGUAGE

Which three questions test phrasal verbs?

*For questions **1–8**, read the text below and decide which answer (**A, B, C** or **D**) best fits each gap. There is an example at the beginning (**0**).*

Should we stay at home?

Travel can yield many benefits. There is the challenge of having to (0) __A__ with novel and unexpected situations, learning about the world and (1) _____ to different customs. It is something that is meant to forge our character and make us more flexible individuals, confronting our prejudices along the way. Of course, travel isn't (2) _____ to do any such thing. It might, in reality, create expense and discomfort whilst merely reinforcing our existing (3) _____ of the world. What is meant to be quality time with the family can (4) _____ to be more stressful than life at home and instead of taking every (5) _____ to learn about local customs, we may end up hanging out with our compatriots.

Although there remains a lingering feeling that an unwillingness to travel might (6) _____ a lack of curiosity about the world, some people still feel that what drives their curiosity is closer to home. (7) _____ from being a problem, this can be an advantage if it means what thrills and stimulates them is cheaper and doesn't (8) _____ up the world's finite resources.

0	A deal	B survive	C manage	D face
1	A accommodating	B adapting	C familiarising	D accepting
2	A promised	B assured	C pledged	D guaranteed
3	A belief	B view	C sight	D thought
4	A turn out	B come about	C show up	D keep on
5	A convenience	B possibility	C opportunity	D prospect
6	A indicate	B hint	C point	D disclose
7	A Contrary	B Far	C Rather	D Despite
8	A waste	B exploit	C spoil	D use

Language development 1

➤ **CB** p. 109, **EG** p. 183

Cleft sentences: emphasis with *what*, *the thing*, *the reason*, *the place*, *all* ...

1 Complete the sentences with words and phrases from the box.

---
all   the job   the month   the one thing   the person
the place   the reason   what
---

1 _____ that used to drive me mad was his loud music.
2 _____ that we ask our son to pay us rent is because it teaches him to be responsible.
3 _____ we'll have to talk to about it is your uncle.
4 _____ I get most fed up with is shopping for food and ironing.
5 _____ we usually go off to when the kids are having friends round is the cinema.
6 _____ I ask in life is for my family to be happy and healthy.
7 _____ he'd love to apply for would involve moving to Australia.
8 _____ they're expecting to move out is March.

2 Rewrite the sentences.

1 I phoned Joe and then drove round to see him.
   What I did _____ .
2 The car in front of me stopped suddenly and I went into it.
   What happened _____ .
3 I'd really love to visit Venice one day.
   The place _____ .
4 We asked them to leave in the end because it was too much work for us.
   The reason _____ .
5 You'll find the most suitable university course for you is at York.
   The place _____ .
6 I'd really love to go hang-gliding just once in my life.
   What _____ .
7 She wishes she'd found a job nearer home.
   What she wishes she _____ .
8 My ambition has always been to work with endangered species.
   All _____ .

Emphasis with *it* + *be*

3 Complete the responses using *it* and the words in brackets.
   A: I heard you'd moved to the States.
   B: No, (1) _____ .
       (my brother / move / there)
   A: Didn't you use to play tennis with Lucy?
   B: No, (2) _____ .
       (squash / play / with her)
   A: And you must have left the company when I did, in 2005?
   B: No, (3) _____ .
       (not until 2009 / leave)
   A: I hear you and your wife met in New York.
   B: No, (4) _____ .
       (Philadelphia / meet)
   A: So, are you going to move back to Manchester?
   B: No, (5) _____ .
       (my parents / want / move back here)
   A: And will they move here straightaway?
   B: No, (6) _____ .
       (only by selling their other house / be able to / afford / move)

4 Rewrite the sentences so that the emphasis is on the information in *italics*.

1 We only realised she wasn't with us *when we were nearly home*.
   It was _____ .
2 *A friend of mine* suggested we called the police.
   It was _____ .
3 The council won't do anything about the roads *until the end of the year*.
   It won't be _____ .
4 I love lots of things about this country but the thing I love most is *the weather*.
   It's _____ .
5 I was finally able to hand in the work *on Wednesday*.
   It wasn't _____ .
6 *Until I saw her*, I didn't realise how bad she was.
   It was _____ .

Use of English (Paper 1 Part 2)

Open cloze

1 Read the title of the text and think about what you are going to read.

2 Read the whole text quickly to get the general meaning.

3 Read the text again carefully and think about the type of word that will fit in each gap.

4 Do the task.

5 Read through the text again, with your answers in place. Does it make complete sense?

HELP

➤ Q2 Which word completes this expression meaning 'like'?

➤ Q3 You need a quantifier here.

➤ Q5 Which modal verb fits best here?

EXPERT LANGUAGE

Find three compound nouns connected with education in the text.

*For questions **1–8**, read the text below and think of the word which best fits each gap. Use only **one** word in each gap. There is an example at the beginning (**0**).*

No place like home

In my first few weeks (**0**) _as_ a university student, living alone in a strange city, I horrified one new-found friend by saying I was 'going home', referring to the student residence in (**1**) _____ we were living. (**2**) _____ common with many of my classmates, she was going through the pain of homesickness and the institutional residence bore very (**3**) _____ resemblance to the home she was missing.

Meanwhile, on a nearby street, I spotted a sticker on the window of a VW camper van that read *Home is where you park it*. This minimalist slogan appealed to me, suggesting that grand mansions or chic apartments were all very well, but all you actually needed in (**4**) _____ to feel at home was a little van and the few possessions it (**5**) _____ accommodate. In some sense, home has always been somewhat portable for me. (**6**) _____ said that, it was only (**7**) _____ 20 years of adult life that I finally lived in a house that provided me (**8**) _____ anything like the warmth of my parental home.

Listening (Paper 3 Part 2)

Sentence completion

EXPERT STRATEGY

Remember that you won't hear exactly the same words and phrases as you read in the sentences – but you will hear the same ideas expressed in a different way.

HELP

➤ **Q2** Listen for a number and another word for *countries*.

➤ **Q4** Listen for what Ruby says is *the best policy*.

➤ **Q6** Ruby talks about three *safeguards*. Listen for the first one.

EXPERT LANGUAGE

Look back at the task. How did you know which answers were:
1 numbers?
2 nouns?

EXPERT WORD CHECK

age bracket   non-profit
off the beaten track
overstay your welcome   plus points
resource-sharing   safeguards
target user   vouch for

1 Read the instructions for the task. Who is going to be speaking? What will that person be speaking about?

2 Read the sentences in the task. How much do you find out about the topic?

3 Try to predict the type of information that you need to listen for in each gap.

4 🎧 08 Do the task.

You will hear a radio presenter called Ruby Eversden talking about an international hospitality network known as couchsurfing. For questions 1–8, complete the sentences with a word or short phrase.

Couchsurfing

Ruby explains that members do not have to have a(n) **(1)** _____ in order to offer accommodation.

There are couchsurfing members in as many as **(2)** _____ different countries.

Ruby uses the term **(3)** _____ to describe the wider category of activities that couchsurfing belongs to.

Ruby stresses the need for **(4)** _____ when creating a couchsurfing profile.

Groups of hosts can cooperate in producing something called a(n) **(5)** _____ for the website.

Ruby points out that new members have to provide **(6)** _____ before they are allowed to sign up.

Ruby recommends consulting what are known as **(7)** _____ before making arrangements with a member.

Ruby feels that **(8)** _____ is essential when you are a couchsurfing guest.

Vocabulary development 2

▶ **CB** p. 112

Travel

1 Complete the text with words from the box.

> challenge danger nowhere rough self-reliant
> spur stranded tricky

When I left university, I went backpacking around
South America for a year. My family and friends
thought I was mad because I wanted to do it on
my own and they said it would be fraught with
(1) _____ . But I wanted to be able to get right
away from everything I knew for a while.

I found myself in many **(2)** _____ situations. For
example, once when I was on the road in Brazil, a
long-distance bus I was on broke down in the middle of
(3) _____ and we were completely **(4)** _____
until it got fixed. We did all sleep **(5)** _____ that
night, but it was fine – we rose to the **(6)** _____
and survived to tell the tale!

The trip taught me many things. I became much
more **(7)** _____ and better at doing things on the
(8) _____ of the moment. And I made lots of
friends along the way.

Travel: collocations and phrasal verbs

2 Complete the sentences with the correct form of
the verbs in the box.

> blow face fend go pack run soak stem

1 Going on my travels was the first time I've really had
  to _____ *for myself*.
2 I was a bit nervous beforehand but that largely
  _____ *from* my lack of experience.
3 I knew I would _____ *the risk* of failing but
  that's all part and parcel of the experience.
4 I was _____ *away* by some of the places I
  visited.
5 I did have to _____ *up to* certain difficult
  situations.
6 I managed to _____ *in* a lot of activities in a
  short time.
7 Some things did _____ *wrong*.
8 I enjoyed having time to _____ *up* the
  atmosphere.

3 Look at your answers to Exercise 2 and match
the phrasal verbs and collocations (1–8) with their
meanings (a–h).

a do a lot in a limited time _____
b develop as a result of something _____
c very pleasantly surprised _____
d take responsibility for oneself _____
e have a bad outcome _____
f be in a situation where there's a possibility
   that something bad will happen _____
g enjoy something as much as possible _____
h accept and deal with something difficult _____

Travel and transport: idioms

4 Choose the correct answer (A, B or C).

1 If I were you, I wouldn't _____ all my boats
  just yet. You may want to come back.
  A abandon   B burn   C destroy
2 I'm a bit worried about Kay's daughter. She seems to
  be going off the _____ now she's left school.
  A rails   B track   C road
3 I wish I could say next term would be plain
  _____ but I think it's going to be even tougher.
  A sailing   B driving   C flying
4 I think we should _____ the boat out and have
  a lovely meal out tonight.
  A send   B sail   C push
5 Amanda likes to sail close to the _____ and
  hand her work in at the last moment.
  A shore   B wind   C coast
6 OK, shall we hit the _____ ? It's late.
  A path   B highway   C road
7 You were supposed to apply last month. I think
  you've missed the _____ .
  A train   B boat   C plane
8 She _____ off the handle and accused me of
  lying to her.
  A flew   B drove   C sailed

Reading (Paper 1 Part 7)

Gapped text

1 Read the title of the text and the introductory sentence. What do you think the text will be about?

2 Read the main text quickly and answer the questions.
1 How does the writer travel?
2 What do we learn about the place where he is staying?
3 Why is this place popular with celebrities?
4 Find the names of two aircraft.

3a Read the task and the paragraph before gap 1. What do you think the writer is waiting for? What do you think the red dot is?

b Now read the paragraph after gap 1. What do you think *my taxi* refers to? Read the whole paragraph to be sure. Read the options and decide which fits in this gap. What tells you that each of the other options doesn't fit in this gap?

4 Do the rest of the task.

EXPERT STRATEGY

Underline the links as you choose an answer so that you can go back and double check. Keep reading all the options even if you think you've fitted one into an earlier gap. You may want to go back and change your mind.

HELP

➤ Q2 In the text before gap 2, John was frustrated. Which option includes something which changed that?

➤ Q3 The text before the gap talks about the land in the past. Which option contains a reference to what has happened to it more recently?

➤ D Look at the word *too* in the first line of this option. What is it referring to?

EXPERT LANGUAGE

Look back at the main text. Find sentences that begin with a time reference — a word or phrase related to time.

EXPERT WORD CHECK

aviator   featherweight   mossy ground
nimble   propeller   rendezvous
rock face   sandbars   skims low
soars upwards   stake a claim   veers

---

*You are going to read a newspaper article. Six paragraphs have been removed from the article. Choose from the paragraphs **A–G** the one which fits each gap (1–6). There is one extra paragraph which you do not need to use.*

A 'Hey, don't panic,' says Paul. 'We fly you to the top. Easy! From there, you hike for a couple of hours to the edge of the rock face, where we come and pick you up again, two by two. Deal?'

B It grows, its buzzing becoming audible as it veers left and right following the curves of the Chitina river, until, after several minutes, a shiny red De Havilland Otter swoops down and lands before me on the gravel.

C Meanwhile, other family members are cooking dinner, a large salmon caught locally by one of the team. As she chops vegetables from the garden, Ellie tells me that as well as flying planes here, her husband Ben is also a helicopter pilot.

D Planes are central to the activities on offer for guests too, providing an easy way to reach the best locations for walking, skiing, wildlife-spotting, sightseeing or simply having a picnic. There are five in all, ranging from the nine-seater Otter, to a three-seater Piper Super-cub that weighs less than 450 kg.

E Since then, five two-bedroom cabins accommodating a maximum of 12 guests have been constructed on it, and the whole family is involved with the business. Paul's daughters Ellie, Logan, son Jay and son-in-law Ben all work at the lodge. Like their grandfather, now retired and living in Anchorage, all are skilled bush pilots.

F Then he learnt to fly and found the doors to the wilderness suddenly thrown open. He continued teaching but used his spare time to explore by air, landing on plains and river sandbars where no one had touched down before.

G When he spots a good piece of grass, Paul circles and prepares to land the tiny aircraft. Then, after only a few bumpy metres on its gigantic rubber tyres, the plane comes to a halt. 'Out you get,' he says. 'I've got other guests to pick up!'

Flight-seeing in ALASKA

In the wilds of America's largest national park, the best way to get around is by plane.

My rendezvous with the wilderness is set for 6 p.m., on the edge of a remote Alaskan village with a population of just 150. 'Park alongside the log cabin and wait, but stay away from the stretch of ground beside the car
5 park,' were the instructions in the email. I've driven four hours from Anchorage to get to the village of Chitina and stand staring at the cloudy sky. In the distance, a red dot appears.

1

My taxi has arrived, with Paul Claus at the wheel –
10 aviator, adventurer and owner of Ultima Thule, a lodge 100 miles from the nearest road, where I am to stay for the next three days. We board the plane and leave civilisation far behind. Paul's father, John, was a teacher in Anchorage, eager to climb in the Alaskan mountains
15 but frustrated by how hard it was to access them.

2

John staked a claim to a patch of land beside the Chitina river, and was granted five acres, where he and his wife Eleanor set about building a modest wooden cabin and landing strip. Decades later, when the Wrangell-St Elias
20 National Park was established, the Claus family were allowed to keep their land, one of only a handful of private properties within a park the size of Switzerland.

3

When the lodge runs out of supplies, one of the family hops into a plane and flies out to get them. 'Lots of
25 celebrities like coming because they can be absolutely sure that no paparazzi can get up here,' says Paul, as the Otter passes miles of mountainous nowhere. He tells me about the time he took the actor Jim Carrey, a regular guest, on an emergency flight to carry diesel to
30 some stranded trekkers. 'I'll never forget their faces.'

4

'How do you fancy a hike up the mountain behind the lodge tomorrow, weather permitting?' asks Paul, over dinner on the first night. I look up at the peak apprehensively.

5

35 Flying in the Super-cub, as we do this time, turns out to be an experience in itself. It has no electric motor, so the propeller has to be manually spun to start it. Once airborne, the featherweight plane skims low across the river and then soars upwards, as nimble as
40 a buzzing bee.

6

While he flies off to fetch them, I stand waiting beside my guide, enjoying the silence. Around us there is nothing but wild Alaskan nature; snowy peaks and glaciers disappear into the far distance. We walk
45 for several hours over mossy ground, with no trees, occasionally snow, a few wild sheep and, according to the guide, a brown bear in the distance.

Language development 2

➤ **CB** p 114, **EG** p. 183

Past tenses for hypothetical meanings: *wish/if only*

1 Choose the correct answers.

1 I wish I *worked / would work* somewhere less stressful.
2 If only I *didn't eat / hadn't eaten* those prawns last night.
3 I wish I *would go / were going* to that gig with you.
4 If only you *had all stopped / would all stop* talking and get on with your work!
5 I wish the train *wouldn't / couldn't* always be late.
6 I wish my sister *didn't keep / wouldn't have kept* borrowing my make-up.
7 If only we *were having / had* the party today when it's so sunny, rather than tomorrow.
8 I wish he *left / had left* a message if he knew he was going to be late.

2 Write sentences using *I wish* or *If only*. More than one answer may be possible.

1 I'd love to go backpacking round the world, but I can't afford it.
I wish _____ .
2 The builders have turned up the radio really loud and it's distracting me from my work.
If only _____ .
3 Unfortunately, I haven't got my purse with me, which is a nuisance.
I wish _____ .
4 I'd prefer to be taller than I am.
I wish _____ .
5 I regret giving up maths at the first opportunity.
If only _____ .
6 It's a pity I didn't see that documentary.
I wish _____ .
7 My only criticism of him is that he leaves wet towels everywhere.
If only _____ .
8 Sometimes I regret having a dog because I can't go away for long.
I sometimes wish _____ .

Other expressions

3 Complete the sentences with the correct form of the verbs in the box.

be	*cry*	*give*	*leave*	*not criticise*	*see*	*start*	*stop*

1 I'd much rather you _____ me a chance to explain before losing your temper like that.
2 It's about time you _____ to fend for yourselves a bit more at your age.
3 I'd much prefer it if the teacher _____ us all the time – she's never happy with anything we do!
4 Supposing we _____ for lunch early, how would that sound?
5 He looked as if he _____ . His eyes were red.
6 What if we just _____ our jobs? It would be great to disappear for a while!
7 I'd sooner you _____ the film than me. You've wanted to see it for ages.
8 Ken kept staring at me, as though I _____ a complete stranger.

4 Rewrite the sentences using the words in brackets. More than one answer may be possible.

1 I've only been here for six months but it feels like years.
(as if)
_____
2 I'm thinking about inviting your ex-girlfriend. How would you feel about it?
(suppose)
_____
3 Please don't ask me to drive all that way!
(rather)
_____
4 We really should leave now – it's after midnight.
(time)
_____
5 Why didn't you ask me for directions rather than getting lost?
(sooner)
_____
6 It would be lovely to stay in a hotel for once.
(prefer it)
_____
7 We could call in and apologise to her – what do you think?
(what if)
_____
8 Sometimes you behave in the same way as an old man would.
(as though)
_____

Use of English (Paper 1 Part 4)

Key word transformations

1   Read the instructions for the task and look at the example. Think about how the two sentences are different and notice how the meaning hasn't changed.

2   Do the task.

HELP
> ➤ Q1   You need to use the verb *decided*.
> ➤ Q2   You need to use the causative here.
> ➤ Q4   You need to use the key word twice in your answer.

EXPERT LANGUAGE

Look back at the questions. How many test conditional structures?

*For questions **1–10**, complete the second sentence so that it has a similar meaning to the first sentence, using the word given. **Do not change the word given**. You must use between **three** and **six** words, including the word given. Here is an example (**0**).*

0   Drew is not happy with my decision.
    APPROVE
    Drew _does not approve of_ my decision.

1   Jonas regrets his decision to live in a student residence.
    WISHES
    Jonas _____ to live in a student residence.

2   A local company cuts the grass while the family are away on holiday.
    GETS
    The family _____ a local company when they are away on holiday.

3   Frances had absolutely no idea that her brother had decided to leave home.
    ABACK
    Frances was _____ her brother's decision to leave home.

4   Only students with a valid ID card are allowed to use the library.
    AS
    Students may use the library _____ possession of a valid ID card.

5   If the weather doesn't improve, the building is unlikely to be completed on time.
    LITTLE
    Unless _____ chance of the building being completed on time.

6   If any delegates require parking, they should contact the conference organiser.
    TOUCH
    Any delegates _____ with the conference organiser.

7   If I could choose, I'd much rather travel by train than by air.
    FAR
    Given _____ travel by train than by air.

8   Sandra appears to be enjoying her first term at university.
    AS
    It looks _____ her first term at university.

9   Glen thought that it would be better if Clare knew as little as possible.
    LESS
    Glen thought that _____ , the better.

10 In the end, Graeme spent a lot of money on taxi fares.
    UP
    Graeme _____ deal of money on taxi fares.

Writing (Paper 2 Part 2: Letter)

➤ **CB** pp. 116–117, **EW** p. 195

Analysing the task

1 Read the task and answer the questions.
  1 Who are you writing to?
  2 What style of language will you use?

You work for an overseas voluntary organisation and have been asked to write to the prinicipals of secondary schools and universities to inform them about your programme and encourage young people to volunteer. Your letter should:

  • *summarise the type of work available*
  • *say what, if any, experience is needed to do the work*
  • *outline the benefits for participants.*

*Write your **letter** in 220–260 words.*

Choosing what to include

2 Look at the notes and decide which of the information is not relevant to the task.

  1 participants must pay own flights
  2 skills sometimes needed (e.g. to teach languages or sports); not always necessary, and training available
  3 voluntary work useful for CV/university applications
  4 accommodation usually shared rooms, basic
  5 variety of opportunities include teaching, healthcare, childcare, community projects, conservation
  6 programme helps personal development (independence, teamwork, confidence)

Topic sentences

3 Read a student's answer and complete it with these topic sentences. Ignore the words in *italics* at this stage.
  a For some placements – for example, in the field of medicine or construction – a degree or a particular skill set may be necessary.
  b Volunteering will change a student's life. Moreover, it helps the average job-seeker or university applicant to stand out from the crowd.
  c There are a wide range of opportunities, the most common of which are teaching and education, healthcare, animals and natural resources, conservation and the environment, community and social development.

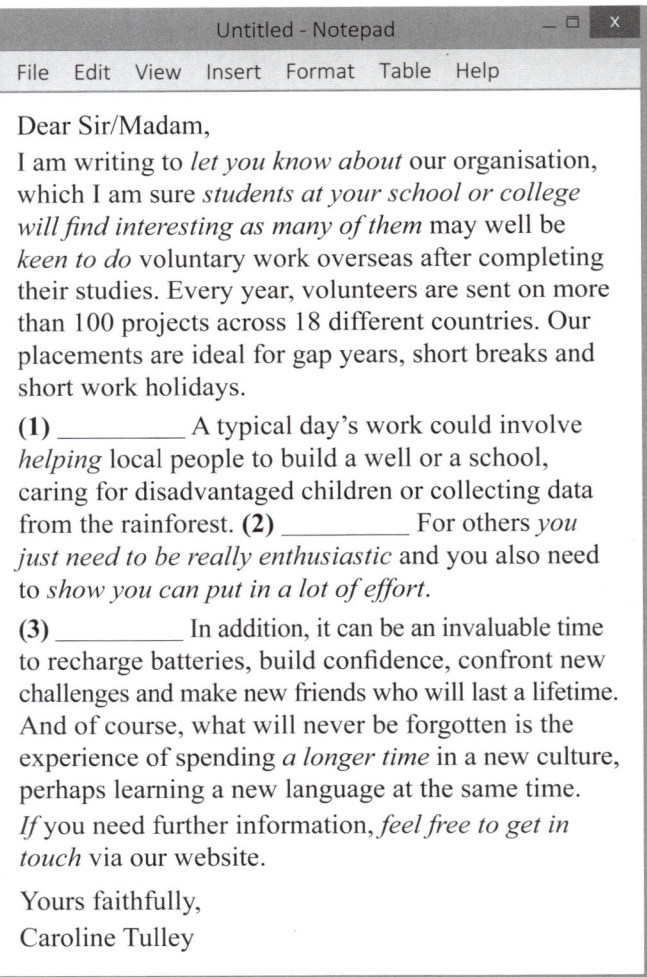

Dear Sir/Madam,

I am writing to *let you know about* our organisation, which I am sure *students at your school or college will find interesting as many of them* may well be *keen to do* voluntary work overseas after completing their studies. Every year, volunteers are sent on more than 100 projects across 18 different countries. Our placements are ideal for gap years, short breaks and short work holidays.

(1) _____ A typical day's work could involve *helping* local people to build a well or a school, caring for disadvantaged children or collecting data from the rainforest. **(2)** _____ For others *you just need to be really enthusiastic* and you also need to *show you can put in a lot of effort*.

(3) _____ In addition, it can be an invaluable time to recharge batteries, build confidence, confront new challenges and make new friends who will last a lifetime. And of course, what will never be forgotten is the experience of spending *a longer time* in a new culture, perhaps learning a new language at the same time. *If* you need further information, *feel free to get in touch* via our website.

Yours faithfully,
Caroline Tulley

Using appropriate language

4 Replace the phrases in *italics* in the letter with these more formal ones.
  1 demonstrate a capacity for hard work
  2 many of whom
  3 do not hesitate to contact us
  4 is likely to be of interest to students at your school or college
  5 interested in taking part in
  6 should
  7 assisting
  8 make you aware of
  9 little more than a high level of commitment is required
  10 an extended period

Features of good writing

5 Find an example of the following structures in the letter.
  1 impersonal/passive forms
  2 emphasis/hypothesis
  3 relative clauses
  4 formal linking expressions

Writing task

6 Now do the task in Exercise 1.

Vocabulary development 1

➤ CB p. 122

Business: phrasal verbs

1 Complete the sentences with the correct form of a verb from A and a preposition from B.

A	B
lay start take (x2) turn wind	down off (x2) out over up

1 As soon as Marco left school, he _____ his own stationery business.
2 Unfortunately, although he struggled for several years, the business never really _____ .
3 Eventually, he had to _____ some of his staff.
4 However, he then met someone who wanted to _____ his own business _____ so that he could retire.
5 He asked Marco if he would like to _____ it _____ as a going concern.
6 The gamble _____ very well and he's now a successful businessman.

Verb + noun collocations

2 Complete the sentences with the correct form of the verbs in the box.

do   give   make (x2)   play   run   take (x2)

1 After being made redundant, Anna decided to _____ a gamble and set up on her own.
2 She had never dreamed of _____ a company before.
3 However, she decided to _____ it a try.
4 At first, the company didn't _____ any profit.
5 However, she preferred to _____ it safe rather than _____ any risks.
6 It's now _____ very well indeed, and _____ a lot of money.

Business: prepositions

3 Choose the correct answers.

1 I've always wanted to go *in / into* business with Ben.
2 We've just embarked *in / on* a new project together.
3 Tony has gone away *on / in* business, I'm afraid.
4 That's none *of / on* your business.
5 That firm has gone *out / down* of business.
6 We're working very hard to stay *with / in* business.

Compounds

4 Choose the correct answer (A, B or C).

1 The _____ of the big retail firm caused shockwaves.
   A take-up   B takeover   C takeout
2 The _____ from my customers was very positive.
   A comeback   B talkback   C feedback
3 My _____ last year was more than I'd hoped for.
   A turnover   B turn-out   C turnround
4 We were obviously affected by the _____ in the economy.
   A downfall   B downturn   C downgrade
5 I've got a really heavy _____ at the moment.
   A workload   B jobload   C taskload
6 It's really important for a business to have a _____ of contacts.
   A groupwork   B teamwork   C network

Business

5 Complete the text with words from the box.

balance   disaster   disillusioned   entrepreneurs   let lucrative   running   sailing   service   stumbled

Do you have what it takes to be an entrepreneur?

Every year in the UK, more than half a million people start up a business. Some are clearly natural **(1)** _____ who have come up with or **(2)** _____ across a fantastic idea they turn into a successful new product or a(n) **(3)** _____ they can sell. Some are looking for greater flexibility or a better work-life **(4)** _____ . It can end up being **(5)** _____ if you are fortunate, but there are no guarantees and it rarely turns out to be plain **(6)** _____ . Some ideas are a recipe for **(7)** _____ and never really get up and **(8)** _____ . Some businesspeople go from strength to strength: far more will eventually get **(9)** _____ and have to **(10)** _____ their dream go.

Use of English   (Paper 1 Part 1)

Multiple-choice cloze

1   Read the whole text quickly to get the general meaning.

2   Read the text again carefully and think about the type of word that will fit in each gap. Can you predict the answer without looking at the options?

3   Do the task.

4   Read through the text again, with your answers in place. Does it make complete sense?

HELP

➤ **Q2** Which word completes this idiomatic expression with *hands*?

➤ **Q5** You need to make a phrasal verb that means 'becomes extinct'.

➤ **Q6** Read the two sentences before the gapped one. You need to make a contrast with them.

EXPERT LANGUAGE

Find two examples of the future in the past in the text.

---

*For questions **1–8**, read the text below and decide which answer (**A**, **B**, **C** or **D**) best fits each gap. There is an example at the beginning (**0**).*

The demise of the bookstore

As I was leaving the vast New York bookstore, feelings of guilt **(0)** __A__ in. I'd spent 45 minutes inside, treading the thick green carpets, **(1)** _____ the wooden shelves but, as usual, I'd left empty-handed. The only money to **(2)** _____ hands was in the store's coffee shop, where I'd **(3)** _____ through a biography which I'd be downloading later. I'd even taken a **(4)** _____ photo of the cover with my smartphone, to ensure I located the correct edition online.
For me, a visit to a good bookstore has long been one of life's great pleasures and I'm desolate at the thought that they might be **(5)** _____ out. Should more be done to save them?
(6) _____ , did I want the inconvenience of lugging the heavy tome around with me all day? The sad fact is that in the age of the digital download, the bookstore is no longer a **(7)** _____ business model – its fate sealed long ago, when the first Kindle **(8)** _____ on to the market and consigned it to history.

0	A kicked	B jumped	C popped	D slipped
1	A seeking	B glancing	C leafing	D browsing
2	A move	B change	C swap	D join
3	A skimmed	B glimpsed	C scrolled	D gazed
4	A surreptitious	B disguised	C hidden	D secluded
5	A ceasing	B closing	C dying	D expiring
6	A What's more	B Indeed	C There again	D Consequently
7	A loyal	B virtuous	C sincere	D viable
8	A appeared	B came	C released	D brought

Language development 1

➤ **CB** p. 125, **EG** pp. 184–185

Emphasis using negative introductory expressions

1 Tick (✓) the correct sentences. Correct the mistakes in the wrong ones.

1 Under any circumstances could I ever run a company.

2 Rarely has a business of this kind taken off so quickly.

3 After only borrowing from my family was I able to achieve my dreams.

4 Under no circumstances I ever want to work that hard again!

5 Not since was I a child had I been so afraid of something.

6 Never will I see such a fantastic place again.

7 Hardly had he taken his coat off when the phone went.

8 At no time you must never touch that switch.

2 Rewrite the sentences in Exercise 1 in a non-emphatic way.

1 _____
2 _____
3 _____
4 _____
5 _____
6 _____
7 _____
8 _____

3 Rewrite the sentences beginning with the words in brackets.

1 You must never try to launch a business without doing market research. (Under no circumstances)
_____

2 I would never have given up my day job before being sure that the business would make money. (Never)
_____

3 Investors won't be interested in putting money into the business until they've seen a detailed business plan. (Not until)
_____

4 You shouldn't assume that you will be given a loan from the bank. (At no time)
_____

5 My website was only just up and running when enquiries came flooding in. (Barely)
_____

6 I have hardly ever felt more relieved than when I began to make some money. (Rarely)
_____

4 Rewrite the sentences beginning with a word or phrase from the box.

---
little   no sooner   not only   on no account   only after
only now   rarely   under no circumstances
---

1 You should never have signed that contract.
_____

2 I didn't realise how difficult the process would be.
_____

3 I will have to write a business plan and talk to the bank as well.
_____

4 He'd already set off for the airport when he remembered he'd left his passport behind.
_____

5 I'd only just arrived at the park with the dog when it started to rain.
_____

6 We hardly ever eat out in places like this.
_____

7 You mustn't open the door while we're out, whatever happens.
_____

8 We are only just ready to leave.
_____

Emphasis through fronting parts of the sentence

5 Rewrite the sentences beginning with the words in bold.

1 The film has been **so popular** that we're going to have a repeat showing.
_____

2 The scenery is **even more impressive than the wildlife**.
_____

3 The sun came **out**, just in time for the picnic.
_____

4 It may be **lovely**, but it's also very expensive.
_____

5 James drove **up**, just as we were about to leave.
_____

6 He was **annoyed** but he finished the talk.
_____

7 Her confidence in her ability was **such** that we were all amazed.
_____

8 An old man in a dark coat was **outside the hotel**.
_____

Use of English (Paper 1 Part 3)

Word formation

1 Read the title of the text and think about what you are going to read.

2 Read the whole text quickly to get the general meaning.

3 Read the text again carefully and think about how to change the word that will fit in each gap.

4 Do the task.

5 Read through the text again, with your answers in place. Does it make complete sense?

HELP

➤ Q1 Add a suffix and check the spelling carefully.
➤ Q2 Add a prefix and a suffix to change this word into an adjective.
➤ Q4 Add a suffix and check whether you need a singular or a plural word here.

EXPERT LANGUAGE

Find three examples of compound adjectives in the text.

*For questions **1–8**, read the text below. Use the word given in capitals at the end of some of the lines to form a word that fits in the gap **in the same line**. There is an example at the beginning (0).*

The origin of plastic payment cards

In 1954, Stanley Dashew's company was facing serious
(0) _financial_ difficulties. With a large tax bill to pay   FINANCE
and a **(1)** _____ demanding immediate payment,   SUPPLY
it looked **(2)** _____ to meet its next payroll.   LIKE
However, not only did the California-based Dashew
Business Machines survive its cash-flow crisis, it went
on to bring the world one of the banking sector's most
(3) _____ successful innovations: the embossed   ENDURE
plastic card.
In those days, most everyday consumer **(4)** _____   TRANSACT
were settled in cash, whilst larger payments involved
the use of handwritten cheques. Although charge
cards were already in **(5)** _____ , these were   EXIST
paper-based, and so **(6)** _____ torn or defaced.   EASY
At the time, Dashew Business Machines was making
data-imprinting equipment for the US government
and Stanley saw a possible new **(7)** _____ of the   APPLY
existing technology. He developed a machine that could
emboss a plastic bank card with the account holder's
name and other details, a technological **(8)** _____   BREAK
which was to lead directly to the development of the
world's first credit card.

Listening (Paper 3 Part 4)

Multiple matching

1 Read the instructions for the tasks. How many extracts are you going to hear? What are the speakers going to talk about?

2a Look at Task One. What are you listening for? Mark the key words in the options and think about them in relation to the task.

b Now look at Task Two. What are you listening for? Mark the key words in the options and think about them in relation to the task.

3 🎧 09 Do the tasks. Remember that you must choose one option from each task for each speaker.

You will hear five short extracts in which businesspeople are talking about running a retail shop.

TASK ONE	TASK TWO
*For questions **1–5**, choose from the list (**A–H**) each speaker's main reason for starting a business.*	*For questions **6–10**, choose from the list (**A–H**) how each speaker feels about the business now.*

While you listen, you must complete both tasks.

A the encouragement of friends	A disappointed with performance so far
B a family tradition	B cautious about the future
C having some funds to invest Speaker 1 [1]	C unwilling to accept defeat Speaker 1 [6]
D having a product to promote Speaker 2 [2]	D frustrated by the attitude of suppliers Speaker 2 [7]
E a wish to change career Speaker 3 [3]	Speaker 3 [8]
F a dislike of being an employee Speaker 4 [4]	E keen to learn from mistakes Speaker 4 [9]
G seeing others doing well Speaker 5 [5]	F surprised by how demanding the work is Speaker 5 [10]
H perceiving a gap in the market	G resentful of a competitor's strategies
	H grateful for support received

HELP
➤ **Q1** Listen to what the speaker says about his children – the answer comes soon afterwards.
➤ **Q2** Which option talks about receiving some money?
➤ **Q7** Listen to the end of Speaker 2 to get the answer.
➤ **Q8** Listen to what the speaker says about his former colleagues.

Reading   (Paper 1 Part 5)

Multiple choice

1 Read the title of the text and the introductory sentence. What do you think the text will be about? Can you predict the writer's attitude to the topic?

2 Read the text quickly to see if you were right.

3 Read question 1 and mark the key words. Then read the text carefully to find the section which contains the answer.

4 Choose the option that best answers the question according to the text.

5 Repeat the procedure for the other questions.

EXPERT STRATEGY

In this task, you need to distinguish between similar viewpoints or reasons in the options. Read the question and study the text to find your own answer before comparing the options.

HELP

➤ Q1   You need to read the whole paragraph to answer this question.
➤ Q2   Look at the end of the paragraph to find the answer.
➤ Q4   Look in the previous sentence to find the point of reference.

EXPERT LANGUAGE

Look back at the first paragraph. Find the words and phrases the writer uses to sequence the argument.

EXPERT WORD CHECK

aesthetically   *equilibrium*   *existential*
fleeting   *hedonic*   *homespun*
pedigree   *underpin*   *yin yang*

---

*You are going to read an article about the relationship between material possessions and happiness. For questions 1–6, choose the answer (**A, B, C** or **D**) which you think fits best according to the text.*

1   In the first paragraph, the writer is
   A   giving reasons why an accepted truth is so widely believed.
   B   exposing the weaknesses in a commonly held assumption.
   C   providing examples in support of her personal viewpoint.
   D   questioning the logic of a popularly accepted theory.

2   The writer gives the example of her smartphone to illustrate
   A   how difficult it would be to live without certain key possessions.
   B   how superficial is our feeling of attachment to pieces of technology.
   C   how quickly we become accustomed to the advantages of certain gadgets.
   D   how the usefulness of consumer goods affects our view of their lasting value.

3   In the third paragraph, the writer suggests that fear of losing certain material goods
   A   is a natural reaction to their intrinsic value.
   B   is a reflection of the cost of having to replace them.
   C   is a symptom of placing too much importance on them.
   D   is a logical response to our emotional attachment to them.

4   The word *it* in line 47 refers to
   A   an important change.
   B   an everyday object.
   C   a serious mistake.
   D   a strong feeling.

5   In the fourth paragraph, the writer quotes from Alexandre Dumas in order to
   A   provide a contrast to the ideas of Plato.
   B   show how mistaken her uncle's words were.
   C   demonstrate why a popular folk theory is misguided.
   D   clarify a point of view which she only partially agrees with.

6   In the final paragraph, the writer is encouraging us to
   A   guard against complacency in our attitudes to life.
   B   be prepared for both good times and hardships in life.
   C   strive to improve both our own lives and those of others.
   D   accept the positive contribution of consumer goods to our lives.

Is better off really better?

Do material possessions really make us happy?

It's a well-known fact that material possessions don't ultimately make us happy. There are a number of reasons for this. First of all, it is things such as connection with people and meaningful activity that make a big difference
5 to our well-being. Additionally, there are various factors that underpin the fleeting nature of the thrill that comes from getting the stuff we crave. One is that the acquisition of material goods is often quickly followed by anxiety about losing or damaging them; think of the
10 first scratch on a new car. Another is that if something makes you happy, more of it won't necessarily make you even happier. Then there is what's known as hedonic adaptation: the fact
15 that we simply get used to having the things that make us feel good and so stop noticing their beneficial impact.

That's all true. And yet, I've come to think that the issue is slightly more
20 nuanced. There seem to be certain things that continue to make a little bit of difference to daily life for a long time. In my case, the prime example is my smartphone, which never ceases to amaze me. I don't live in fear of losing or damaging it, nor have I stopped noticing its benefits.
25 One distinction that can be made is whether the item is functional and something we really grow to rely on, rather than just own. An expensive watch, for instance, wouldn't in itself necessarily make the same kind of difference. You only really get a thrill when it's new.

30 Another important point is whether we manage to keep material goods in perspective and avoid giving them more value than they deserve. Apart from the fact that they can often be replaced, we should aim to enjoy things in the genuine understanding that they will not last forever nor
35 will they give meaning to our life. If we do this, we may be able to avert excessive fear of losing them. It would be completely wrong to let our well-being hang on an electronic device or to think that it could bring about a deep existential
40 transformation. But there's nothing wrong with noticing and appreciating what it can do for us, practically and aesthetically.

And what is happiness, anyway? As my uncle always used to say, 'Laughing always
45 turns to crying.' He may not have known that his homespun wisdom had a classical pedigree. Plato thought that if we feel pleasure, we will inevitably feel a corresponding pain as we regain equilibrium; and if we feel pain, we will feel pleasure
50 when we are restored to normality. One popular folk theory to explain this, often dignified by references to Taoism, is that the yin of happiness requires the yang of misery. 'He who has felt the deepest grief is best able to experience supreme happiness,' as Alexandre
55 Dumas put it. From this principle many draw the same conclusion he did: that happiness and misery have a measure of relativity. 'There is neither happiness nor misery in the world; there is only
60 the comparison of one state with another.' There is some truth in this, but good and bad cannot be defined purely relative to expectation and experience. Many things or states
65 of affairs really are better or worse than others. Poverty, for example, is terrible, even when people around you are even poorer.

Nothing has the power of the first time, so as we get
70 used to good things, it is inevitable that many will have less impact. But familiarity need not make us lose sight of their real value. Remembering how lucky you are to eat well every day and how easily things could be different, for instance, can lead to more,
75 not less, satisfaction with life. The way to appreciate improvements in life is never to allow ourselves to get so used to them that they are no longer noticed.

Vocabulary development 2

➤ **CB** p. 128

Phrasal verbs: money

1 Match the sentence halves.

1 At the moment I'm **scraping** _____
2 I **got** totally **ripped** _____
3 I've just **taken** _____
4 Most of my money **is tied** _____
5 I've **put** some money _____
6 I managed to **beat** _____
7 If I **came** _____
8 I would **help** you _____

a **out** a subscription to that new nature magazine.
b **into** a fortune, I'd start a business.
c **by** on very little money as it's the end of term.
d **out** financially if I could, but I'm broke again.
e him **down** in the end but I had to haggle for ages.
f **off** at that new restaurant I went to last week.
g **up** in investments.
h **by** for an emergency.

2 Match the phrasal verbs in bold in Exercise 1 with their meanings.

1 be unavailable for anything else _____
2 save money to use later _____
3 have only just enough money to live on _____
4 persuade someone to reduce their price _____
5 be charged too much money _____
6 inherit _____
7 make a financial arrangement _____
8 give assistance _____

Prepositions

3 Complete the sentences with prepositions from the box.

beyond   by   for   in   into   of   on (x2)

1 Was there a discount or did you have to pay _____ full?
2 Most students at this college are _____ a grant.
3 Are you allowed to pay _____ card at that restaurant?
4 I've just paid my salary _____ my account.
5 Sarah is always short _____ money at this time of the month.
6 Unfortunately, this car is only _____ loan while mine's being repaired.
7 My friend is often hard-up because she tends to live _____ her means.
8 I think that trip is excellent value _____ money.

Collocations

4 Complete the sentences with words from the box.

bargain   cause   costs   deal   earth   even   regular   savings

1 He doesn't earn a fortune but he has a(n) _____ income.
2 We usually have to be careful what we spend at the end of the month but we usually manage to break _____ .
3 That handbag she bought cost the _____ even though it was in the sale.
4 In order to cut _____ , we're going to change our power supplier.
5 Tony got a good _____ at the currency exchange.
6 I love spotting a _____ and saving myself money.
7 I am happy to donate a monthly sum to a worthy _____ .
8 She'll never be well-off because she can't resist dipping into her _____ .

5 Choose the correct answers.

Tips for managing money

💬 **Sam:** If we're staying in, we sometimes get an Indian takeaway or something to **(1)** *share / divide*. If we go out for a drink, we usually just **(2)** *split / cut* the bill between us.

💬 **Emily:** When you go out to a restaurant or a club, you sometimes get special **(3)** *charges / rates* if you're a student, so look out for them. When I go out with a friend, I prefer to pay my own **(4)** *way / part*.

💬 **Vanessa:** When you rent a student flat, be careful there are no hidden **(5)** *additions / extras*. And it's generally better to pay **(6)** *upright / up front* than on credit, as long as you get a receipt.

💬 **Jesse:** I am much better at **(7)** *dealing / handling* money than I was at the beginning of term. My tip is to **(8)** *withdraw / extract* only a certain amount every week from the bank – then you know where you are.

Language development 2

➤ **CB** p. 130, **EG** p. 183

Modifying comparisons

1   Complete each gap with one word or phrase from A and one from B.

A	B
about considerably	as less more
nothing like slightly	the same

> **Is it cheaper to be a woman than a man?**
>
> You would expect that clothes for both sexes would cost **(1)** _____ if they're identical but although this is true in some shops, others charge men **(2)** _____ , which may seem unfair, given that their clothes often use more material. Only a tiny bit, true, but it's the principle that counts.
>
> However, women over the year do spend **(3)** _____ on clothes – nearly twice the amount, in fact. And predictably, men spend **(4)** _____ much on shoes as their wives or girlfriends do – again, around half the average sum.

A	B
a great deal	less more
easily somewhat	the biggest

> It seems that hairdressers charge **(5)** _____ for women's haircuts than men's – women are paying almost double, unless they know someone who will cut it at home. And of course, the cost of make-up means that women are **(6)** _____ spenders as regards spending on appearance. However, women do pay **(7)** _____ for the same brands of moisturiser, which many men have now started wearing.

A	B
anywhere near	as much likely
far more just	the same

> Women are **(8)** _____ to compare prices and wait before making a purchase, whereas men tend just to buy on impulse.
>
> But men don't donate **(9)** _____ to charity as women, who are very generous. Men and women spend **(10)** _____ on entertainment. There is very little difference.

Other ways of making comparisons

2   Tick (✓) the correct sentences. Correct the mistakes in the wrong ones.

1   It was too hot for us lying on the beach.
2   I'm getting more and more worried.
3   She works like a waitress at weekends.
4   It was so successful company that it expanded all over the world.
5   I'd prefer giving up the business than risk losing all our money.
6   The little you know, the better.
7   He'd sooner be unemployed than work with that company again.
8   I wasn't quick enough applying for the job.

3   Choose the correct answers.

Ways to make money from home

Rather than do extra hours at work in these difficult times, it makes **(1)** *a great deal / far more* sense to try and get something for nothing. For example, you could rent out your driveway for someone to park on during the day. **(2)** *By far / Considerably* the biggest demand is for parking near an airport, and if you act **(3)** *as / like* a taxi-driver and drop clients off at the airport, you would earn even more.

If that idea won't work, why not rent out a spare room? There are **(4)** *nowhere near / somewhat* enough affordable places to rent available for young people, who will be grateful just for a room. If you'd prefer **(5)** *to rent / rent* to an overseas student, you can improve your linguistic skills at the same time – many people find it **(6)** *such a / so* good experience and make so many new friends that they say they would do it without being paid.

If your house isn't big enough **(7)** *to accommodate / accommodating* somebody else, you could sell your good quality, rarely worn clothes online to make money. The more clothes you have, the **(8)** *fewer / less* you wear them, so clear some space and it will **(9)** *easily / decidedly* be the best decision you have made!

(10) *Slightly / Barely* more preparation is required to set up a car boot sale, but this way you can get rid of all the rubbish in your house. Give it a go and watch the money roll in!

Use of English (Paper 1 Part 4)

Key word transformations

1 Read the instructions for the task and look at the example. Think about how the two sentences are different and notice how the meaning hasn't changed.

2 Do the task.

*For questions 1–10, complete the second sentence so that it has a similar meaning to the first sentence, using the word given. **Do not change the word given.** You must use between **three** and **six** words, including the word given. Here is an example (0).*

0 Do you think you could help me lift the table?
HAND
Would you mind _giving me a hand_ to lift the table?

1 My brother managed to get a place at a prestigious business college.
SUCCEEDED
My brother _____ at a prestigious business college.

2 Despite the poor economic climate, the company increased its sales.
MANAGED
The company _____ spite of the poor economic climate.

3 Dan didn't realise he'd forgotten his passport until he arrived at the airport.
DID
Only when _____ Dan realise that he'd forgotten his passport.

4 Very few businesses are profitable in their first year.
MAKE
Hardly _____ in their first year.

5 Ken's family persuaded him to ask for a salary increase.
TALKED
Ken was _____ in salary by his family.

6 The end of the film was completely unpredictable.
COULD
Nobody _____ would end.

7 Very few club members bothered to attend the Annual General Meeting.
EFFORT
Hardly _____ to attend the Annual General Meeting.

8 A multinational corporation has recently acquired the local company.
OVER
The local company _____ by a multinational corporation.

9 Many fewer shoppers have been visiting the mall lately.
SHARP
There has been _____ number of shoppers visiting the mall lately.

10 Students may not use the staff entrance under any circumstances.
MAKE
Under _____ of the staff entrance.

Writing (Paper 2 Part 2: Review)

➤ CB p. 126, 132–133, **EW** p. 197

Planning your answer

1   Read the task and then look at two possible paragraph plans. Which one do you prefer? Why?

You see this advertisement on a college website.

> Have you recently seen the film version of a book you have read? Compare the film and the book, including your opinions on how the main characters are portrayed and say which you preferred.

*Write your **review** in 220–260 words.*

A

para 1: introduction
para 2: what you liked/disliked about the film
para 3: what you liked/disliked about the book
para 4: summary and recommendation

B

para 1: introduction
para 2: compare and contrast (e.g. story, structure)
para 3: compare and contrast (e.g. portrayal of characters)
para 4: summary and recommendation

Introduction and conclusion

2   Read a student's answer and choose the best sentence (A or B) to complete the introduction and conclusion. Give reasons for your choice.

1   introduction
   A The much-loved novel *One Day* was written by David Nicholls.
   B If you haven't read the runaway best-selling book *One Day*, you're in a minority!

2   conclusion
   A All in all, after all the hype, I thought it fell a bit flat and I certainly wouldn't rush out and see it.
   B The film is now available on DVD and well worth a watch.

One Day

(I) _____ Selling millions of copies worldwide, I thought it was somewhat overrated but there was still no question of me missing the film version when it came out.

What I found most original about the book was the way it was structured. Telling the story of the close friendship between Emma and Dexter, which started at university and continued over a period of 20 years, we learn about the relationship by reading about what happened one day every year in their lives. However, in my view, that doesn't really come across as well in the film, partly because it feels as if it is moving far too fast. After all, 20 years has to be crammed into two hours. Despite this, the screenplay keeps pretty much to the book and nothing too vital is left out.

Perhaps more important was the lack of chemistry between the two main characters in the film. I just didn't find Emma as convincing as in the book, and not just because of the dodgy Yorkshire accent. Oddly, though, it was Dexter who I didn't warm to in the novel, whereas I much preferred his character in the film; he came over as altogether more likeable. The rest of the cast were quite strong, too, particularly Rafe Spall, who added a touch of humour as Ian. And of course, the ending was just as heartbreaking as in the book.

(2) _____ However, if you haven't read it yet, you might like to give the novel a go.

Using appropriate language

3   Find examples in the review of language which:
   1 compares and contrasts.
   2 balances an opinion.
   3 expresses preferences.
   4 summarises.

4   Find examples of descriptive language in the review that match these meanings.
   1 not as good as it was said to be
   2 made to fit into something small
   3 not very good
   4 like
   5 a bit of fun
   6 very sad
   7 didn't work very well
   8 try

Writing task

5   Now do the task in Exercise 1.

9 The world of science

9A Personal challenges

Vocabulary development 1

➤ **CB** p. 138

Word formation: science

1 Complete the sentences with words formed from the words in brackets.

1 My son is hoping to study _____ (chemist) at university.
2 The _____ (invent) of the internet is still a relatively recent one.
3 I've always been interested in the idea of _____ (astronomy) research.
4 They've set off on an _____ (explore) trip into space.
5 To be a scientist, you need quite an _____ (analyse) brain.
6 I believe that _____ (engineer) is a very popular subject these days.
7 They have said that _____ (atmosphere) pressure is very high today.
8 Before our child was born, we went to speak to a _____ (genetics).

Expressions connected to space

2 Choose the correct answers.

1 I don't know why you're having so many problems with those instructions. Putting a blender together is not exactly *space / rocket* science!
2 My daughter sometimes looks at me as though I'm from another *planet / star*.
3 We only go to expensive restaurants once in a blue *sky / moon*.
4 Unless we book the flights soon, prices are going to *rocket / fly*.
5 I did study some physics once but that's many *suns / moons* ago.
6 I haven't slept well for a couple of days, so I'm feeling a bit *spaced / shuttled* out.

Ways of seeing

3 Complete the sentences with the correct form of the words in the box.

gaze   glance   glimpse   peer   sight   view

1 We should get a great _____ of the moon.
2 I know Liz by _____ but I've never met her.
3 She only got a quick _____ of the singer as he was rushed into the car.
4 Astonished, Tom just sat and _____ into space.
5 I could see her _____ at the menu, obviously unable to see it very well without her glasses.
6 I _____ at her quickly but she didn't meet my eyes.

Idioms with *like*

4 Match the sentence halves.

1 It's hard to tell her daughters apart. They're _____
2 Don't talk to Deb about her ex-husband. It's _____
3 I had nothing in common with anyone at the conference. I felt _____
4 The teacher stressed to him how important the homework was but it was _____
5 He never looks where he's going. He's _____
6 Jo is determined to get what he wants. He's _____

a like a bull in a china shop.
b like a dog with a bone.
c like a fish out of water.
d like a red rag to a bull.
e like two peas in a pod.
f like water off a duck's back.

Prepositional phrases

5 Choose the correct answers.

1 A small bright light appears low in the sky *at / from* time to time.
2 For a small handful of people, that dot *on / at* the horizon is a place called home.
3 The spacecraft flies *at / in* 17,500 mph.
4 If you are there for a week or two, you are *on / at* a high the whole time.
5 *On / In* time, people can perfect the skill of flying around the spacecraft.
6 The faces *from / on* the other side of the hatch are always pleased to see you.
7 *In / At* orbit, things are weightless.
8 *By / On* the downside, many astronauts lose their sense of smell and taste.

94

Use of English (Paper 1 Part 1)

Multiple-choice cloze

1 Read the whole text quickly to get the general meaning.

2 Read the text again carefully and think about the type of word that will fit in each gap. Can you predict the answer without looking at the options?

3 Do the task.

4 Read through the text again, with your answers in place. Does it make complete sense?

HELP

➤ Q2 You need a phrasal verb that means *happened*.

➤ Q3 Read the whole sentence carefully. Only one of these linking words fits grammatically.

➤ Q4 Only one of these words can be followed by *to*.

EXPERT LANGUAGE

Find an example of an auxiliary verb used for emphasis in the text.

For questions 1–8, read the text below and decide which answer (A, B, C or D) best fits each gap. There is an example at the beginning (0).

The search for extra-terrestrial intelligence

On a misty April morning in 1960, a young US astronomer called Frank Drake **(0)** _A_ a radio telescope at a nearby star. He was listening for signals from any alien civilisation that might inhabit its planetary system. On this occasion, Drake **(1)** _____ up a strong radio signal that he thought couldn't have come from a natural source. As it **(2)** _____ out, however, it actually emanated from a secret terrestrial source: a defence radar establishment.

(3) _____ this disappointment, Drake went on to develop a whole new area of research called astrobiology, **(4)** _____ to the task of finding alien intelligence. Since then, although the amount of data has expanded immensely, the story **(5)** _____ one of radio silence, punctuated by occasional **(6)** _____ alarms. Yet, as a crop of new books shows, this **(7)** _____ of research has never been more active. Evidence is **(8)** _____ that many stars in our galaxy have planets on which life might have originated, and advances in technology are making it easier to detect alien life if it does exist. So it could just be a matter of time before something is discovered.

0 A pointed	B steered	C posed	D shone
1 A spotted	B caught	C picked	D brought
2 A showed	B turned	C worked	D ended
3 A Whilst	B Albeit	C Although	D Despite
4 A devoted	B concentrated	C specialised	D focused
5 A persists	B continues	C remains	D keeps
6 A fake	B wrong	C mistaken	D false
7 A zone	B province	C scope	D field
8 A enlarging	B growing	C swelling	D expanding

Language development 1

➤ **CB** p. 141, **EG** p. 185

Review of reported speech

1 Report the direct speech.

1 'The world belongs to you.'
Frances's father told her _____ .

2 'I've always believed that nobody should have to clean houses.'
Frances said _____ .

3 'I'm going to build a house to help disabled people.'
Frances said _____ .

4 'The house took me 40 years to complete.'
Frances told us _____ .

5 'I have no idea what will eventually happen to the house.'
Frances said _____ .

6 'Would you like to come and see the house?'
Frances asked us _____ .

7 'Did you know I have been nominated as one of the US' top inventors?'
Frances asked us _____ .

8 'I might spend more time doing sculptures.'
Frances told us _____ .

Patterns after reporting verbs

2 Report the statements using the reporting verbs in the box.

accuse agree apologise invite offer regret remind suggest

1 'Remember you have to phone the bank today,' Jo told her husband.
Jo _____ .

2 'I'll get you a coffee,' my mother said.
My mother _____ .

3 'I wish we'd gone by train,' said my husband.
My husband _____ .

4 'Why don't we visit the Science Museum next week?' said my friend.
My friend _____ .

5 'You're always late,' my son told me.
My son _____ .

6 'You must come and stay with us next week,' they said to us.
They _____ .

7 'Yes, it's true that the presentation wasn't very interesting,' he said.
He _____ .

8 'I'm really sorry I forgot about the meeting yesterday,' I said.
I _____ .

3 Tick (✓) the correct sentences. Correct the mistakes in the wrong ones.

1 My friend blamed me for I lost her phone.
2 They refused to leave unless I went with them.
3 The assistant recommended me to buy the larger size.
4 I complained to the waiter about having to wait so long for my food.
5 He advised me to speak to my teacher.
6 Becky flatly denied to break the jug.
7 We insisted to see the manager.
8 They explained her how to get there.

Impersonal report structures

4 Report the statements using an impersonal structure. Begin with the words in brackets.

1 Many people expected that families would be going to the moon on holiday by now. (It)
_____

2 Some space travel companies have promised that by 2018, flights to space will be available for ordinary people. (It)
_____

3 There is a belief that some rich people have paid in excess of $20 million to go into space. (Some rich people)
_____

4 Some scientists have claimed that we may soon be able to go to within 100k of the moon. (It)
_____

5 I have read a report which says that classes in space tourism are taking place in the US and Japan. (Classes in space tourism)
_____

6 Some people have alleged that there is a waiting list of people wanting to make the first flight. (It)
_____

7 We know that some space tourists have also done research while they were there. (Some space tourists)
_____

8 Environmentalists claim that space tourism is sure to accelerate global warming. (It)
_____

Use of English (Paper 1 Part 3)

Word formation

1 Read the title of the text and think about what you are going to read.

2 Read the whole text quickly to get the general meaning.

3 Read the text again carefully and think about how to change the word that will fit in each gap.

4 Do the task.

5 Read through the text again, with your answers in place. Does it make complete sense?

HELP

➤ Q1 Add two suffixes to make this noun into an adverb.

➤ Q3 Read carefully to see whether this word should be singular or plural.

➤ Q4 Add both a prefix and a suffix to this word.

EXPERT LANGUAGE

Find an example of a passive infinitive in the text.

*For questions 1–8, read the text below. Use the word given in capitals at the end of some of the lines to form a word that fits in the gap **in the same line**. There is an example at the beginning (0).*

The colour of gold

It has long been possible to modify the **(0)** appearance of precious metals by adding a layer of another material, such as an alloy, to the surface. For example, what is known as 'rose gold' is **(1)** _____ made by adding copper. Nanotechnology **(2)** _____ at Southampton University have now discovered how to produce gold and silver in any colour you please, by making microscopic **(3)** _____ in the surface that affect the way the material reflects light.

(4) _____ , much of the allure of a material such as gold lies in its **(5)** _____ colouring, which has led people to ask what is to be gained by the newly discovered process. However, it seems there are quite a number of possible applications for the technique, where another colour would be **(6)** _____ . For example, you could add coloured branding to a piece of silver **(7)** _____ or design a gold watch face on which the hours are denoted in different colours. Another **(8)** _____ application might be security tagging because the modified surfaces would be extremely hard to forge.

APPEAR

TRADITION
RESEARCH

ALTER

DOUBT
DISTINCT

DESIRE

JEWEL

SIGNIFY

Listening (Paper 3 Part 2)

Sentence completion

HELP
➤ **Q1** You are listening for the exact place the gadget was fixed to.
➤ **Q3** Listen for the name that the manufacturers gave to this.
➤ **Q4** Listen for the expression *the last straw*. The answer comes soon afterwards.

1 Read the instructions for the task. What type of text are you going to hear? What will it be about?

2 Read the sentences in the task. How much do you find out about the topic?

3 Try to predict the type of information that you need to listen for in each gap.

4 🎧 10 Do the task.

*You will hear a radio report about the Knee Defender, a controversial gadget used by some airline passengers. For questions **1–8**, complete the sentences with a word or short phrase.*

The Knee Defender

The gadget was designed to be attached to a passenger's **(1)** _____ on certain planes.

Users pointed to the fact that the gadget was both **(2)** _____ and easy to use as key advantages.

The gadget was sold with what was called a **(3)** _____ to be given to the passenger in front.

Moves to ban the gadget arose after a flight was **(4)** _____ following a violent conflict between two passengers.

A total of **(5)** _____ airline passengers took part in an online survey about the gadget.

Some supporters of the gadget mentioned the need to do **(6)** _____ on long-haul flights.

Some opponents of the gadget felt that airlines should issue a **(7)** _____ about the use of the gadget.

The company has also developed a gadget called a **(8)** _____ , which passengers find useful during airport security procedures.

Vocabulary development 2

> **CB** p. 144

Expressions with *mind*

1 Complete the sentences with the correct form of the verbs in the box.

cross keep make put (x2) speak take wander

1 I should have phoned you. I'm so sorry – it never _____ *my mind* that you'd be worrying.
2 I'm going to go out – it'll _____ *my mind off* the news.
3 That woman appears to be able to _____ *her mind to* almost anything.
4 Jessica always _____ *her mind* at staff meetings. She's not afraid to say exactly what she thinks about the situation.
5 I wish you'd _____ *up your mind* – just choose one and let's go!
6 *My mind was* _____ – I couldn't concentrate.
7 You must _____ *it out of your mind* – it's no use worrying about something that might not happen.
8 I think we should _____ *an open mind* about the restructuring.

2 Match the expressions in Exercise 1 (1–8) with their meanings (a–h).
a say what you think   _____
b stop thinking about it   _____
c distract me   _____
d wait until you know the facts before making a decision _____
e occur to me   _____
f apply yourself   _____
g not pay attention   _____
h decide   _____

3 Match the sentence halves.
1 I was out of my mind with worry _____
2 It was a huge weight off my mind _____
3 I carried on going out but at the back of my mind _____
4 No one in their right mind   _____
5 My mind tends to go blank   _____
6 My car has a mind of its own; _____

a would do something so stupid.
b when I was told I'd been accepted.
c it sometimes refuses to start for no reason.
d when there was an earthquake in my daughter's town.
e whenever I am asked a question.
f I knew I should be doing more studying.

Remembering and forgetting

4a Complete the sentences with *recall*, *remind* or *memorise*.
1 I am trying to _____ these French verbs for my test.
2 Can you _____ me which episode we saw last time?
3 Do you _____ where she lives?

b Complete the sentences with *reminder*, *mind* or *memory*.
1 Did the reconstruction jog your _____ at all?
2 What I was just saying has completely slipped my _____ .
3 I'll keep that idea in _____ for next time.
4 That note will serve as a _____ for when you need to take your pills.
5 They say an elephant has a really long _____ , like you!
6 That day is etched in my _____ for ever.

Words connected to the mind or brain

5 Complete the text with words from the box.

able dense feet gifted half knowledgeable loss precocious uptake witted

Some of my old classmates were unforgettable. For example, I remember someone in my class called Fred. He was extremely quick-**(1)** _____ and made us all laugh a lot. He may not have been the most **(2)** _____ student but because he could think on his **(3)** _____ and was never at a **(4)** _____ for words, he would always do well. He was very popular.

Then there was Charlie. He was not always very quick on the **(5)** _____ with academic subjects and one or two unkind people called him **(6)** _____ . However, he was incredibly **(7)** _____ at sports and we all admired him.

Elena must have been a bit **(8)** _____ because she was much younger than the rest of us and yet very **(9)** _____ about all sorts of things. Some people said she was too clever by **(10)** _____ but I liked her.

Reading (Paper 1 Part 6)

Multiple matching

1 Read the title of the text and the introductory sentence. What are you going to read?

2 Read the task and mark the key words in each question.

3 Read all the sections quickly to get an idea of what the reviewers are saying about the book.

4 Do the task.

EXPERT STRATEGY

There will be some reference to the ideas in the questions in each of the sections. Underline these and keep reading them together with the question wording until you find the correct match.

HELP

➤ Q1 Look for one other reviewer who expresses the same idea as 'aren't worth the hassle' in C.

➤ Q3 Reviewer A says the ideas are not 'new and challenging'. Which other reviewer thinks they are unoriginal?

➤ Q4 Only one reviewer makes a positive comment about this.

EXPERT LANGUAGE

Find an example of a colon and a semicolon in the text. Why have these punctuation marks been used?

EXPERT WORD CHECK

*a drag   commonplace   dabbles
hassle   in triplicate   losing the thread
maxim   multitasking   take stock
well-worn   woefully*

*You are going to read four reviews of a book about how people organise their lives and possessions. For questions **1–4**, choose from the reviews **A–D**. The reviews may be chosen more than once.*

Which reviewer:

shares Reviewer C's view regarding the usefulness of complicated systems for storing things like those featured in the book? | 1 | |

holds a different view to Reviewer B regarding the extent to which the book makes the reader think? | 2 | |

holds a similar view to Reviewer A regarding the originality of some of Levitin's advice? | 3 | |

holds a different view to the others regarding how well the book is structured? | 4 | |

Vocabulary

5a Choose the correct answers. Then find the verbs in the text and check.

1 aspire *to do / on doing* something _____
2 expand *on / for* something _____
3 approve *to / of* something _____
4 engage *to / with* something _____
5 go about *doing / to do* something _____
6 jot something *over / down* _____

b Match the verbs in Exercise 5a (1–6) with their meanings (a–f).

a think that something is good, right or suitable
b become involved in and try to understand something
c want very much to do or achieve something
d write something quickly so that you remember it
e add more details or information to something you have already said
f begin to do or deal with something

c Complete the sentences with the correct form of the verbs in Exercise 5a.

1 His parents didn't _____ him leaving school but he did it anyway.
2 Hang on – let me _____ Jill's number so we can call her later.
3 How can we _____ solving this problem?
4 Could you _____ on your last point, please? I'm not sure I understand.
5 As a child, she _____ be a great artist — she would spend most of her time painting and drawing.
6 The book helped me to _____ the idea of taking responsibility for my own actions.

The Organized MIND

Four reviewers comment on Daniel Levitin's book.

A In his book *The Organized Mind*, Daniel Levitin's somewhat unfocussed discussion aspires to provide a comprehensive account of the way we think about organising everything that we regard as possessions, but I kept losing the thread of the argument. He
5 offers plenty of psychological detail to make us reflect in new and challenging ways about our mental categories, yet frequently dabbles in dispensing practical tips that couldn't be described as either new or challenging. Whilst agreeing with the maxim that everything should have a place and be put back in that place, Levitin
10 expands on that, seeming to approve of devising overly complex organisational systems for a complex world, even describing one in which letters are printed in triplicate to allow filing chronologically, according to topic and by correspondent. I would suggest we can do without most of our paperwork; even love letters become a drag
15 if you hoard every single one.

B Daniel Levitin's book *The Organized Mind* has both its strengths and weaknesses. There are tens of thousands of words on topics that are perfectly interesting in isolation, and yet they do not seem to fit together and you keep wondering where it's all leading. Levitin
20 is strongest when he's making us take stock of why we do what we do. Organising my study is a different problem to organising a library and Levitin forced me to engage with that truth. Where the book falls down, however, is in its desire to suggest intricate ways of organising things to its readers. Levitin's approach to computers
25 illustrates this. He makes the familiar argument that multitasking is a distracting problem, but he goes for a novel solution. He suggests buying several computers, each with a single purpose: one is for work, one for domestic tasks, one for social networking, etc. Whilst he's apologetic about the cost, one wonders if many people will try
30 out this simple fix.

C Daniel Levitin's book *The Organized Mind* is great on fact, but keeps returning to universal themes and ideas so that the reader begins to build up a clear picture of the issues. Along the way, we learn a great deal about different ways of organising
35 things, and some handy techniques are described in enough detail for you to adopt them if you wish. The book is a bit light on insight, however, and seems to miss the valid point that too much organisation is also a trap. Instead of getting rid of things we don't need, we buy more stuff in order to organise the stuff we
40 already have. Most of the complex filing solutions which Levitin advocates aren't worth the hassle. They are a poor fit for the rich mess that is reality.

D The challenge of 'getting organised' is both commonplace and oddly particular. How we go about organising our possessions
45 can be practical to the point of banality, but it can also be philosophically deep, something Levitin keeps reminding us of in his thought-provoking book *The Organized Mind*. Having said that, it is his desire to be comprehensive that weighs on the book. It is long and, while it does include a great deal to intrigue and
50 entertain, the rather random parade of disparate topics makes it less than the sum of its parts. Levitin offers sensible practical ideas, but these tend to be rather well-worn, such as: 'Why not carry a notebook to jot down ideas so that you don't forget them?' And when he admiringly describes the way that Joni Mitchell has
55 a customised drawer for Scotch Tape, another for masking tape, a third for string, we realise how woefully inadequate our own arrangements would seem to him.

Language development 2

> **CB** p 146, **EG** p. 186

Verbs + prepositions

1 Complete the text with prepositions from the box.

against at by for from (x2) of on (x5) to with

Men and women's brains: how are they different?

On the whole, scientists tend to agree **(1)** _____ each other **(2)** _____ the biological differences between men and women's brains. There is general consensus, for example, that connections are wired differently between and within each side of the brain.

However, what they can't always agree **(3)** _____ is the extent to which this might explain the differences in behaviour and skills which are often seen in men and women. Men often blame women **(4)** _____ their lack of spatial awareness and women accuse men **(5)** _____ not remembering faces or paying attention to detail. Perhaps we should blame it **(6)** _____ the way our brains are structured instead.

Some scientists, however, are keen to discourage people **(7)** _____ thinking that biology is the only answer. They object **(8)** _____ the emphasis being put on connections in the brain, believing that any differences which result **(9)** _____ this are tiny. For these scientists, behavioural differences are primarily influenced **(10)** _____ the different expectations of society, which is still based largely **(11)** _____ traditional stereotyping. For this reason, they advise parents **(12)** _____ giving dolls to girls, for example, as they may feel they have to keep **(13)** _____ taking up jobs in the caring professions, which are traditionally lower paid, instead of going for careers in areas more traditionally aimed **(14)** _____ boys, such as engineering or physics.

2 Choose the correct answers.

1 The success of the project depends on everyone *work / to work / working* together.
2 We insisted *on giving / giving / to give* him a lift home at the end of the evening.
3 When nobody took any notice of him, he resorted *to shouting / to shout / shouting* at them.
4 He couldn't prevent *that I go / me from going / me to go* on the trip.
5 We are relying on Anna *she reminds / to reminding / to remind* us.
6 My friends tried to discourage *me entering / me from entering / that I enter* the competition.

Adjectives + prepositions

3 Replace the words in bold with a preposition and an *-ing* form. Make any changes necessary.

1 Clare was really upset **not to get** an invitation to the wedding.
2 He phoned to say he was sorry **he had taken** my car without asking.
3 She had started to feel afraid **to go** out alone at night.
4 He's really excited **that he's won** the match.
5 I know she's really proud **that she came** first in the competition.
6 I hadn't done anything like it before, so I was really worried **I'd make** mistakes.
7 She was angry **that she had** to wait for an hour to see a doctor.
8 I was thankful **that I'd found** a place to stay.

Nouns + prepositions

4 Choose the correct answers.

1 The prospect *of / at* working overtime didn't fill me with great enthusiasm.
2 The delay *of / in* the arrival of the Madrid train was caused by a tree on the line.
3 I thought Guy's belief *in / with* human nature was really touching.
4 Their insistence *on / of* leaving early was really very unusual for them.
5 There is absolutely no point *of / in* worrying about it now.
6 I think our surprise *in / at* what they had achieved pleased them.
7 The effect *of / on* what had happened *on / in* the whole family was devastating.
8 I have recently developed a fascination *of / for* modern art.

Use of English   (Paper 1 Part 2)

Open cloze

1   Read the title of the text and think about what you're going to read.

2   Read the whole text quickly to get the general meaning.

3   Read the text again carefully and think about the type of word that will fit in each gap.

4   Do the task.

5   Read through the text again, with your answers in place. Does it make complete sense?

HELP
➤ Q1   You need a word that means 'having the ability or qualities for something'.
➤ Q5   You need a preposition to complete this multi-word verb.
➤ Q7   The word *unobtrusive* helps you to know what is needed here.

EXPERT LANGUAGE
Find an example of a compound adjective in the text.

*For questions **1–8**, read the text below and think of the word which best fits each gap. Use only **one** word in each gap. There is an example at the beginning (**0**).*

Clean jeans that wash away pollution

An unusual collaboration (**0**) _between_ chemists and fashion experts has produced pollution-busting clothes, which are (**1**) _____ of cleaning up urban air as people walk around. The researchers produced prototype jeans in (**2**) _____ the denim was laden with nanoparticles of titanium dioxide. These particles catalyse the destruction of nitrogen oxides, the main cause of low level urban pollution. The technology is not new, but the application is. Catalytic clothing, (**3**) _____ it's known, was first exhibited at science and fashion shows, with the particles sprayed onto the denim. In (**4**) _____ to bring the idea to a mass market, scientists came (**5**) _____ with a laundry additive to add the titanium in a domestic washing machine. This means that there's now a good chance of (**6**) _____ a real difference to air quality. Clothes need only be washed once with the laundry product because the unobtrusive nanoparticles grip tightly on to fabric fibres (**7**) _____ affecting the look or feel of the clothing. (**8**) _____ best suited to denim and other cottons, they also work with other materials.

Writing (Paper 2 Part 1: Essay)

➤ **CB** pp. 148–149, **EW** pp. 191–192

Structuring paragraphs

1a Read the task and three paragraphs from students' essays. Match each paragraph with one of the reasons for studying science given in the task. Ignore the words in *italics* in the paragraphs at this stage.

> *Your class has attended a discussion on the reasons for studying science at university. You have made the notes below.*
>
> Reasons for studying science at university
> * interesting and relevant
> * career prospects
> * importance to society
>
> Some opinions expressed in the discussion:
>
> 'These days scientists have a particularly vital role to play in society.'
>
> 'Science graduates find it easier to get high-paying jobs.'
>
> 'It is more fun to study subjects such as languages or the humanities.'
>
> *Write an essay for your tutor discussing **two of the reasons** in your notes. You should **explain which reason you think is more important**, **giving reasons** in support of your answer. You may, if you wish, make use of the opinions expressed in the discussion, but you should use your own words as far as possible. Write your **essay** in **220–260** words.*

A

(1) *Whilst / Because* science subjects have a reputation for being dry and specialised, this is not necessarily the case. (2) *Nevertheless / In fact,* the knowledge and skills acquired, (3) *such as / just like* problem solving, are fascinating and applicable to any profession, (4) *for example / not only* science-related jobs.

B

It is beyond doubt that there are many issues which need scientific input these days if our planet is to survive, (5) *due to / because* the ever-increasing demands we make on the world's resources. Future scientists will face huge challenges, (6) *whether / if* it is developing new communications systems (7) *and / or* contributing towards making the world a better place.

C

(8) *In addition / As well* to being highly employable, it has been shown that science graduates are more likely to achieve greater rewards in monetary terms. It is common knowledge that chemistry and physics graduates earn well above the average salary and (9) *what's more / although* that is not the only reason to study these subjects, it is without doubt a strong incentive. (10) *Consequently / Nevertheless,* one would expect science to gain in popularity.

b Now match each paragraph with one of the opinions in the task. Does each student agree or disagree with each opinion? Have they used the same wording/expressions as in the task?

2 Underline the topic sentence in each paragraph.

3 Choose the correct linking words or phrases in the paragraphs in Exercise 1.

Introduction

4 In the introduction, the language is usually impersonal. Rewrite these sentences to make them less personal.

1 People generally agree that science is a good subject to study at university.
Science _____ .
2 People used to feel that careers in science and maths would be more suitable for boys.
It used _____ .
3 Many schools have claimed that science is where the future is.
It _____ .
4 Students often assume that science is too difficult.
Science _____ .

Conclusion

5 Complete these concluding phrases with words from the box.

all	in	on (x2)	overall	up

1 To sum _____ , ...
2 _____ conclusion, ...
3 _____ the whole ...
4 _____ balance, I feel ...
5 _____ things considered, ...
6 _____ , I believe that ...

Writing task

6 Now do the task in Exercise 1.

Vocabulary development 1

> **CB** p.154

Word formation: fitness

1 Complete the text with words formed from the words in brackets.

A day in the life of a footballer

After getting up at about six, I do a bit of yoga, which is essential to **(1)** _____ (sure) my body is warm and flexible. My breakfast is usually the same: I **(2)** _____ (vary) have porridge with fruit. Then I drive to work, drinking the first of my five daily bottles of water on the way – it's really important to avoid **(3)** _____ (hydrate).
On the way to the football ground, I just switch off and listen to music. My **(4)** _____ (fit) programme begins as soon as I get to the ground. This will involve exercises to build up core **(5)** _____ (strong), as well as a lot of **(6)** _____ (resist) work in the gym, which focuses **(7)** _____ (specify) on different groups of muscles at a time. We then move on to football training. All of this work **(8)** _____ (able) us to have the stamina to go on and play matches without getting injured or exhausted. It's a huge **(9)** _____ (commit) but I love every minute.
At lunchtime I will eat protein such as chicken, lots of vegetables and some carbs – bread and potatoes – and will then have a rest. Sleep is very important with all the training we do. In fact, it is fairly **(10)** _____ (exception) if I go to bed later than 9.30. Not very glamorous, but it keeps me fit and well.

Verb + noun collocations

2 Complete the sentences with the correct form of the verbs in the box.

burn   catch   come   hold   make

1 Although sportspeople _____ a lot of calories, they still have to watch their diet.
2 Being an athlete involves _____ a lifelong commitment.
3 It must be hard to _____ to terms with injury when it means giving up your career.
4 Jessica Ennis _____ my attention at the 2012 Olympics. I hadn't heard of her before.
5 Usain Bolt currently _____ the record for the 100-metre sprint.

Prepositional phrases

3 Choose the correct answers.

1 Most sportspeople probably feel *in / under* pressure much of the time.
2 We have varied and interesting lives, but it's *at / in* the expense of our personal relationships.
3 In order to be *on / by* top form, we have to train every day.
4 We have a fitness coach who's *in / at* charge of our programmes.
5 *On / To* an extent, his reputation was based on his public image.
6 It's important to keep your emotions *at / in* check while performing.
7 *On / In* terms of nutrition, the important thing is a healthy diet.
8 It's important to be *with / in* good hands, so choose the best coach you can find.

Sport metaphors

4 Match the sentence halves.

1 Antonia is always on _____
2 I heard that your favourite sports player's in _____
3 Because they moved _____
4 As expected, Adam sailed _____
5 When he speaks to me, he tends to skate _____
6 You took the wind out of his _____
7 He made the decision on the spur of _____
8 We have all had to rein in _____

a the goalposts without informing me, I am behind with my work.
b the moment, taking us all by surprise.
c through the rugby trials with flying colours.
d the ball, so I let her deal with all the complaints at work.
e our spending habits during the recession.
f sails by accusing him outright like that.
g the running for another award this year.
h around the topics that he doesn't want to discuss.

Use of English (Paper 1 Part 1)

Multiple-choice cloze

1 Read the whole text quickly to get the general meaning.

2 Read the text again carefully and think about the type of word that will fit in each gap. Can you predict the answer without looking at the options?

3 Do the task.

4 Read through the text again, with your answers in place. Does it make complete sense?

HELP
➤ **Q1** You need a word that means 'official name'.
➤ **Q2** You need to create a phrasal verb with *up*.
➤ **Q3** Only one of these words can be followed by *to*.

EXPERT LANGUAGE
Find three examples of relative clauses in the text.

*For questions **1–8**, read the text below and decide which answer (**A**, **B**, **C** or **D**) best fits each gap. There is an example at the beginning (**0**).*

Formula One development driver

I'm one of 580 team members whose job it is to **(0)** ___A___ that our Formula One cars are as competitive as possible. My job **(1)** _____ is Development Driver, a role which involves both helping to **(2)** _____ the cars up for races and testing new parts on a simulator. I drive a mock-up car, under an egg-shaped dome, surrounded by 3D computer screens, which are **(3)** _____ to a team of engineers sitting behind a glass partition. I can **(4)** _____ up 100 laps a day, at up to 300 kilometres an hour, in an environment of total secrecy at the team factory. What the engineers want is the most precise description of how the car is performing on the track, **(5)** _____ they can convert that information into faster laptime. At a Grand Prix, I always have my headset on, listening to the **(6)** _____ from the drivers. If they have any **(7)** _____ with the way the car is handling, the engineers can make suggestions **(8)** _____ on the techniques we've tried in the simulator.

0	A ensure	B enable	C enforce	D encourage
1	A heading	B title	C topic	D subject
2	A set	B make	C get	D put
3	A observed	B shared	C connected	D monitored
4	A record	B sum	C count	D clock
5	A apart from	B in order to	C so that	D as well as
6	A backlog	B setback	C backup	D feedback
7	A issues	B matters	C bothers	D questions
8	A according	B based	C following	D related

Language development 1

➤ **CB** p. 157, **EG** p. 183

Participle clauses

1 Choose the correct answers. Sometimes both options are possible.

1 *As soon as / When* she walked into the room, she saw what had happened.
2 *Because / If* she had trained really hard, she was disappointed not to be chosen for the team.
3 People *who / when* arrive early are more likely to get a place.
4 *Since / As* we left the theatre later than we expected, we missed the last train.
5 I knew it was going to be really icy on the roads, *so / because* I refused to let my daughter drive.
6 *If /When* it is eaten hot, it tastes even more delicious.

2 Match the sentences in Exercise 1 (1–6) with the functions (a–e). You need to use some of the functions more than once.

a reason   c relative clause   e result
b time   d condition

3 Rewrite the sentences in Exercise 1 using participle clauses.

1 _____
2 _____
3 _____
4 _____
5 _____
6 _____

4 Complete the sentences with the present or past participle form of the verbs in the box.

convince   invite   learn   not be able   realise   rescue
want   wear

1 _____ my boss for a barbecue, I then remembered that I was supposed to be going to a concert the same evening.
2 _____ that I would be really tired, Mark had booked us a table at a lovely restaurant.
3 The family _____ from the rainforest last night spoke of their ordeal to *BBC News*.
4 _____ that I'd failed, I didn't even bother to look at the results.
5 _____ with boots and a jacket, those jeans can look quite elegant.
6 _____ to see more of the country, Andy extended his visa.
7 _____ French at school, I decided I'd like to give Spanish a go next.
8 _____ to swim, Alex stayed by the shore and watched us surfing.

5 Join the sentences using participle clauses. Make any changes necessary.

1 I'm a member of the club. That's why I get priority booking for home matches.
_____

2 She needs to be given a lot of support. If this happens, she could be a really good player.
_____

3 I ran out of the office. I then hailed a taxi and jumped in.
_____

4 I'm a bit lazy. Because of that, I'd never make a world-class tennis player.
_____

5 I quickly realised my team weren't going to win. I decided to leave.
_____

6 I knew he wanted to see the game. I bought tickets for both of us.
_____

to-infinitive clauses

6 Join the sentences using *to*-infinitive clauses to replace the words in bold. Make any changes necessary.

1 My personal trainer phoned me. **He wanted to arrange** a session.
_____

2 I finally got to the football ground. **Then I discovered** that my son hadn't been chosen for the team.
_____

3 **You should see him play**. If you did, you'd think he was a professional.
_____

4 I set off to meet Richard at the cinema. **Only then did I realise** I'd got the wrong date.
_____

5 I travel **a lot. I know** that delays are inevitable.
_____

6 I spent ages writing a proposal. **I had to present it** at the meeting.
_____

Use of English (Paper 1 Part 2)

Open cloze

1 Read the title of the text and think about what you are going to read.

2 Read the whole text quickly to get the general meaning.

3 Read the text again carefully and think about the type of word that will fit in each gap.

4 Do the task.

5 Read through the text again, with your answers in place. Does it make complete sense?

HELP

➤ Q1 You need a preposition here.
➤ Q5 Which word completes this fixed phrase that expresses contrast?
➤ Q8 Is the answer a relative pronoun or a conjunction? Read carefully to be sure.

EXPERT LANGUAGE

Look back at the text. Find three examples of adverbs used to describe the extent or degree of something.

*For questions **1–8**, read the text below and think of the word which best fits each gap. Use only **one** word in each space. There is an example at the beginning (0).*

E-health

What is known **(0)** __as__ e-health is one of the most interesting developments of the electronic age. The term is applied to a range of devices designed to help us manage our personal health. A growing number of apps and wearable devices are now **(1)** _____ the market, allowing the individual to monitor **(2)** _____ things as the burning of calories and fertility cycles. Yet scientists say that these wearable devices barely scratch the surface of **(3)** _____ will eventually be possible. They see much greater potential **(4)** _____ direct therapeutic intervention as **(5)** _____ to passive monitoring.

One hand-held device is already delivering treatment for migraine headaches, through the use of electronic pulses **(6)** _____ of drugs. The device, which looks **(7)** _____ an electric razor, is placed against the neck, where it stimulates the vagus nerve. The electronic pulses help control a substance called glutamine, **(8)** _____ has been linked to migraines. In one clinical trial, the device provided effective pain relief in 43 percent of cases.

Listening (Paper 3 Part 3)

Multiple choice

1 Read the instructions for the task and answer the questions.

  1 How many speakers are you going to hear?

  2 What are they going to talk about?

2 Look at the questions and mark the key words in the stems and options.

3 🎧 11 Do the task.

> *You will hear an interview with a skydiver called Jennie Parks, who recently took part in a record-breaking formation jump, and Paul Grimes, a skydiving instructor. For questions **1–6**, choose the answer (**A, B, C** or **D**) which fits best according to what you hear.*

1 What motivated Jennie to take part in the record-breaking jump?
- A a desire to set herself new challenges
- B a determination to prove somebody wrong
- C a feeling that she should support other female skydivers
- D a sense of dissatisfaction with her own skydiving performance

2 Paul disagrees with Jennie's point that
- A a skydiver's first jump is the hardest.
- B experience lessens the thrill of skydiving.
- C learning to turn in the air takes a lot of skill.
- D women are better suited to skydiving than men.

3 What does Paul suggest about the success of Jennie's record-breaking jump?
- A It reflected the thoroughness of the planning.
- B The design of the parachutes was the key factor.
- C The individual skydivers didn't need to be particularly skilled.
- D Controlling the speed of the fall was the greatest achievement.

4 What does Jennie say about the record-breaking jump?
- A The international make-up of the team caused communication problems.
- B Coordinating the work of the pilots led to unexpected delays.
- C It was frustrating not to have succeeded at the first attempt.
- D It was achieved in less time than had been anticipated.

5 For Jennie personally, the hardest aspect of the jump was
- A dealing with unreliable radio equipment.
- B remembering the correct sequence of moves.
- C following the lead of the designated 'superfloater'.
- D knowing which teammates to make physical contact with.

6 How did Jennie feel during the second formation?
- A concerned that she'd made a technical error
- B confused by some of the leader's instructions
- C aware of her individual responsibility to the group
- D worried about the judges' attitude towards her group

EXPERT STRATEGY

Listen to the interviewer's questions carefully — they help you to know which question you should be looking at in the task.

HELP

➤ **Q1** Listen to the end of Jennie's turn to hear the answer.

➤ **Q2** You need to listen to what both Paul and Jennie say to find the answer.

➤ **Q4** Listen to what Jennie says about the approach the team adopted.

EXPERT LANGUAGE

Find two adjectives with negative prefixes in the questions.

EXPERT WORD CHECK

*aptitude   heightened   incremental
manual   meticulous   parachute
prowess   put time aside   transcend
waned*

Reading (Paper 1 Part 8)

Multiple matching

1. Read the title of the text and the introductory sentence. What do you know about orienteering?

2. Read the task and mark the key words in each question.

3. Read the text quickly to get an idea of how it is structured and what issues are discussed in each section. What is the main focus of each section?

4. Look at question 1 and find the sections of the text that talk about the skills needed for the sport. Look for sentences about people doing the sport for the first time. Write the question number next to these sections so you can find them again quickly. Then read these sections carefully and decide which section matches the exact wording of question 1.

5. Repeat the procedure for the other questions.

*You are going to read an article about the sport of orienteering. For questions **1–10**, choose from the sections (**A–D**). The sections may be chosen more than once.*

In which section does the writer mention:	
the typical skills profile of a novice at the sport?	1
being advised of the best way to avoid getting lost?	2
a growing awareness of certain features of the landscape?	3
the need to bear an important safety requirement in mind?	4
proof that her choice of course had been appropriate?	5
seeking to justify an error of judgement?	6
another context to give an idea of the level of challenge in one course?	7
a way of measuring the aptitude of individuals for the activity?	8
seeing participants adopting very different attitudes towards the activity?	9
being amused by the use of certain terminology?	10

Vocabulary

6. Match the sentence halves to form sentences with collocations from the text.

1. In the forest, it's easy to lose _____
2. If you get into difficulties, you should raise _____
3. If you need help, ask the marshal to give _____
4. If someone goes missing, we'll send _____
5. The runners set off at _____
6. If you get lost, try to retrace _____
7. The checkpoint was tucked _____
8. As an orienteer, it's important to pay _____
9. If you're feeling confident, why not lay _____

a. out a search party.
b. your bearings.
c. down the gauntlet.
d. you a few tips.
e. your steps.
f. attention to interesting paths.
g. out of view.
h. regular intervals.
i. an alert.

EXPERT STRATEGY

Be careful: similar ideas may be expressed in different sections of the text. You need to look for the one that matches the wording of the question exactly.

HELP

➤ Q2 Be careful: the words *getting lost* appear in Section C but this may not be the answer.
➤ Q3 Look for words describing hills, plants, etc. These are all features of the landscape.
➤ Q4 Which section deals with a situation where participants' safety becomes an issue?

EXPERT LANGUAGE

Find a verb formed by adding a suffix to a noun in section C of the text.

EXPERT WORD CHECK

attuned checkpoints compass countdown beeps fan base hollow overshoot retrace my steps shrubbery twiddle

The ART of orienteering

Our reporter gets her first taste of the sport.

A The aim of orienteering is to navigate cross-country between a series of points marked on a map in the fastest time possible, and it has a growing fan base. I attended a club event which offers courses at a range of levels. The easiest is simple to follow, safe for families with young children and has control points at every turn, whereas the most challenging is physically demanding and navigationally complex – think military-level map skills. I'm competing on the 2.5-kilometre moderate 'orange' course and although the length is the direct distance between the nine control points, the distance you actually travel might be considerably more. 'Most people can run much quicker than they can map-read, at least when they're starting out,' says Ian, one of the friendly marshals at the registration tent. 'If you can do a kilometre in ten minutes, you know what you're doing.' Ian reckons the Orange should take newbies like me an hour.

B The set-up for taking part in an orienteering event is simple. I've brought my own compass, but hire an electronic 'dibber' card that will record my arrival time at each control point and the organisers provide the map. Because I'm a beginner, Ian gives me a few tips on technique: 'Orientate the map first, then move yourself and have an idea of what distance you need to travel to the next feature – it's easy to overshoot and lose your bearings. Always report back to the start or finish, even if you don't complete the course. Otherwise you'll raise a "missing-person" alert and the organisers will send out a search party.' An orienteering map isn't entirely intuitive. Woodland is marked as white unless it's dense woodland, which is green. Fields are yellow, earthworks are brown, green stripes mean 'undergrowth – slow run', narrow green stripes are 'undergrowth – fight'. I like a map legend with a sense of humour. There's no mass start in orienteering. Competitors set off at timed intervals. I get ten countdown beeps and set off. I align the map with north, twiddle myself around and identify the path I need to follow into the woods to get to Control 1, an orange and white flag.

C There are two elements to getting lost: the first is realising, the second is to work out where you actually are. Five minutes later, when I fail to reach my first goal, I stop, check the compass, make sure I'm not holding the map upside down and scrutinise the terrain. I discover I'm closer to Control 7 than Control 1, so retrace my steps downhill, almost back to

the beginning. There go my vainglorious hopes of beginners' triumph. But the sun is shining, the woodland is beautiful and I decide that going the long way around is surely part of the fun. I work out the direction and distance to the next point. Control 2 is only a few hundred metres away, tucked out of view in a little natural hollow off the path, but I find it pretty quickly. My delight is childlike – I found the treasure! I feel a deep sense of satisfaction. I've never paid as much attention to intersecting paths and changes of shrubbery as today. My senses are attuned, the blood is flowing through the grey matter as much as it is through my legs. I spot fellow orienteering fans navigating their way through the woodland in different directions. It's a lovely way to enjoy the countryside.

D As I 'dib' the finish, sweaty and triumphant, I see my first stab at orienteering has taken just under 65 minutes. Without that initial detour, I'd have been well inside my one-hour target. The gauntlet is laid down: I'm hooked. Finishing ahead of us are a family who took an hour to walk the shorter 'white' course, stopping en route for a picnic in the woods; rushing up behind us is an elite runner who's completed the eight-kilometre 'brown' course with 22 checkpoints in 50 minutes. Orienteering can be the adventure sport you want it to be. There's the thrill of the treasure hunt, the physical challenge of heading out cross-country over unprepared ground. It exercises both mind and body, is both sociable and inexpensive and, if my club is anything to go by, incredibly welcoming to newcomers.

Vocabulary development 2

➤ **CB** p. 160

Word formation: leisure activities

1 Complete the text with words formed from the words in brackets.

My mother has always wanted to do amateur
(1) _____ (drama). After going for an audition with
a local group, she was given her first part, much to her
(2) _____ (amaze). She finds it very **(3)** _____
(reward) and at least it's better than spending the whole
time **(4)** _____ (garden), which is what she used to do.

Myself, I do very little in my free time – I'm somewhat
of a couch potato – although I've done a course in
(5) _____ (create) writing. It was very interesting
and I made a whole new **(6)** _____ (friend) group
but I also found it **(7)** _____ (incredible) time-
(8) _____ (consume), so I gave it up in the end.
What I quite fancy doing next is some furniture
(9) _____ (restore), although I am not
(10) _____ (optimism) that I will be very good at it. I
would feel very **(11)** _____ (anxiety) if the furniture
was **(12)** _____ (value). I think it may be safer to stick
to playing computer games and watching TV!

Phrasal verbs with *get*

2 Complete the conversation with prepositions from the box.

around   away   back   into   out   over   round   through

A: I haven't seen you for ages. What have you been
   up to?
B: Well, actually, I've really been getting **(1)** _____
   cycling recently.
A: I thought you hadn't been feeling too good. Liz told me.
B: Oh, I've got **(2)** _____ that. It was only a cold.
A: It saps your energy, though.
B: I know. I got **(3)** _____ loads of vitamin
   supplements.
A: I used to cycle once but never get **(4)** _____ to it
   any more.
B: I know, it's tricky – you have to make the time, really.
A: I can't usually get **(5)** _____ from the office before
   6.30 and then it takes me an hour to get home.
B: I go in really early in the morning and then leave early.
A: What happens if you have a meeting?
B: I try and get **(6)** _____ of it!
A: I hear you've also taken up yoga.
B: Wow, news certainly gets **(7)** _____ !
A: Anyway, you've inspired me. I'll get **(8)** _____ to it
   as soon as the weather is better.
B: Good luck!

3 Match the phrasal verbs in Exercise 2 (1–8)
   with their meanings (a–h).
   a use up   _____
   b start doing again _____
   c escape from   _____
   d start being involved _____
   e spread   _____
   f recover from   _____
   g find the time   _____
   h avoid   _____

Reading

4 Complete the text with words from the box.

_bookworm   browse   caught   compulsive   dip
fiction   go   paperback   ranging   swap   switch
trashy   value   widely   works_

I'm always reading and read quite **(1)** _____ .
I often get through a couple of books a week,
(2) _____ from fairly **(3)** _____ novels to
more serious **(4)** _____ of literature. I usually
get totally **(5)** _____ up in books; it helps me
to **(6)** _____ off.
I like novels best and I find psychological thrillers
quite **(7)** _____ . So much so that I often
stay up till all hours reading them. But I also
(8) _____ into biographies and other non-
(9) _____ , though I may not read them from
cover to cover. I just **(10)** _____ , really, and
read up on things I feel I should know.
I normally wait until the **(11)** _____
versions of books come out because they're
cheaper and also get quite a lot from the
library and local charity shop, which is really
good **(12)** _____ . My friends and I also
(13) _____ books a lot. I'll give anything
a **(14)** _____ – I suppose I am a bit of a
(15) _____ .

Language development 2

➤ **CB** p 162, **EG** p. 183

Modals and semi-modals (Part 2): certainty, willingness and characteristic behaviour

1 Replace the words in bold with a word from the box. Make any changes necessary. More than one answer may be possible.

shall   will   won't   would

1 My friend and I **used to** clean people's cars to earn money when we were kids.
2 The dishwasher **isn't working**. I don't know why.
3 I think that this new information **is sure to change** your mind.
4 **Is it possible for you to** shut the door, please? It's cold.
5 **Let me** help you.
6 **Can you possibly** move your car, please?
7 My brother **never takes** the dog for a walk – I always have to do it.
8 **It's typical of her to be** late just when we are in such a hurry.

Modal revision

2 Choose the correct answers.

1 I wish you'd phoned. I *could / should* have come round to your house.
2 I am a member, so I *didn't have to pay / needn't have paid* for the tickets. I just showed them my card.
3 I'll wait for you here, *will / shall* I?
4 That was a bit scary. We *could / would* have been stopped by the police.
5 I am really pleased that I *can / could* see you in Paris next week.
6 It took a while but finally I *could / was able to* get the car started, and we set off.
7 The audience got fed up because they *weren't able to / can't* hear very well.
8 That's really kind, but you really *shouldn't / mustn't* have spent all that money!

3 Complete the sentences with the correct form of the verbs in the box and the modals in brackets.

be   do   have   leave   make   remove   talk   tell

1 It's not important. I _____ (not have to) it straightaway.
2 You _____ (should) me you were coming. I would have picked you up.
3 I'm not sure where she is. I suppose she _____ (might) to Stella downstairs.
4 It's really late and I'm a bit worried. He _____ (could) an accident.
5 As long as you sign this document, there _____ (should) a problem.
6 You _____ (need) a meal for me yesterday. I told you I would be going out.
7 They _____ (can) already, surely. It's only five o'clock.
8 Books _____ (must) from the library under any circumstances.

Alternatives to modals

4 Cross out the one incorrect option for each sentence.

1 I think _____ switch off your phone.
   A you are obliged
   B you'd better
   C you should

2 Clients _____ sign out before leaving the premises.
   A are required to
   B are to
   C must to

3 You _____ to buy anything.
   A are under no obligation
   B needn't
   C shouldn't feel under pressure

4 It is _____ lock your car if you leave it here.
   A advisable to
   B suggested to
   C recommended that you

5 Visitors _____ to feed the animals.
   A are prohibited
   B are forbidden
   C aren't allowed

6 All books are _____ to be returned to school before the end of term.
   A supposed
   B meant
   C advised

7 The school doesn't _____ students wear uniform on trips.
   A make
   B insist
   C force

8 It _____ for all passengers to clear security check.
   A is required
   B is compulsory
   C is necessary

5 Write sentences using the incorrect options in Exercise 4.

1 _____
2 _____
3 _____
4 _____
5 _____
6 _____
7 _____
8 _____

Use of English (Paper 1 Part 4)

Key word transformations

1 Read the instructions for the task and look at the example. Think about how the two sentences are different and notice how the meaning hasn't changed.

2 Do the task.

HELP

➤ Q1 Change a noun in the first sentence into an adjective.

➤ Q2 How is *ought* different to other modal verbs?

➤ Q4 You need to use an impersonal passive structure here.

EXPERT LANGUAGE

Look back at the task. Find two examples of compound nouns where two words are written as one.

For questions 1–10, complete the second sentence so that it has a similar meaning to the first sentence, using the word given. Do not change the word given. You must use between three and six words, including the word given. Here is an example (0).

0 We need to get a taxi or they will leave before we get there.
   TIME
   Unless we get a taxi, they <u>will have left by the time</u> we get there.

1 By law, airlines are obliged to check each passenger's passport.
   UNDER
   Airlines are _____ check each passenger's passport.

2 'I think we'd better report the incident to the police,' said Vincent.
   OUGHT
   Vincent said that the incident _____ to the police.

3 Almost everybody thinks that the couple will announce their engagement shortly.
   WIDELY
   The couple are _____ point of announcing their engagement.

4 There is a rumour going round that the film star intends to sell his house.
   IS
   The film star _____ to sell his house.

5 Do you mind if I ask you some questions about your free-time activities?
   OBJECTION
   Would you _____ answering some questions about your free-time activities?

6 I don't think the proposal will meet with widespread support.
   UNLIKELY
   In my _____ meet with widespread support.

7 It annoys me that Sandra is always checking for messages on her smartphone.
   WISH
   I _____ keep checking for messages on her smartphone.

8 From the look on Tom's face, you can see the interview probably hasn't gone well.
   IF
   From the look on Tom's face, _____ the interview hasn't gone well.

9 I will only go fishing if the weather improves.
   UNLESS
   I _____ is an improvement in the weather.

10 Harriet could remember very little about her childhood holiday in Spain.
   HARDLY
   Harriet _____ about her childhood holiday in Spain.

Writing (Paper 2 Part 2: Proposal)

➤ **CB** pp. 164–165, **EW** p. 196

Planning content

1 Which of these conventions is *not* important in proposals?

1 a formal/impersonal style
2 a persuasive opinion/recommendation
3 headings
4 descriptive language
5 being concise and direct

2 Read the task and then look at the points below. Which ones should you *not* include in your proposal?

You work in the student services office at an international language college. In a client satisfaction survey, several students have suggested running fitness classes during the lunch breaks.
You have decided to send a proposal to the principal of the college, asking for permission to do this and for practical assistance. Your proposal should include the following information:

• why you think such classes would be beneficial
• what kind of activities could be held
• what kind of help you would need from the college.

*Write your **proposal** in 220–260 words.*

1 suggestions for other research you could do
2 possible reasons as to why students need fitness classes at lunchtime (e.g. gym too far away, nothing to do)
3 other alternatives to fitness activities
4 a list of possible fitness classes (e.g. Pilates, yoga, running club)
5 permission to hold fitness classes somewhere in the college
6 a suggestion for how much students should pay
7 ideas for activities which are run by other colleges
8 how to publicise the classes
9 suggestions for healthy lunches after the classes
10 a request for subsidy from college to pay fitness teachers

Organisation

3 Decide how many paragraphs you will have and what the headings will be. Use the task input to help you organise this and remember to include all the information required.

Using appropriate language

4a Which of these sentence openings are too informal for an introduction?

1 I'm writing this proposal because …
2 The purpose of this proposal is …
3 The aims of this proposal are …
4 The point of writing this proposal is …
5 Why I decided to write this proposal is …
6 In this proposal, I will/intend to address issues raised in …

b Which of these sentence openings for recommendations are too informal for a conclusion?

1 I would suggest/recommend that …
2 I think it would be great if …
3 Why don't we …?
4 How about …?
5 Let's …
6 It would be a good idea to …
7 It is doubtful whether …
8 I strongly urge …

Being persuasive

5 Which of these final paragraphs is the most effective? Why?

A

My recommendations would be as follows:

• to employ a teacher to come in three times a week to teach a class in yoga, Pilates and jazz dance
• to introduce a small fee (£5) for each class, with the college making up the rest of the fee
• classes to take place in the hall
• twice a week, one of the teams to lead a running group

I am confident that if these ideas were to be implemented, we would have a happier and healthier group of students.

B

In my view, we need to do something to keep our students happy and I suggest that the best way is to provide them with the classes they are asking for. This could be a mixture of fitness classes, such as yoga, and outdoor exercise, like running. I feel sure that students would be willing to pay something towards the cost. Let's ask them and then perhaps the college could contribute towards it as well.

Writing task

6 Now do the task in Exercise 1.

Practice exam

Reading and Use of English

Part 1

For questions **1–8**, read the text below and decide which answer (**A**, **B**, **C** or **D**) best fits each gap. There is an example at the beginning (**0**).

Mark your answers **on the separate answer sheet**.

Example:

0 A carried   **B** filled   **C** taken   **D** brought

0	A	B	C	D

Working from home

According to a survey of over 2,000 parents that was **(0)** _____ out recently, homeworking was the most attractive type of flexible working that could be offered to employees – with the main reason being that it allowed parents to take their children to school in the morning and **(1)** _____ them up at the end of the day. This rated **(2)** _____ as an incentive than other factors, such as saving time and money on commuting.

Clearly, however, there are certain **(3)** _____ to homeworking. The survey showed, for example, that most homeworkers use their own equipment, with only seven percent having use of smartphones supplied by their employers. **(4)** _____ , the majority of homeworkers have to **(5)** _____ out any technical problems themselves, with only 36 percent being able to call on technical support from their employers if they get into trouble – something very much taken for **(6)** _____ in an office environment. Many employees still lack **(7)** _____ confidence in remote communications tools, **(8)** _____ their desire to work from home.

1	**A** lift	**B** fetch	**C** pick	**D** collect
2	**A** greater	**B** higher	**C** larger	**D** better
3	**A** outcomes	**B** downfalls	**C** upshots	**D** drawbacks
4	**A** What's more	**B** Instead	**C** On the contrary	**D** Otherwise
5	**A** deal	**B** sort	**C** cope	**D** work
6	**A** given	**B** read	**C** normal	**D** granted
7	**A** whole	**B** entire	**C** utter	**D** complete
8	**A** despite	**B** nonetheless	**C** although	**D** however

Part 2

For questions **9–16**, read the text below and think of the word which best fits each gap. Use only **one** word in each gap. There is an example at the beginning (**0**).

Write your answers **IN CAPITAL LETTERS on the separate answer sheet**.

Example: | 0 | W | H | Y | | | | | | | | | | | | | |

Tree-hugging koalas

Australian researchers have discovered (**0**) _____ it is that koalas hug trees. Thermal imaging shows that the trunks of some acacia and eucalyptus species are as (**9**) _____ as five degrees cooler than their surroundings in hot weather. The research team (**10**) _____ use of a thermal camera and a portable weather station in (**11**) _____ to assess the conditions available to the koalas in different places within the woodlands they inhabit. (**12**) _____ the team discovered was that during heatwaves, the animals were more likely to hug the trunks and lower branches than in cooler weather, (**13**) _____ they tended to live higher in the canopy. Also, in times of extreme heat, the animals tended to abandon eucalyptus trees in (**14**) _____ of acacias, the species with the coolest trunks.

Koalas are vulnerable to thermal stress and (**15**) _____ to a quarter of some populations have died in heatwaves. What's more, the findings (**16**) _____ well turn out to be significant to a wider range of tree-dwelling animals, as climate change brings more extreme weather.

Part 3

For questions **17–24**, read the text below. Use the word given in capitals at the end of some of the lines to form a word that fits in the gap **in the same line**. There is an example at the beginning (**0**).

Write your answers **IN CAPITAL LETTERS on the separate answer sheet**.

Example: | 0 | E | X | T | E | N | S | I | V | E | L | Y | | | |

Aboard the flight simulator

Flight simulator machines are **(0)** _____ used in the training of airline pilots.   **EXTEND**

Members of the public can now sample the experience, **(17)** _____ by a   **COMPANY**

working pilot in the role of instructor. Although you never leave the ground,

sitting in the simulator cockpit, the combination of sound, movement

and computer-generated images makes for an uncannily **(18)** _____   **REALISM**

experience. Your logical mind keeps telling you it's not for real, but

something deep in your subconscious mind responds to the **(19)** _____ of   **AUTHENTIC**

the sensory environment and you feel a real sense of **(20)** _____ for your   **RESPONSIBLE**

actions. This is fine at first, when you're simply cruising the skies, learning

how to steer the plane. **(21)** _____ by the thousands of buttons and dials,   **DETER**

you may even start to **(22)** _____ about your chances in the airline's next   **FANTASY**

(23) _____ campaign. The moment of truth, however, comes as you take   **RECRUIT**

the plane in to land. **(24)** _____ , people have been known to get so terrified   **APPEAR**

that they burst into tears at this point – so real does the experience feel.

Part 4

For questions **25–30**, complete the second sentence so that it has a similar meaning to the first sentence, using the word given. **Do not change the word given.** You must use between **three** and **six** words, including the word given. Here is an example (**0**).

Example:

0 **I don't think many local people will support the campaign.**

 UNLIKELY

 In my opinion, _____ get much support locally.

The gap can be filled by the words 'the campaign is unlikely to', so you write:

Example:	0	THE CAMPAIGN IS UNLIKELY TO

Write **only** the missing words **IN CAPITAL LETTERS on the separate answer sheet**.

---

25 At first, the speed of the new computer system greatly impressed the office manager.

 INITIAL

 The speed of the new computer system _____ the office manager.

26 Gerry seems to have no understanding whatsoever of the importance of politeness in his job.

 LACK

 Gerry seems to _____ important politeness is in his job.

27 If you can think of some original ideas, your proposal is more likely to be accepted.

 BEING

 In order to increase the _____ , you should think of some original ideas.

28 Danny persuaded his friend to enrol for the outback survival course.

 TALKED

 Danny _____ up for the outback survival course.

29 'Don't forget that you promised to get some ink cartridges for the printer,' said Amy's sister.

 REMINDED

 Amy's sister _____ promised to get ink cartridges for the printer.

30 Far from putting him off running, Clive's ankle injury made him determined to continue with it.

 BEING

 Far from _____ ankle injury, Clive became determined to continue with it.

Part 5

You are going to read an article about women in top management positions. For questions **31–36**, choose the answer (**A**, **B**, **C** or **D**) which you think fits best according to the text.
Mark your answers **on the separate answer sheet**.

The mummy juggle

Should more women be going after top corporate jobs?

Sheryl Sandberg became the first female board member at Facebook, having previously worked for both Google and the US Treasury Department. I remember speaking to her on Skype one Wednesday afternoon as she sat in her glass office, wearing a pink and black sports jacket. She'd had a busy day at work and in a few minutes, she explained with a broad grin she'd be leaving for a baseball match with her son. 'I've got cupcakes and pizza – he'll love it!' she said, looking every inch the baseball-mum with tousled hair, make-up-free face and sporty top. 'How does she do it?' I wondered momentarily, with a sense of awed envy, and then mentally scolded myself in shame. As someone doing the 'mummy juggle' myself, I hate being asked that question. Indeed, when I'd first met Sheryl two years earlier at a media dinner I was hosting, we'd laughed about this. Everyone knows that being a working mum is challenging: the reason we were chatting on Skype, not meeting up, was because our schedules were so packed. But millions of other women – and men – are juggling today, except the men are rarely grilled on how they combine the joys of parenthood with ambition or handle the inevitable flashes of guilt or inadequacy.

In any case, it seemed rather redundant to ask Sandberg how she 'does it'. The previous month she'd published her first book, *Lean In*, which describes in breathless detail how she made family and career work – and appeals for more mums to do the same. Although western women have entered the workforce and education in record numbers in recent decades, this achievement hasn't filtered through to the top corporate jobs, of which only 14 percent are held by women in the USA. Depressingly, that low statistic has remained flat for a decade. And at six percent, the figure is lower still in the UK.

What's more, if there is stagnation, it seems few people are talking about it. Some women see it as a result of male prejudice or institutional impediments. But Sandberg thinks that women's minds are at fault. Most notably, she believes they sabotage themselves by 'leaning back' in their careers, both prior to having children and on their return to work after maternity leave. By this she means failing to make their voices heard and refusing to make men take on an equal share of domestic tasks. So she wants more women to 'lean in' at work, pushing for success, even as they attend baseball matches with their children.

This message infuriated some people who point out that Sandberg is wealthy enough to afford domestic staff and powerful enough in her office to set the rules. For other women, the battle looks tougher. Indeed, Anne-Marie Slaughter, the professor at Princeton who chose to leave a job at the state department in 2011 when she found the 'juggle' too tough, has criticised Sandberg for not paying enough attention to institutional problems. Sandberg herself is at pains to play down any slanging match. *Lean In* topped the bestseller list and she's committed to promoting her message not just to women but to men as well, including those who sit in the (largely female-free) senior corporate echelons.

And in response to anyone who thinks there's a danger of US corporations simply jumping aboard the latest public relations trend – after all, almost every corporate leader today claims to like equality – Sandberg insists there are bigger reasons why CEOs are open to her message. Companies shouldn't be changing as a favour to women, but rather because getting more women engaged makes sense because it's good for a company's competitiveness. There is, she feels, a second, less obvious, factor, too. 'There are a lot of senior men out there with daughters. In particular, high-flying fathers are now realising that if they want their own daughters to fly, it's not enough simply to put them into a good college or entry job. Women are outstripping men in education, but this isn't reflected at the top. It's time it was.'

31 During their Skype conversation, the writer remembers feeling

    A embarrassed because she said something inappropriate to Sandberg.

    B annoyed with her own reaction to what Sandberg told her.

    C resentful of how well-organised Sandberg appeared to be.

    D disappointed not to have had Sandberg's full attention.

32 In the first paragraph, the writer says that men are less likely than women

    A to be expected to combine childcare with a career.

    B to feel torn between the demands of work and family life.

    C to be asked how they balance work and family commitments.

    D to feel concerned if their work means that they see little of their children.

33 What do we learn about Sandberg's book in the second paragraph?

    A It contains rather predictable arguments.

    B It encourages other women to emulate her.

    C It was written in a relatively short space of time.

    D It seeks to explain why there are so few women in top jobs.

34 For Sandberg, women who tend to 'lean back' in their careers

    A are to blame for their own lack of career advancement.

    B are unfortunate victims of entrenched male attitudes.

    C need to reach top positions before having children.

    D should negotiate better maternity leave conditions.

35 In the fourth paragraph, we learn that Sandberg's ideas have come in for criticism because

    A her privileged position is regarded as untypical.

    B she has made quite a lot of money writing about them.

    C she is fortunate to work for a particularly enlightened employer.

    D it is felt that she doesn't put them into practice with her own staff.

36 In the final paragraph, the writer agrees with Sandberg's point that

    A there are now better educational opportunities available to women.

    B women from certain families stand more chance of getting the best jobs.

    C public opinion is leading to a change of attitudes amongst corporate bosses.

    D there are sound economic arguments for having more women in top positions.

Part 6

You are going to read four reviews of an exhibition on the subject of bridges. For questions **37–40**, choose from the reviews **A–D**. The reviews may be chosen more than once.

The role of bridges in the city landscape: an exhibition of drawings, paintings and photos

A Anita McKay

This exhibition is much more than a collection of images of bridges: it asks enduring and relevant questions about the purpose of these structures and highlights their central role in defining the cities which they grace. As you make your way through the gallery, you're confronted with unexpected and surprising juxtapositions. Atmospheric photos appear next to precise scale drawings of the same bridge. What's more, you're not just visually challenged but also forced to consider familiar structures in a new light as you undertake this fascinating journey. For me, the absence of any sense of chronological or geographical progression in the exhibits was liberating. Instead of being led to see similarities between bridges or trace lines of development in bridge design, you're encouraged to marvel at their great diversity and individuality. In terms of the range of bridges depicted, the exhibition is an unapologetically eclectic selection that makes no attempt at coverage of styles or regions. It is all the better for it.

B Brian Makepeace

This exhibition is devoted to bridges of different types and deftly illustrates the significance of these structures to the image of a city, brilliantly capturing the vitality of the river as an urban artery. The inclusion of a mixture of both familiar and less familiar bridges helps to hold your interest as you make your way round. But anyone hoping to come away with a potted history of the bridge from an architectural or engineering perspective will be disappointed. The ancient and modern pop up next to each other in a seemingly random fashion, as do structures from the four corners of the globe. But this is a strength rather than a weakness because, to its great credit, this exhibition makes you look at bridges from an aesthetic viewpoint. This is ultimately much more engaging than either the technical or the historical perspective that could so easily have been laboured here.

C Chloe Forbes

For centuries, bridges have been a marker for urban ambition. Cities around the world commissioned architects to create distinctive bridges to act as icons. This delightful exhibition showcases some of these structures, though, sadly, some of the most iconic have been overlooked in favour of somewhat undistinguished alternatives. There is little here, however, to make you ponder the deeper social significance of bridges, nor are we shown how central the bridges are to their respective city's image of itself. Instead, we're treated to a feast of stunning visual images that excites the senses in all sorts of unexpected ways. Fortunately, the exhibits aren't arranged in date order, nor do we have rooms devoted to specific locations or cultures, so we're spared any discussion of the technical background. This is an exhibition that appeals to the eyes rather than the intellect.

D David Braintree

Architects regard bridges as more than the functional means to an end. Because it tames nature, a bridge can have an aura of power and majesty, and people marvel at the technical achievement. Despite being a rather random collection of visual images, this exhibition captures that aura surprisingly well and makes you reflect on how well functionality and beauty can be combined. Having said that, I didn't come away with any new insights into either bridge building or indeed what bridges do for cities, which is supposedly the focus of the event. Indeed, as we moved from one era to another and one style to another without any sense of progression, I found my attention wandering for want of a coherent thread to latch on to. What's more, some of the world's most interesting examples of urban bridge design didn't get a look in, which was a shame, whilst some far from iconic structures were given centre stage.

Which reviewer

has a different view to McKay concerning how effective the order and positioning of the exhibits is? **37** ⬚

shares Makepeace's opinion of how well the exhibition shows the importance of urban bridges? **38** ⬚

has a similar view to Forbes regarding the choice of bridges which appears in the exhibition? **39** ⬚

has a different opinion to the others about how thought-provoking the exhibition is? **40** ⬚

Part 7

You are going to read a newspaper article about a tiger reserve in India. Six paragraphs have been removed from the article. Choose from the paragraphs **A–G** the one which fits each gap (**41–46**). There is one extra paragraph which you do not need to use.

Mark your answers **on the separate answer sheet**.

Hidden tigers

The elusive big cats are the star attraction in India's Pench National Park.

In 1894 Rudyard Kipling's novel *The Jungle Book* was published, partly set in what is now Pench National Park in the central Indian state of Madhya Pradesh. The story tells of Mowgli, a man-cub raised by wolves, and his adventures with various animals he befriends. But the star of the story, and the film which followed, is undoubtedly Shere Khan, a ferocious, crotchety tiger.

41	

India has 42 such reserves, with Pench among the more popular, as it has 30 to 35 tigers prowling its 758 square kilometres. A friend had returned triumphant from a trip the previous weekend, having seen two. Tigers invite superlatives – the king of the jungle, nature's masterwork and so on – but they are solitary, elusive animals, and I have heard many more stories about fruitless attempts to spot one.

42	

Despite the best efforts of our amiable guide, our first drive through the park is pleasantly uneventful. We toddle around in the evening sunlight, cooing over the park's numerous spotted deer and black-faced langur monkeys. There are scant signs of tigers, but we return contentedly enough four hours later, ready for the Italian supper cooked by the lodge's friendly chef.

43	

We see little evidence of such troubling behaviour during our visit, but Pench does have a reputation as one of India's better-managed reserves. Its tiger population has increased in recent decades too, as part of a major national conservation effort called Project Tiger, launched in the 1970s.

44	

If more are born, the result is often a fight for territory. If they survive, the losers often leave and must fend for themselves outside the area protected by the park. It explains why India's tiger population is just holding steady, despite years of intensive conservation projects. 'Sometimes I feel these animals are cursed,' Kassim says, with an air of genuine sadness. 'At least lions hang around in packs and help each other. Tigers need so much space; they just can't live together.'

45	

As the freezing air rushes by, Kassim yells back to explain that tigers often walk on the roads early in the morning, to avoid getting their paws wet on the morning dew. Then he stops the jeep suddenly, killing the engine. Apparently, one of the park's female tigers often sits near this spot, with her cubs. We listen intently, as the morning light comes up around us.

46	

Despite these wild imaginings, nothing emerges and we trundle off reluctantly to try our luck elsewhere. It is a pattern that sadly repeats itself on subsequent drives: we hear the odd alarm call but the tigers keep themselves well hidden. The trips are relaxing and enjoyable nonetheless, and we see a fine array of other wildlife.

A But visitors like us are not universally given such a warm welcome in the National Park. Some people view tourists as harmful, claiming that they annoy the tigers and contaminate the reserve with discarded plastic and so on. What's more, at the moment these voices seem to be winning the debate.

B 'Creating such a safe habitat means fending off poachers and displacing villagers,' says our guide, shouting to be heard against the wind as we rattle off into the park next morning. But tigers also require space, meaning even well-run parks find it hard to increase numbers much.

C Even so, we begin to feel a touch sorry for him, especially when he tells us of the pressures that come with his occupation: '95 percent of guests are just all about tigers, tigers, tigers!' he says at one point, with a rueful smile. 'If I tell them something I know about a tree, they aren't really that interested.'

D Little has changed much since then, at least judging by the approach to the modern-day park. We pass signs for tiger tours, tiger hotels and tiger restaurants; the effect leaves little doubt what visitors have in mind.

E The thick forest around us is silent. Our hearts racing, we listen out for 'alarm calls' from other nearby animals, alerting each other to the tiger's presence. Using binoculars, I peer hopefully through the dense vegetation and find myself almost willingly hallucinating tigers in the distance. Far-off logs take on feline form, while tree stumps seem suddenly to exhibit distinctive, symmetrical orange and black stripes.

F Such gloomy thoughts are banished a few minutes later, however, as fresh paw prints (called 'pug' marks) are spotted on the road ahead. Suddenly elated, we speed up and follow the trail down the road, convinced a first sighting is imminent.

G To improve our own chances, as part of a short stay at a luxurious safari lodge we've booked four drives into the park led by Kassim, a local naturalist. In Kipling's day, estimates put India's tiger population at 40,000. Today it is roughly 1,700, according to official figures, a decimation wrought by a combination of habitat destruction and hunting.

Part 8

You are going to read an article about attitudes towards wearing clothing made out of animal fur. For questions **47–56**, choose from the sections (**A–D**). The sections may be chosen more than once.

Mark your answers **on the separate answer sheet**.

In which section does the writer mention

an example of inconsistent attitudes to related issues?	47
continuing to feel slightly uncomfortable with a decision?	48
an image that made a lasting impression on her generation?	49
an unintended side-effect of a successful protest movement?	50
a way of justifying a practice that was once heavily criticised?	51
an acknowledgement of the practical value of an item of clothing?	52
a technological development that has allowed a softening of public attitudes?	53
being influenced by a particularly effective attempt to change public attitudes?	54
how one particular garment is indistinguishable from those designed to imitate it?	55
examples of production methods that have addressed some of the concerns of campaigners?	56

The fur debate goes full circle

A

A couple of months ago I inherited some items that had once belonged to my mother. Most of these boxes invoked poignant joy. But one produced a moral dilemma. I found a collection of fur garments, wrapped in plastic, which my mother had inherited from her mother. This included a fabulous floor-length mink coat of the sort that wealthy women once commonly wore around New York or Geneva and still sport in some places. Should I wear it, toss it away or simply sell it on eBay? 20 years ago my answer would have been clear: I would've conducted a ritual burning of the mink while enveloped in a smug glow of political correctness. I started my adult life as an anthropology student and back then the animal rights movement was running such a slick anti-fur campaign that mink seemed taboo to westerners of my age. Who can forget those shots of fur-clad ladies being doused in red paint in the streets by angry protesters? In those days sporting fur in public seemed like an act of deliberate provocation – even before you factored in the issues of privilege and wealth. Indeed, fur was so controversial that I'd forgotten my mother even had a mink coat because she barely wore it.

B

But today my view of fur – like that of many western consumers – has become less black and white. Having lived in Russia, I now realise that fur is extraordinarily effective at combating extreme cold. I have also become increasingly aware of the capricious nature of political campaigns and concepts of political correctness. The more I think about it, the odder it seems that someone should throw a paintball at a fur coat but still wear leather or eat factory-farmed meat. In any case, fur isn't always associated with animal cruelty: these days, designers in places such as Vermont are making fur coats out of road kill. Indeed, the social ecosystem of fur is more complex than it might seem. As fur prices have tumbled in recent years due to the anti-fur campaign, it's not the rich who have suffered but rather the indigenous groups in places such as Canada who were at the centre of the fur trade – so much so that some anthropologists are now lobbying against the anti-fur campaign.

C

The other complicating factor is advances made in the science of synthetic materials. It's now extremely easy to produce a fake fur coat. Sometimes these are fashioned to look as artificial as possible – such as the peppermint-green fake fur that was a must-have item one year – but often such items look identical to my mink. Either way, the trend has made furry images ubiquitous. This, in turn, has stealthily lessened the stigma around fur and helped make the real items more acceptable again, boosting fur prices. In some ways this is deeply ironic. In centuries past fur was valuable because it seemed so exclusive and natural. Now its acceptability and price are rising because of fakes. If nothing else, this should remind us all of just how malleable many of our symbols and value systems can be. What is deemed ultra-precious today may be less so tomorrow. Our reactions to symbols can shift in subtle ways – even when they feel natural or inevitable.

D

I am a case in point. For many weeks that mink sat untouched in my closet in New York while I uneasily pondered what to do. Then my young daughters stumbled on the bags and it suddenly occurred to me that wearing that coat, whatever its origins, could be an ecologically positive act. I was recycling something and, in a sense, honouring the past. So when the temperature plunged, I finally swathed myself in the sensual layers of mink. Part of me still feels a touch uneasy sporting it in the street. But I keep reminding myself that, as one of my daughters acerbically pointed out, nobody knows if it's actually real or not. I can't say what my grandmother would've made of that, but I prefer to chuckle at the irony – and hope the next generation of fur coats can be produced in the most humane way possible.

Part 1

You **must** answer this question. Write your answer in **220–260** words in an appropriate style.

1 Your class has watched an online panel discussion about the effect of globalisation on life in the 21st century. You have made the notes below:

> **The effect of globalisation**
>
> - travel
> - living standards
> - culture

> **Some opinions expressed in the online discussion:**
>
> 'The world has become much more accessible.'
>
> 'We are losing our national identity.'
>
> 'There is much more choice of products to buy as a result.'

Write an essay for your tutor discussing **two** of the points in your notes. You should **explain which effect has been greater, giving reasons** in support of your answer.

You may, if you wish, make use of the opinions expressed in the online discussion, but you should use your own words as far as possible.

Part 2

Write an answer to **one** of the questions **2–4** in this part. Write your answer in **220–260** words in an appropriate style.

2 You have just been on a cultural exchange visit overseas with your college. The college has never done this exchange before. All students have been asked to write a report on the positive aspects of the visit and suggest any improvements that could be made for future visits.

Your report should give details about the activities provided, the host family and the location.

Write your **report**.

3 You have received an email from a friend who will shortly be having her first job interview.

> ...
>
> I'm really nervous about the interview. Can you tell me about your experiences and give me advice on things to remember to say and avoid saying? Also: what could I wear? I really want this job!

Write your **email**.

4 You see the following announcement in an online magazine called *TV World*.

> **The end of TV?**
>
> It is often claimed that TV is on its way out and nobody watches it any more. We are not convinced and we want to know about the most and least popular television programmes or series that you have seen.
>
> Write us a review of the best and worst TV programme or series you've seen. Remember to give reasons for your choices!

Write your **review**.

Part 1

🎧 12 You will hear three different extracts.

For questions **1–6**, choose the answer (**A**, **B** or **C**) which fits best according to what you hear.

There are two questions for each extract.

Extract One

You hear two guests on a chat show talking about visiting the Grand Canyon in the USA.

1 How did the man feel during his first visit to the canyon?

   A frustrated by unforeseen events

   B disappointed by the quality of the light

   C annoyed with himself for planning it badly

2 The woman suggests that we would have appreciated the canyon more if he had

   A gone there in a different season.

   B arrived at a different time of day.

   C viewed it from a different perspective.

Extract Two

You hear part of a consumer programme in which mattress toppers, a new fashion in bedding, are being discussed.

3 When talking about the toppers, the woman is

   A questioning their overall effectiveness.

   B expressing her personal dissatisfaction with them.

   C reporting certain reservations people have about them.

4 The man says that horsehair filling

   A is the most economical of the available alternatives.

   B offers greater long-term comfort than other materials.

   C has a particularly beneficial effect on the user's sleep patterns.

Extract Three

You hear two friends talking about modern-day reading habits.

5 The woman suggests the first title discussed by Mark Zuckerberg's online book club

    A may not have been selected for its readability.

    B must have attracted lots of new members.

    C would have become popular in any case.

6 The friends agree that it is a mistake to

    A rely on the internet for analysis of current affairs.

    B read too much into falling newspaper sales.

    C assume that book clubs promote reading.

Part 2

🎧 13 You will hear a man called Matt Selby talking about the sport of stand-up paddleboarding. For questions **7–14**, complete the sentences with a word or short phrase.

Stand-up paddleboarding

Matt decided to take up the sport following an injury to his **(7)** _____ .

Matt took lessons from a company with the name **(8)** _____ .

Matt's lessons took place at a venue known as **(9)** _____ .

The venue is good for learners because there are no **(10)** _____ in the water.

Matt found learning how to **(11)** _____ on his board quite straightforward.

Matt says that the sport gives participants a good **(12)** _____ .

Matt heard that some celebrities practise **(13)** _____ on their paddleboards.

Matt's inflatable paddleboard looks like a **(14)** _____ when he's travelling.

Part 3

🎧 14   You will hear an interview in which two British novelists called Julian Mearsby and Lois Ridge are talking about the role of fiction in the modern world. For questions **15–20**, choose the answer (**A**, **B**, **C** or **D**) which fits best according to what you hear.

15 Lois feels that recent research into children's reading habits

    A supports a view that she has long held herself.

    B has been largely misinterpreted by commentators.

    C reveals how misguided parents' attitudes to reading can be.

    D shows how counterproductive it is to force children to read.

16 Julian says that the research lends weight to his own view that

    A stories are an intrinsic part of general education.

    B everybody needs the escapism that stories provide.

    C not all stories are equally worthy of our admiration.

    D people who don't read stories often lack key language skills.

17 What does Julian think about reading on screen?

    A Readers are more likely to get distracted.

    B Readers find it less enjoyable than a physical book.

    C It's been shown to discourage the reading of fiction.

    D It's useful for developing the ability to read and write.

18 Lois regards differences between boys' and girls' reading habits as

    A a result of their biological make-up.

    B surprisingly uniform across cultures.

    C a product of their social environment.

    D exaggerated by recent research findings.

19 Lois feels that the public's view of authors

    A has been affected by undue criticism in the media.

    B reflects the status of storytelling in society in general.

    C is disproportionately influenced by a few successful individuals.

    D suffers from unfair comparison with other creative people in society.

20 Julian and Lois both feel that it's unfortunate that many writers

    A don't share their own astute business skills.

    B are unwilling to fight for better financial rewards.

    C fail to appreciate the complexity of the publishing industry.

    D seem unaware that their falling incomes are part of a wider trend.

Part 4

🎧 15 You will hear five short extracts in which university students are talking about doing voluntary work on wildlife projects. While you listen, you must complete both tasks.

Task One

For questions **21–25**, choose from the list (**A–H**) the reason each speaker gives for deciding to do the work.

A to please a friend

B to make useful contacts

C to keep up a family tradition

D to help a charitable organisation

E to have an inexpensive holiday

F to gain specific skills

G to improve employment prospects

H to gather useful data

Speaker 1	21
Speaker 2	22
Speaker 3	23
Speaker 4	24
Speaker 5	25

Task Two

For questions **26–30**, choose from the list (**A–H**) what disappointed each speaker about the experience.

A the accommodation provided

B the initial training programme

C the level of ongoing support

D the catering arrangements

E the attitude of fellow volunteers

F the degree of challenge offered

G the unexpected costs

H the health and safety policy

Speaker 1	26
Speaker 2	27
Speaker 3	28
Speaker 4	29
Speaker 5	30

Part 1 (2 minutes)

Answer two questions from the following:

- Where are you from?

- What do you do here/there?

- How long have you been studying English?

- What do you enjoy most about studying English?

Now answer two more questions from the following:

- Do you enjoy going to the cinema with friends? Why/Why not?

- Is there anything in particular that you would like to learn in future? Why/Why not?

- Do you prefer listening to music at home or going to a live concert? Why?

- Have you always lived in the same place?

- Do you generally prefer to go shopping with friends or alone? Why?

- What kind of holidays do you enjoy? Why?

- How do you usually spend your free time at the weekends?

- If you could live anywhere in the world, where would you choose? Why?

Part 2 (4 minutes)

Interlocutor: In this part of the test, I'm going to give each of you three pictures. I'd like you to talk about **two** of them on your own for about a minute, and also to answer a question briefly about your partner's pictures.

Candidate A: It's your turn first. Here are your pictures. They show **people listening in different situations**. I'd like you to compare two of the pictures and say **why the people might be listening in these situations, and how important it might be for them to listen carefully**. All right?

Candidate B: *[Approximately 1 minute]*

Interlocutor: Thank you. *(Candidate A)*, **in which situation do you think it would be most difficult to concentrate**? (**Why**?)

Candidate B: *[Approximately 30 seconds]*

Interlocutor: Thank you.

Interlocutor: Thank you. Now, (*Candidate B*), here are your pictures. They show **people and visual images**. I'd like you to compare two of the pictures, and say **what feelings the people might have about the images they are looking at**. All right?

Candidate B: [*Approximately 1 minute*]

Interlocutor: Thank you. (*Candidate A*), **which person do you think feels most attached to their visual image**? (**Why**?)

Candidate A: [*Approximately 30 seconds*]

Interlocutor: Thank you.

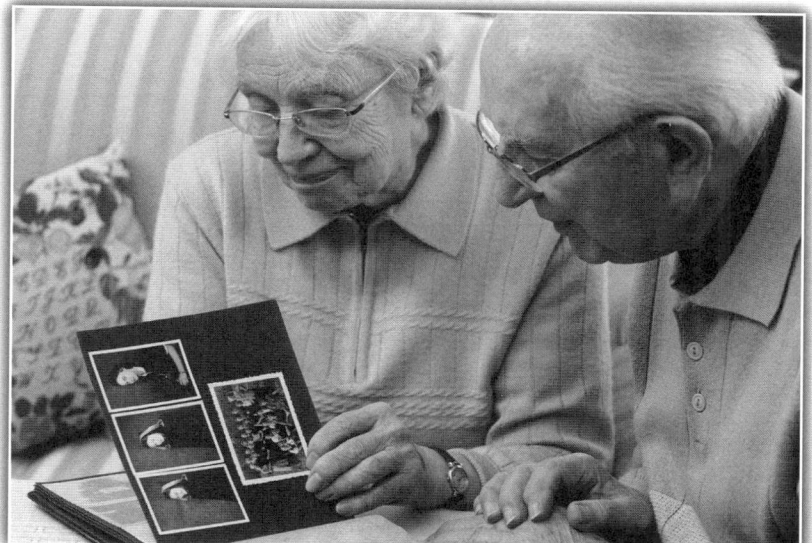

Part 3 (4 minutes)

Interlocutor: Now, I'd like you to talk about something together for about two minutes.

Here are some things young people often think about when they are trying to decide on their future career and a question for you to discuss. First you have some time to look at the task.

[15 seconds]

Now, talk to each other about **how important these things might be for young people who are trying to decide on their career.**

Candidates: *[2 minutes]*

Interlocutor: Thank you. Now you have about a minute to decide **which one would have the greatest influence on most people's decision about their career.**

Candidates: *[1 minute]*

Interlocutor: Thank you.

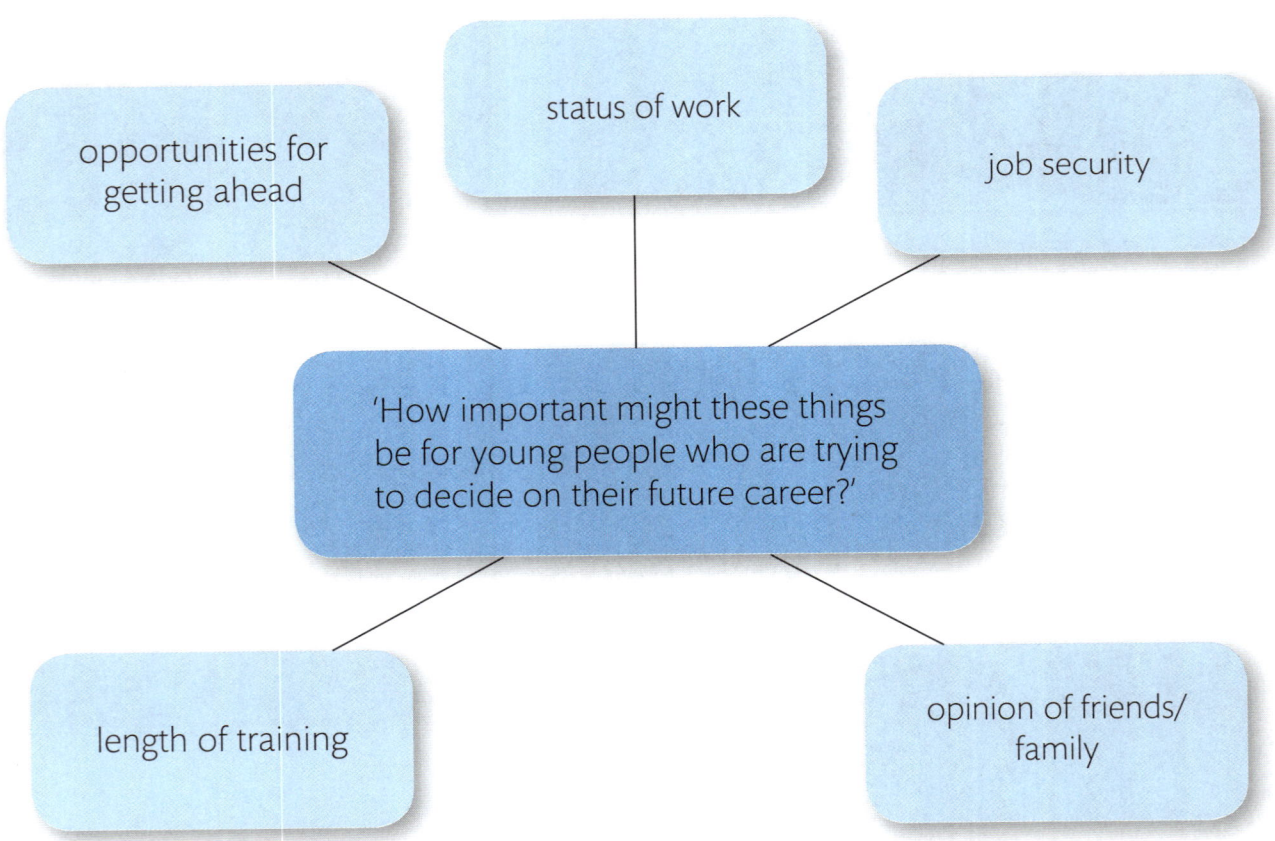

opportunities for getting ahead

status of work

job security

'How important might these things be for young people who are trying to decide on their future career?'

length of training

opinion of friends/ family

Part 4 (5 minutes)

- Is it always necessary to plan a career nowadays or is it better to just take opportunities as they come up? Why?

- Some people decide on a career when they are very young. Is this a good thing? Why/Why not?

- What can colleges do to help their students choose the most suitable career?

- What should be the priority when choosing a career: the money or the work itself? Why?

- Some people want a career that will enable them to travel. Are there any disadvantages to this?

- Many people choose to start their own business instead of following a career. Why do you think they do this?

CAMBRIDGE ENGLISH
Language Assessment
Part of the University of Cambridge

Do not write in this box

Candidate Name
If not already printed, write name in CAPITALS and complete the Candidate No. grid (in pencil).

Candidate Signature

Examination Title

Centre

Supervisor:
If the candidate is ABSENT or has WITHDRAWN shade here

Centre No.

Candidate No.

Examination Details

0	0	0	0
1	1	1	1
2	2	2	2
3	3	3	3
4	4	4	4
5	5	5	5
6	6	6	6
7	7	7	7
8	8	8	8
9	9	9	9

Candidate Answer Sheet

Instructions

Use a PENCIL (B or HB).

Rub out any answer you wish to change using an eraser.

Parts 1, 5, 6 and 7:
Mark ONE letter for each question.

For example, if you think **B** is the right answer to the question, mark your answer sheet like this:

0 A B C D

Parts 2, 3 and 4:
Write your answer clearly in CAPITAL LETTERS.

For Parts 2 and 3 write one letter in each box. For example:

0 EXAMPLE

Part 1

1	A	B	C	D
2	A	B	C	D
3	A	B	C	D
4	A	B	C	D
5	A	B	C	D
6	A	B	C	D
7	A	B	C	D
8	A	B	C	D

Part 2

Do not write below here

9		9 1 0 u
10		10 1 0 u
11		11 1 0 u
12		12 1 0 u
13		13 1 0 u
14		14 1 0 u
15		15 1 0 u
16		16 1 0 u

Continues over →

FCE R

DP802

Part 3

Do not write below here

17		17 1 0 u
18		18 1 0 u
19		19 1 0 u
20		20 1 0 u
21		21 1 0 u
22		22 1 0 u
23		23 1 0 u
24		24 1 0 u

Part 4

Do not write below here

25		25 2 1 0 u
26		26 2 1 0 u
27		27 2 1 0 u
28		28 2 1 0 u
29		29 2 1 0 u
30		30 2 1 0 u

Part 5

31	A	B	C	D
32	A	B	C	D
33	A	B	C	D
34	A	B	C	D
35	A	B	C	D
36	A	B	C	D

Part 6

37	A	B	C	D	E	F	G
38	A	B	C	D	E	F	G
39	A	B	C	D	E	F	G
40	A	B	C	D	E	F	G
41	A	B	C	D	E	F	G
42	A	B	C	D	E	F	G

Part 7

43	A	B	C	D	E	F
44	A	B	C	D	E	F
45	A	B	C	D	E	F
46	A	B	C	D	E	F
47	A	B	C	D	E	F
48	A	B	C	D	E	F
49	A	B	C	D	E	F
50	A	B	C	D	E	F
51	A	B	C	D	E	F
52	A	B	C	D	E	F

denote Print Limited 0121 520 5100

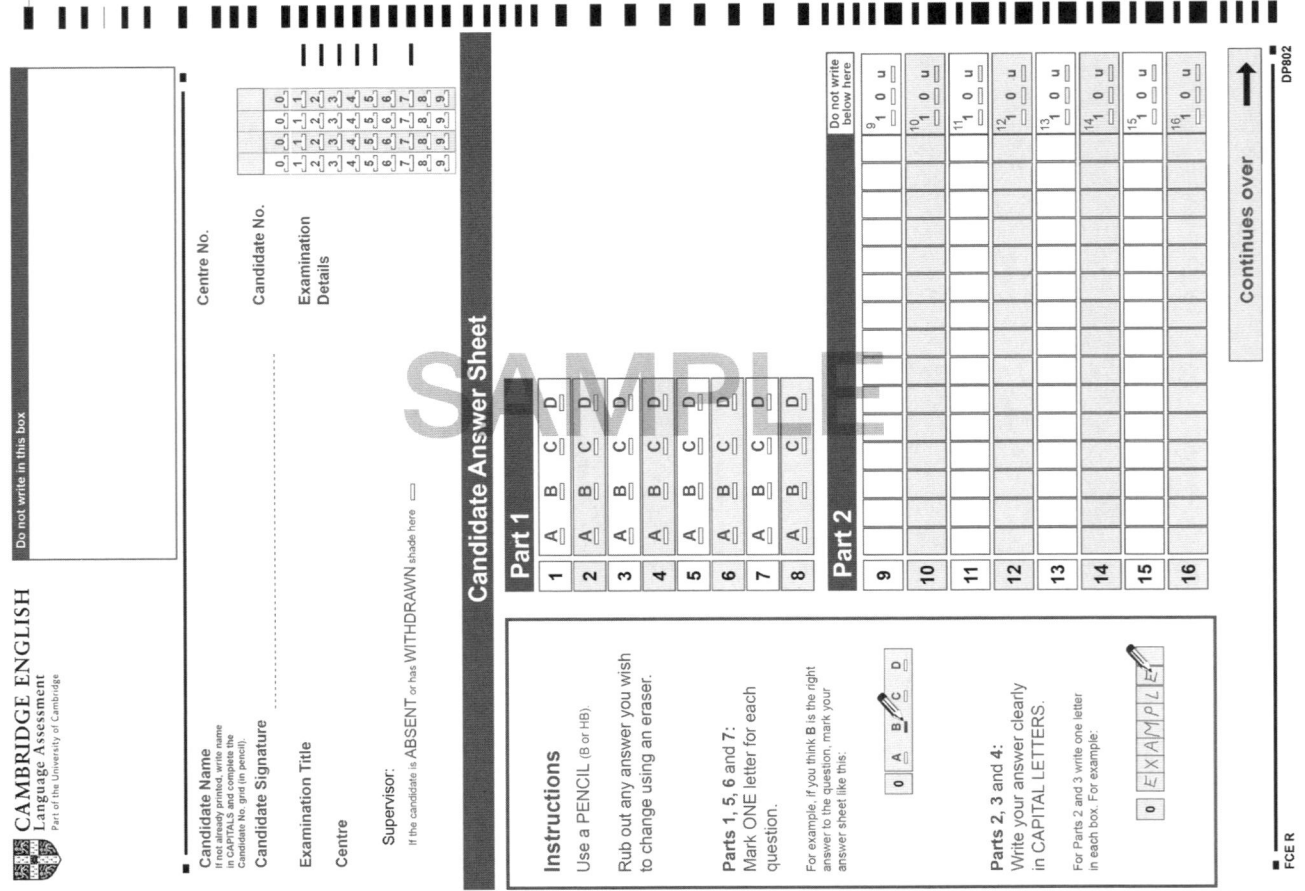

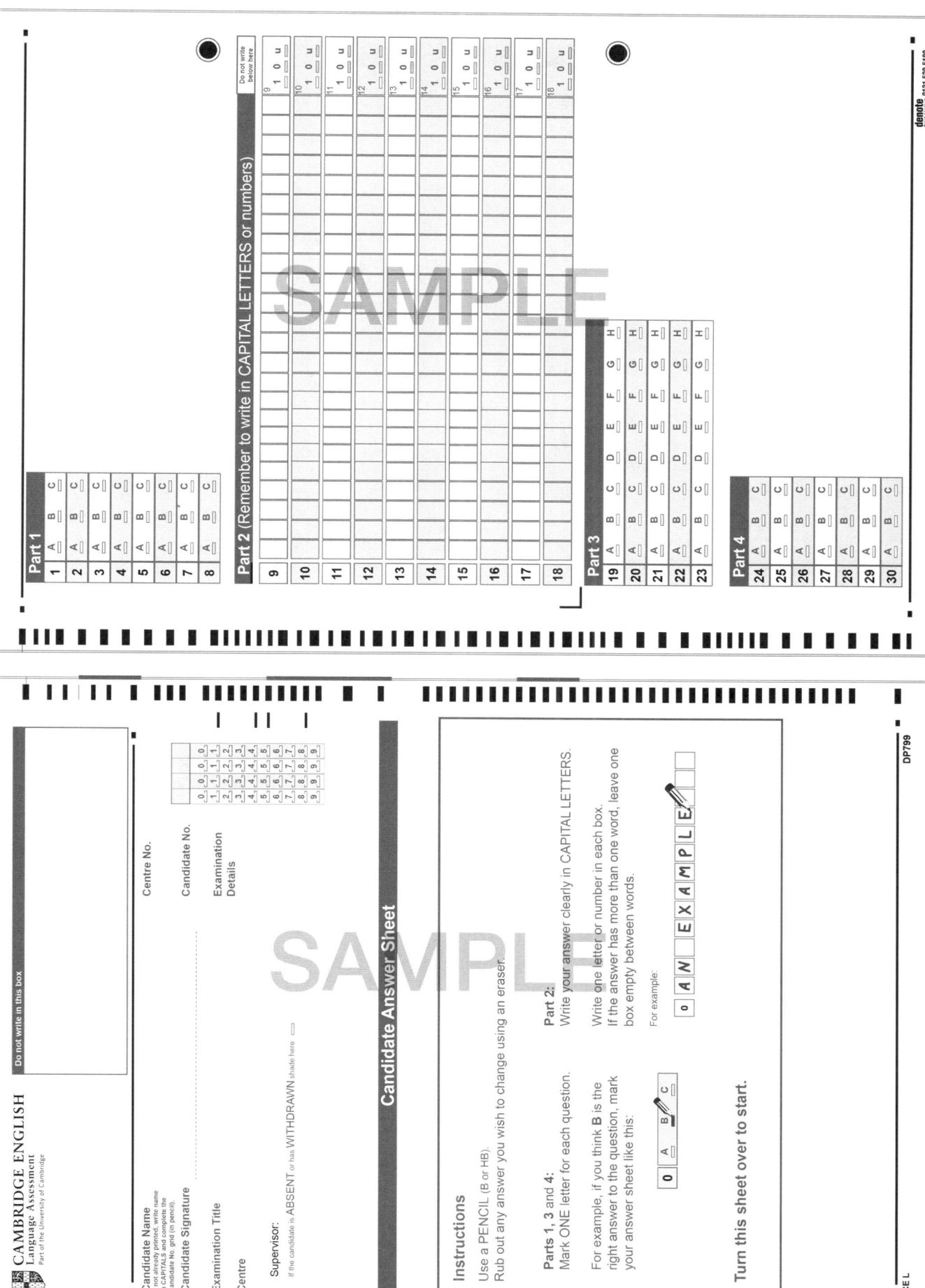

Exam countdown – top tips

Nine months before

- You've already built up a good knowledge of English and now you're starting on the final year of preparation for the *Cambridge English: Advanced* examination. Work consistently, study conscientiously and above all, enjoy learning!
- Establish good habits from the outset.
- Keep vocabulary lists in your notebook that include derivations, opposites, useful phrases, etc.
- Note down any word formations that might present a problem.
- Read widely outside the classroom. Use the resources of the internet to help you (online newspapers, magazines, etc.) plus official Cambridge ESOL guidelines and advice.
- Make use of communication websites to listen to interesting talks in English in order to develop your listening skills further.

Six months before

- Start looking back at what you've learnt over the previous three months. Constant revision is essential to successful learning. It's no use leaving it all until the last minute! The more often you study a new word or phrase, the more likely it is to remain fixed in your memory.
- Go through your written work. Are you developing your use of language sufficiently? Make a conscious effort to use new language in your written work.

Three months before

- By now, you should have acquired a comprehensive understanding of the exam and its requirements and you should be completely familiar with all the exam tasks.
- Revise your vocabulary and word formation lists, highlighting any areas that you feel need special attention. Spend as much time as possible on your English.
- Start to practise the exam tasks under exam conditions: whenever you do an exam task, time yourself so that you can finish it within the time limit.

On the day

- Make sure you take your identification. It must have your photo on it and must be the original document, not a copy.
- You will also need a pen, an HB or B pencil and an eraser.
- You should feel confident, knowing that you have prepared as well as you can for the exam.
- There will be a clock in the exam room but wear a watch if possible and time each section of the exam very carefully. There won't be very much time to spare, so it's important that you know exactly how much time you have. Try not to run over your timing for each part.
- Answer all questions as you work through the paper since you might not have time to check your answers at the end. Ideally, however, you should plan to spend time at the end of each paper checking your answers so that you can change them if necessary.

The day before

- You should have a quick look through your most important notes, the highlighted points in your vocabulary and word formations, together with any other important areas. Do not try to cram in new material that you haven't managed to cover before.
- Know when to say, 'Enough is enough,' and get a good night's sleep. Your brain cannot work efficiently on five hours' sleep!

One month before

- Having done so much exam practice and preparation, you should by now feel confident in your knowledge of the language and your ability to cope successfully in the exam.
- You know that lexical chunks (verb phrases, prepositional phrases and so on) make up a large part of language learning. Revise all the phrases you have learnt, highlighting any particular ones that you find difficult to remember.
- Do a mock exam under exam conditions, whether through your school or on your own at home, if you are following a course of self-study. Check your performance according to timing, word count, etc.

Module 1

Vocabulary development 1

1
1	strong preference	4	wide variety
2	high salary	5	long hours
3	main priority	6	impressive CV

2
1	set	5	gain
2	taken	6	achieve
3	put	7	seize
4	overcome	8	make

3
1	pleasure in	5	notice of
2	pity on	6	pride in
3	aback by	7	advantage of
4	exception to	8	in, stride

4
1 successful, applicant, confident
2 qualifications, evidence, interested
3 disappointment, optimistic, determined
4 reliability, communicator, flexibility

Use of English

3 1 B   2 D   3 C   4 A   5 A   6 D   7 C   8 B

Expert language
2 (meet deadlines)

Language development 1

1
1	've gained	5	hasn't worked
2	was	6	finished
3	has made	7	had decided
4	had never had	8	had met

2
1 **a** was travelling; **b** travelled
2 **a** have been reading; **b** read
3 **a** stays; **b** is staying
4 **a** had eaten; **b** had been eating
5 **a** will probably be leaving; **b** will leave

3
1	am working	11	left
2	have been writing	12	had
3	gives	13	had been working/was working
4	am	14	applied
5	feel/have felt/have been feeling	15	had told
6	don't get/am not getting	16	promised
7	realise	17	hadn't seen
8	has been/is	18	was spending/had spent
9	have acquired/am acquiring	19	landed
10	still think	20	had gained

Use of English

3
1	who	4	make	7	more
2	on	5	out	8	before
3	though/if	6	what		

Expert language
2 (**switched** her **on** to the legal profession) and 5 (**figuring out** problems)

Listening

1
1 three
2 Extract One: two law graduates talking about their education and career; Extract Two: an interview with a recent graduate; Extract Three: a discussion programme about career choices

2 We know that the speakers are law graduates and that they will be talking about their education and career. We know that one of the speakers is surprised about something, and that they both appreciate a particular aspect of studying law.

3 1 A   2 B   3 A   4 C   5 A   6 B

Expert language
present: 2, 6   past: 1, 3, 4, 5

Vocabulary development 2

1a
1 tense, intimidated by
2 motivated, distracted
3 apprehensive, daunted
4 frustrated, overwhelmed by

1b
1 keep up (with)
2 take in
3 put (me) off
4 dropped out (of)

2
1	Professors	4	Teachers	7	Trainers
2	Tutors	5	Lecturers		
3	Instructors	6	Coaches		

3
1	at, on	3	with, from	5	by, in
2	by, of	4	to, under	6	about, by

4
1	top	4	status	7	key
2	clear	5	investment	8	outcomes
3	pay	6	value		

Reading

4–5 1 C   2 D   3 A   4 B   5 C   6 A   7 D   8 A   9 C   10 B

6
1	frazzled	6	trumpeting
2	supplementary	7	enhance
3	stirred up	8	steered (towards)
4	flux	9	dropped
5	tap into	10	foster

Expert language
science, technology, engineering, maths, English literature and composition, (American) history, calculus, US politics and government, psychology, (world) history, biology, chemistry, computing science, physics, poetry, humanities, English, French, art, social anthropology, literature

Language development 2

1
1 will be/is going to be
2 were/had been
3 was
4 is being
5 is
6 is

2
1 is located
2 are always taught
3 was originally opened
4 have been developed
5 will be guaranteed
6 is continually being invested

3
1 I think you should be taught by a reputable driving instructor rather than your parents.
2 Some models of vehicle can't be used for the test.
3 Your test might be cancelled if you don't have the right documents.
4 I should have been taken on the big roundabout before I took the test.
5 You may be shouted at (by the instructor) sometimes.
6 Your provisional licence has to be shown to the instructor on your first lesson.

4
1 ... is being ~~criticise~~ criticised for ...
2 ... be prepared to be ~~asking~~ asked some ...
3 ... insisted on being ~~tell~~ told ...
4 ... resent ~~be~~ being made ...
5 ... want to be ~~keep~~ kept informed ...
6 ... expecting to be pick**ed** up ...

5
1 He is said to have been a truly inspirational teacher.
2 They are expected to be arriving at around six o'clock.
3 It is now known that the situation is far worse than had been first thought.
4 It is believed that the Education Secretary will be handing in his resignation later today.
5 There is understood to be very little chance of a peace agreement at this stage.
6 It is hoped that they will have more news before the end of the evening.

Use of English

2
1 came as a great/big surprise to
2 had great difficulty (in)
3 was on the point of accepting
4 matter how hard she works
5 did not/didn't meet with her parents'
6 was a source of disappointment to
7 no circumstances should/may/can students
8 lived up to Gina's
9 (really) took his studies very seriously
10 priority is the repayment

Writing

1
1 your cousin
2 to give advice
3 informal
4 advice about whether or not to (1) look for a permanent job (2) get work experience (3) go travelling overseas

3
1 going straight into a permanent job (against)
2 travelling overseas (for)
3 doing work experience (against)
4 going straight into a permanent job (for)
5 travelling overseas (against)
6 doing work experience (for)

4
1 I'd advise you not to ...
2 Why don't you ...?
3 I'd ... if I were you.
4 What I've found great ... is ...
5 I don't recommend ...
6 It might be good for ...

5a
1 In addition
2 Nevertheless
3 In my view
4 In contrast

5b *Suggested answers*
- Why don't you see a bit of the world, which will give you the time and space to think about what to do next? Mind you, the problem is that you'd need to ...
- I'd be careful if I were you. It can be hard work and you may feel resentful if you're not paid for it. Even so, it might be good for your CV ...

6
Opening: 1, 4
Closing: 1, 3, 4, 5

7 *Model answer*

Hi Sara,

It was great to hear from you, and I'm really sorry I haven't been in touch for so long – it's been mad here at work recently! Anyway, you certainly have a tough decision to make!

Personally, I wouldn't think of settling down just yet; once you're in a permanent job, it's hard to leave – and remember: it's for the rest of your life! It's great to be earning money but there's plenty of time for that. After all, you've only just turned 21!

So I'd suggest seeing a bit of the world and having a break after your exams. You could go to Australia – you've always wanted to go there. Of course, unless you manage to find paid work there, you'll have to do some casual work here first to pay for your flight and living expenses. But six months should do it, especially if you can save money by living at home! Why not see if that little restaurant I worked at has any vacancies? The pay wasn't bad and it was quite fun at times.

As for work experience, it's difficult. It's OK if they pay your expenses or give you a small salary but otherwise it's annoying having to work for nothing. Why not think about that when you get back from your travels?

Anyway, good luck with whatever you decide, and hope to see you very soon.

Take care,
Liz

Audio script 02

Extract One

M: Not many kids I grew up with went to university. I mean, they got jobs, learnt to be electricians or carpenters or whatever, but they didn't have horizons beyond that. So for me, it was a really big step. My grandfather was a docker in London – he couldn't ever have imagined that his grandson would go to university to study law – it was like a massive shock to him. So when I got to Manchester, it was, like, really baffling to me to come across students who just seemed to be there to have a good time. I gave them a wide berth, generally.

F: I know what you mean. Basically, it's like an extension of school for some people – they're still growing up – don't really know where they're heading careerwise. I mean, that's the thing about doing a subject like ours – the future's kind of mapped out in many ways and that makes it easier to knuckle down.

M: Well, it's not completely pre-programmed. I mean, either of us could've gone into industry rather than a legal practice, but your goals are more concrete than in a lot of subjects you might study.

F: Sure, there are choices to make along the road, but the road's always there – that's what appeals to me, actually.

Extract Two

F: So how did it feel when your final exams were over and you were out there in the job market?

M: I spent the first couple of weeks letting off steam – getting student life out of my system for the last time – then I got on the internet. I mean, some people'd been going to careers events, lining stuff up all through their final year, but I thought that was tempting fate rather – better to get your results under your belt first, and it wasn't as if I was looking to join a graduate recruitment programme with a big company anyway.

F: So what did you do?

M: I went for the blanket coverage approach. A quick scan of the job ad, attach your CV, then click. Sometimes I only read the full job spec after I'd applied. At the end of the day, applying doesn't commit you to anything. At least you keep things moving and get experience. Like, I got invited to a group interview for an internship and got temporary work writing stuff for a blog – all grist to the mill. Then finally, after seven weeks, I got lucky and landed a paid job in a call centre, which is exactly the sector I was hoping to go into long-term. I was sorted.

Extract Three

F: So was your career path mapped out from the outset, Bob?

M: Hardly. I jumped at the first job opportunity I was given. Not that this is necessarily a bad move if that first opportunity's the right fit. But I chose to become a sales consultant because the salary package was incredible. What I discovered, however, was that this couldn't compensate for the lack of purpose I felt crunching numbers on a daily basis.

F: Sure …

M: Ultimately, I decided to leave that career and pursue something I was truly passionate about: working with children. Though financially I've taken a large hit from this decision, I'd trade that any day for the daily satisfaction I get from changing kids' lives. How about you?

F: Well, I chose English as my major in college, mainly for lack of anything I was more interested in. After trying out a couple of different careers, which were fun but not always fulfilling, I stumbled upon something that's pretty much a perfect fit for me: proofreading. It was pure chance, really, because it's not something I ever thought about as a job while I was in college, so I had no idea I was preparing for it at that time. But it worked out perfectly!

Module 2

Vocabulary development 1

1 **1** e **2** h **3** a **4** g **5** f **6** c **7** d **8** b

All the adjectives are hyphenated, with the exception of *straightforward* and *outspoken*.

2
1	laid-back	**5**	high-spirited
2	level-headed	**6**	outspoken
3	be self-contained	**7**	straightforward
4	is quick-witted	**8**	absent-minded

3
1	tactless, insensitive	**3**	impractical, disorganised
2	unsociable, inconsiderate	**4**	impatient, disloyal
		5	unselfish, insincere

4
1	down	**3**	out	**5**	off	**7**	after
2	down	**4**	on	**6**	down	**8**	over

5
1	supportive	**3**	aggressive	**5**	ambitious
2	passionate	**4**	critical	**6**	hostility

6
1	a	**3**	get	**5**	over/round
2	in	**4**	into	**6**	for

Use of English

3 **1** B **2** C **3** A **4** D **5** A **6** B **7** C **8** D

Expert language
had aroused, had gone, had placed

Language development 1

1
1 … Revell**,** who has just … by the Heart Foundation**,** …
2 hospital**,** where …
3 which/that
4 … end**,** which was …
5 which/that
6 Simon**,** whose stories … book**,** …
7 who/that

2
1 The woman I met at your party inspired me to go into publishing.
2 That singer, whose name I can never remember, was fantastic.
3 I got the idea from my brother, who went there last year.
4 The concert is on 10 March, (which is) when I'm supposed to be going to the dentist's.
5 We're going to Andorra for a couple of days, which should be very interesting.
6 It was after midnight when I finally got to bed.
7 We went to a restaurant I'd never been to before.
8 Fred, who lives over the road, is hoping to be an actor.

3
1 … charity, ~~who~~ **whose** aim is …
2 … bullying, ~~that~~ **which** is so common …
3 … problem, which ~~it~~ needs …
4 ✓
5 ✓
6 ✓
7 … singer, ~~who's~~ **whose** son was …
8 … project, which ~~it's~~ **is** said …

4
1	on which	**4**	Jo's talking to
2	both of which	**5**	Mark applied for
3	I went with	**6**	which

Use of English

4
1	too	**5**	Although/Though/While
2	hardly/barely	**6**	take
3	or	**7**	As
4	how	**8**	them/one

Expert language
signed up, cut back (on)

Listening

1 five

2a what first impressed the speakers

2b how each speaker feels now

3 1 C 2 D 3 E 4 F 5 B 6 D 7 F 8 H 9 G 10 A

> **Expert language**
> **-(i)ty:** modesty, generosity, loyalty, integrity, difficulty (*difficulties* in the task)
> **-tion:** attention, determination, reputation
> **-ce:** patience
> **-ness:** willingness, weakness (*weaknesses* in the task)
> **-ment:** commitment, achievement (*achievements* in the task)

Reading

1 A fly-on-the-wall documentary is one where the people involved behave naturally, as if the camera were not there.

4–5 1 C 2 A 3 D 4 C

6a 1 c 2 a 3 e 4 f 5 b 6 d

6b 1 bring something into the public eye
2 shed light on something
3 go a long way towards (doing) something
4 restore one's confidence in something
5 have a knock-on effect
6 give the go-ahead

> **Expert language**
> ... students who clearly have **little** interest ...

Vocabulary development 2

1 1 possibility   5 occasion
2 chance   6 chance
3 opportunities   7 possibility
4 chance   8 opportunity

2 1 editor   6 creativity
2 imagination   7 products
3 success   8 player
4 rejections   9 failure
5 encouragement   10 shot

3 1 gave himself up
2 let the young offender off
3 got away with it
4 got over
5 broke out of
6 caught the offender out

4 1 charged   5 serving
2 sentenced   6 trouble
3 release   7 bars
4 arrested   8 committed

Language development 2

1 1 ∅   5 the   9 ∅   13 ∅
2 the   6 ∅   10 the   14 a
3 a   7 ∅   11 the   15 ∅
4 ∅   8 the   12 the   16 a

2 1 is   5 is
2 are trying   6 don't like
3 seems   7 show/have shown
4 has/have had   8 want

3 1 ... and ~~all~~ **both** of them were ...
2 ... haven't got ~~neither~~ **either** of those ...
3 ✓
4 ... spent **the** whole day ...
5 ~~None~~ **No one/Nobody** wants to ...
6 ✓
7 A great ~~deal~~ **number** of prisoners ...
8 ✓

4 1 A   6 the whole
2 the Philippines   7 A few
3 the   8 several
4 number   9 Everyone
5 majority   10 how many

Use of English

4 1 catering   5 unpredictable
2 increasingly   6 shortage(s)
3 growth   7 interruptions
4 drawbacks   8 reoffended

> **Expert language**
> despite, nonetheless

Writing

1 1 a school principal
2 formal
3 benefits of exclusion, drawbacks of exclusion, the school council's views

2 1 ✗   4 ✓   7 ✓
2 ✗   5 ✗
3 ✓   6 ✗

3 1 e 2 d 3 c/f 4 f/c 5 b 6 a

5a 1 a 2 d 3 b 4 c, f 5 e

5b 1 iii   4 ii, vi
2 ii   5 ii
3 ii

6 *Model answer*

Report on the benefits and drawbacks of exclusion from school
Introduction
The aims of this report are to:
- summarise the views of students at this school about the policy of exclusion.
- give the opinions of the school council on what should be done next.

In order for us to prepare this report, students were asked to complete a brief questionnaire. This was followed up with a short meeting in which we discussed their views.
Advantages of exclusion
The majority of students in favour of exclusion felt that:
1 concentration in classes was difficult when students were disruptive.
2 teachers had to focus on discipline rather than teaching.
Drawbacks of exclusion
The higher proportion of students were against exclusion as a punishment for the following reasons.
1 It was claimed that this would serve no useful purpose and could even worsen behaviour.
2 It was felt that it should be the responsibility of the school to address the issue rather than transferring the problem to another school.

3 It is believed by many that the students who are misbehaving would behave differently if they were given some individual attention and encouragement.

Recommendations

In the main, students were in favour of investigating options other than exclusion.

In our opinion, the school should attempt to do the following:

- fund an educational psychologist to visit the school on a regular basis and have individual tutorials with the students concerned.
- establish a 'mentoring' system so that older students meet offending students every week and try to help and encourage them.

Audio script 03

Sp 1: My role model was actually my geography teacher at school. Although he wasn't exactly a live wire in the classroom, he took great pride in producing maps and diagrams. He must've spent ages over them because they were incredibly accurate and beautifully presented. Actually, he was like that in almost everything he did, patient and thorough, and it's thanks to him I chose to study cartography. He wasn't without his faults, though. He didn't suffer fools gladly and would get quite angry if your work didn't come up to his exacting standards. It upset me at the time and I think it held him back as a teacher, but now I'm older I don't hold it against him.

Sp 2: The person I most look up to is actually one of my classmates from school. He's a brilliant singer and quite the extrovert. What I've always admired is his ability to stick at things in the face of big setbacks. So I'm not surprised that his singing career's now going so well, after a few ups and downs. It makes me smile to read in gossip magazines that he's regarded as a heartthrob – I mean, I remember him as a skinny teenager with baggy trousers! He made a few mistakes in his choice of friends when he first hit the big time and I was a bit worried about him at one stage, but he's settled down a lot now.

Sp 3: If I had to name somebody who's had a big influence on me, it'd be my cousin Sean. Even today, he's always up for a challenge and seems not to know what fear is, whether he's white-water rafting or giving a TV interview. I wish I could be like that. As he's a couple of years older than me, there was never any chance of me competing with Sean as a kid. But he never made me feel inadequate if I couldn't do everything he did. He'd simply wait for me to catch up or explain carefully what I needed to do – and he was like that with everybody. It was that quality that I responded to in him.

Sp 4: I love my brother to bits, even if you never know what he's going to do next. His mad business projects don't always work out as planned but he'll be the first to take the blame if things do go pear-shaped. That's why I've always looked up to him so much. There's neither pride nor false modesty in his character – he's just an independent spirit who follows his own inclinations. He's been let down by quite a few friends recently and, being his sister, I know how he must be feeling. It's been tough but I'm sure he won't let that stand in the way of his next venture, so I'm not losing any sleep about it.

Sp 5: Although my role model's a professional sportsperson, it's not his Olympic medals that I hope to emulate – exciting as that might be – it's his charity work. I'd never really taken much notice of his sporting achievements – not being into cycling – so he only really came to my attention when I got involved with a charity that organises activities for children with learning difficulties. That's when I realised that he not only provides financial support to countless organisations like ours but also devotes most of his free time to helping others. I never cease to be amazed at the number of charities he works with – however does he find the time? I'm certainly keen to follow his example.

Module 3

Vocabulary development 1

1
| 1 | adaptable | 3 | persistent |
| 2 | perfectionism | 4 | fussy |

2
1	setting up	4	get (something) down
2	come back (to)	5	break through
3	move on	6	come up with

3a move fast: dash, plunge, race, shoot, soar, tear
go somewhere quickly for a short time: nip, pop
move slowly or aimlessly: dawdle, drift, plod, saunter, wander
move quietly in order not to be noticed: crawl, creep, sidle, sneak

3b 1 e 2 c 3 b 4 d 5 f 6 a

4
| 1 | soared | 3 | crawled | 5 | drifted |
| 2 | plodded | 4 | wandered | | |

5
1	realise	4	shoot	7	released
2	motion	5	soundtrack	8	deal
3	budget	6	debut		

Use of English

3 1 D 2 C 3 A 4 B 5 A 6 B 7 D 8 C

Expert language
has been going ahead, have been constructed, has (also) been (heavily) involved in

Language development 1

1 1 B 2 A 3 B 4 C 5 B 6 A 7 A 8 C

2
1 The train is due to arrive
2 I'm about to go out.
3 she's bound to refuse
4 I'm on the point of giving up
5 The talks are on the verge of breaking down.
6 Beyoncé is likely to be headlining

3
1 was going to join
2 wouldn't take
3 was due to hand in
4 was about to sign up
5 wouldn't be
6 were going to offer me

4
1	on the verge of	4	was to
2	would	5	on the point of phoning
3	would have	6	about to

Answer key

Use of English

1 A trophy is given as a prize to the winner of a competition, race, etc.

4
1	outstanding	5	integration
2	prestigious	6	successfully
3	winner	7	vitality
4	influential	8	authenticity

Expert language
came up with

Listening

1 a student; about how leisure activities can influence job prospects

4
1	cultural fit	5	public relations (departments)
2	drive	6	social media
3	leadership	7	strategically
4	(team) captain	8	token hobbies

Expert language
associated with, suitable for

Vocabulary development 2

1
1	version	7	main	13	plot
2	on	8	convincing	14	part
3	strong	9	ovation	15	make
4	broadcast	10	rave	16	gave
5	opened	11	on	17	nominated
6	returns	12	set	18	put

2
1	version	5	was set	7	plot
2	broadcast	6	making a name for himself	8	put (a lot) into
3	convincing				
4	rave review				

3
1	out	4	into	7	off
2	off	5	in	8	on
3	on	6	forward		

4 1 f 2 b 3 d 4 e 5 a 6 c

Reading

2
1 He is a photographer.
2 Chinese tea caddies, miniature televisions, commemorative plates, cigarette cases (decorated with Russian space-dogs), photographic prints, photography books
3 the (12,000) photography books he has collected over the past 35 years
4 books of his own work

3–4 1 F 2 G 3 E 4 C 5 B 6 D

Expert language
Compound nouns: self-portraits, space-dogs, photo-historian
Compound adjectives: best-known, narrow-minded

Language development 2

1
1	don't usually have to	4	had to
2	must	5	must
3	needn't have	6	needn't wait

2
1	must /should/ought to
2	had better/should/ought to
3	can't/mustn't
4	should have/ought to have
5	mustn't/shouldn't
6	couldn't

3
1 I ~~could finally~~ **was finally able to/finally managed to** borrow the car …
2 ✓
3 ✓
4 I ~~could~~ **managed to/was able to** pass my violin exam …
5 ✓
6 Next year we will ~~can~~ **be able to** apply …

4 1 C 2 B 3 A 4 B 5 B

5
1	can't have seen	4	mustn't wear
2	could have been	5	needn't have worried
3	should have told	6	didn't need to explain

Use of English

2
1	used to go running on a
2	is widely expected to
3	than one/a year since Fiona last
4	had finished/was over by the time
5	is thought to be over
6	must have broken the vase
7	should/must/has to/needs to be pressed before coins
8	has not been serviced for
9	came as a complete/total shock/surprise to
10	will be taken into consideration before

Expert language
See underlined passive forms in Exercise 2 above.

Writing

1 4 ✓ 5 ✓

2a 1 C 2 D/A 3 A/D 4 B

2b
1 the first two
2 2nd opinion: disagree; 1st opinion: agree
3 **para A (2nd note):** People are reluctant to take up creative activities because they worry they may fail.
para D (1st note) People feel there is more chance of getting a job if they study something academic.
4 **para A (2nd note):** They should be made to try them and have a wider range of subjects to choose from.
para D (1st note): If more jobs requiring creativity were available, students would be more likely to study them.

3 **Introduction:** 2, 4, 6; **Conclusion:** 1, 3, 5

4 See Coursebook Exercise 2a for a model answer.

Audio script 04

Speaker: Hi there. My name's Aaron Cole and my presentation's going to focus on how your free-time activities can have an impact on your employability. I'm going to outline some research findings that indicate which common hobbies or activities might make you attractive for various types of job.

Now, this may sound a little far-fetched but at least one prestigious management school in the USA has done research to show that employers there are now using information provided on a CV about a candidate's hobbies and leisure interests as a key indicator of what's called cultural fit. In fact, many employers consider this when faced with candidates whose qualifications and experience are pretty much the same.

First up, something lots of students are into: endurance sports. Anything from running to cycling, swimming and so on, suggests that a person has tenacity, perseverance and most of all *drive* – exactly the quality needed to make your mark as a sales executive. That's not to say other sectors wouldn't be interested, of course.

Then there's adventure sports. Activities such as mountain climbing and sky-diving appeal to people who like to push back boundaries and thrive on what are defined as calculated risks. This makes these people very suitable for going into leadership roles, whether it's managing people directly or processes such as product development.

Now, a lot of people play team sports in their student years and although this can provide evidence of your ability to work as part of a team, unless you've done something out of the ordinary, like regularly being chosen as team captain, this is not an area that's going to cut much ice with employers.

And of course, we're not only talking about active leisure pursuits. Hobbies like cooking, painting and photography suggest a creative mind, which obviously makes you more appealing to employers in areas such as product design and marketing. Less predictable, for me at least, was the finding that recruiters in public relations departments are also looking for these kinds of qualities.

Meanwhile, an interest in creative writing – whether fiction or a personal blog – can highlight your strengths as a communicator of ideas. This is highly sought-after when companies are getting into social media and want to establish themselves there, but there are also opportunities for copywriters in advertising and various types of editorial work.

Meanwhile, an interest in games like chess, backgammon or sudoku shows that you enjoy thinking strategically. This type of strength is desirable for positions where policy development is central to the work because of the importance of planning in that sort of role.

But having said all this, there's no point in making untrue claims about an interest in certain activities when you're making an application. Recruiters can spot what they term 'token hobbies' and often try to get applicants talking about the activity to see how deep their interest goes. If it's not genuine, therefore, it could work against you rather than in your favour.

So before I go on to … *[fade]*

Module 4

Vocabulary development 1

1
1	losing, over	5	sent, to
2	put to	6	slept through
3	rough on	7	slept in
4	get to	8	sleeping over

2 1 d 2 e 3 b 4 a 5 f 6 c

3
1	fell through	3	fell behind	5	fall back
2	fell in	4	fall out	6	fell over

4
1	when	3	parcel	5	miss
2	thin	4	large	6	go

5
1	on	4	invaluable	7	extensively
2	onset	5	rituals	8	brought
3	put	6	bear		

Use of English

4 1 B 2 C 3 D 4 D 5 A 6 C 7 A 8 C

Language development 1

1a
1	hesitation	9	defensive	17	apparent
2	hesitant	10	hope	18	widen
3	happy	11	hope	19	width
4	please	12	specification	20	endanger
5	pleasure	13	specific	21	dangerous
6	persistence	14	criticise	22	enjoyment
7	persistent	15	critical	23	enjoyable
8	defend	16	appearance		

1b
1 -ness, -ure, -nce/-ance/-ence, -ion, -th, -ic, ment
2 -y, -ant, -ive, -ful, -less, -ic, -al, -ent, -ous, -able
3 -ify, -ise, -en

2a
1	romantic	8	patient	15	various
2	traveller	9	rewarding	16	useful
3	decision	10	excitement	17	departure
4	broaden	11	awareness	18	comfortable
5	behaviour	12	cultural	19	active
6	similarities	13	confused	20	tolerant
7	differences	14	surroundings	21	flexible

2b (Suffixes that are new in Exercise 2b are underlined.)
1 -er, -ion, -iour, -ity, -ence, -ment, -ness, -ing, -ure
2 -ic, -ent, -ing, -al, -ed, -ous, -ful, -able, -ive, -ant, -ible
3 -en

3a
1 She's (very) impatient with her brother.
2 Marc is a bit over-emotional.
3 She's unwilling to help us.
4 How can I enlarge this picture?
5 I think she has every reason to distrust/mistrust him.
6 I always mispronounce that word.
7 Do we need to pre-book tickets?
8 The work is incomplete.
9 I was undercharged.
10 You can reuse that plastic bag – don't throw it away.

3b
1	redecorate	6	disloyal
2	overrated/underrated	7	unwrap/rewrap
3	overworked/ underworked	8	misunderstand
		9	endanger
4	improbable	10	replace/misplace
5	inedible		

Use of English

4
1	disruption(s)	4	capable	7	insufficient
2	effective	5	exposure	8	highly
3	unavailable	6	treatment		

Listening

1 No, students need to complete both tasks as they listen.

2a each speaker's main reason for joining the group

2b what each speaker has gained most from being part of the group

3 1 D 2 B 3 E 4 C 5 H 6 H 7 A 8 E 9 D 10 B

Reading

4-5 1 A 2 C 3 C 4 A 5 B 6 D

Vocabulary development 2

1
1 She is digging her heels in on this issue.
2 Let's agree to differ on this issue.
3 We had to meet them halfway in order to reach a final agreement.
4 She is sitting on the fence about this problem.
5 We keep going round in circles – we need to make a decision!
6 I'm not convinced but I'll give you the benefit of the doubt.

2
1	have	4	have	7	made
2	put	5	take	8	taking
3	make/take	6	putting		

3
1	come	3	accept	5	settle
2	work	4	be	6	change

4
1	raised	5	put	9	way
2	unanimous	6	went	10	reach
3	consultation	7	opposed	11	petition
4	high	8	basis	12	publicity

Language development 2

1
1 There is no evidence that she was involved in the crime.
2 There is a strong likelihood that he will ask us to work late.
3 It is very sad that pandas may become extinct.
4 My research showed/found/revealed that a high number of people were face-blind.
5 The teacher explained that there was a wide variety of options/that a wide variety of options are/were available to students.
6 It is very encouraging that a lot of young people have joined the programme this year.

2
1	what	5	when	9	where
2	Who	6	who	10	Why
3	which	7	What		
4	how	8	why		

3
1	to set up	5	to rely on	9	working
2	to use	6	providing	10	to persuade
3	to raise	7	to improve		
4	staffing	8	to be		

4
1	Volunteering	4	who, what	7	that
2	to overstate	5	It, to share		
3	that	6	having		

Use of English

2
1	all likelihood Debbie will/is going to	5	calls for a great
2	was (really) looking forward to beginning	6	lent her loyal support to
3	was of particular concern	7	would be highly beneficial
4	traffic prevented us from arriving	8	remains to be
		9	hardly any (of the) protestors
		10	put paid to

Writing

1
1 to mend relations with the local community
2 the college principal
3 formal/semi-formal

2b 2 and 3

3
1	g	5	h	9	c
2	k	6	j	10	a
3	l	7	i	11	d
4	e	8	f	12	b

4
1 examples: good relations can be reestablished; the concerns raised; a good relationship be maintained; the college is located; the noise is kept; It is understood; It has also been noted; takeaway wrappers and empty soft drink cans are often found; a letter of apology to be written … and distributed; contact with our neighbours to be initiated; a system to be put in place; Were the short-term recommendation … to be implemented … and followed; any present tension could quickly be resolved
3 examples: re-established, maintained, located, kept to a minimum, initiated, distributed
5 examples: The principal objective … in the recent survey. Since the college … after a certain hour. Were the short-term recommendation to be … quickly be resolved
6 examples: It is obviously extremely important that …; it is clearly vital that; Were the … to be implemented …; I feel confident that …

5 *Model answer*
Proposal to improve community relations
Introduction
The principal objective of this proposal is to suggest ways in which good relations with our neighbours can be reestablished in view of the concerns raised in the recent survey. It is obviously extremely important that a good relationship be maintained with the local community and at present, this is clearly not happening.
Current situation
Since the college is located in close proximity to residential family homes, it is clearly vital that the noise is kept to a minimum after a certain hour. It is understood that there has been a tendency for students to shout and laugh very loudly when walking back from town late at night, which disturbs young children sleeping. It has also been noted that the following mornings takeaway wrappers and empty soft drink cans are often found littering the street, which does not reflect well on our town.
Recommendations
I would suggest the following course of action:
• a letter of apology to be written by a 'task group' and distributed to local residents.
• contact with our neighbours to be initiated, e.g. hosting an 'international evening' on which we serve typical snacks and drinks from our countries.
• a system to be put in place whereby residents can liaise directly with the students in the event of any further problems.
Conclusion
Were the short-term recommendation – the letter – to be implemented relatively soon and followed by a social event within the month, I feel confident that any present tension could quickly be resolved.

Audio script 05

Sp 1: My parents couldn't believe I'd decided to campaign for the fair trade movement because I've never taken a principled stand on anything before. I went to the meeting out of curiosity. My flatmate was brought up in Africa, so she's seen the good work the fair trade movement does over there. She was going, so I tagged along. The guy who gave the initial address made such a strong case, though, that I was inspired to start campaigning myself. For me, the great benefit's been how it's really opened my eyes to the way people in some countries are exploited, and how we're all part of that. Though I'm still set for a career in engineering, I feel I've gained masses from the experience.

Sp 2: I'm a volunteer with a charity that speaks up for elderly people who wouldn't otherwise have a voice. Basically, I go out at election time and raise questions regarding issues affecting older people at the hustings – you know, the meetings where candidates set out their policies. I thought this would be really useful because I'm studying law and the ability to present an argument in public's pretty central to that. What I've really got out of it, though, isn't just the insight you get into how society works, but a clearer idea of who I am. I thrive on the cut and thrust of those meetings – so who knows, perhaps a career in parliament beckons?

Sp 3: It came as no surprise to friends and family when I joined the green movement here at university. I've been banging on about pollution and climate change ever since they can remember. My father even said it might help me to get a job as an environmentalist one day – as if I'd be so calculating! I'm studying history, so I'm hardly likely to go down that route anyway. What I have found, however, is that my convictions have been reinforced through working together with other committed people and the value of that can't be overestimated. For me, the campaigning's fun. Whether we're influencing local and national policies at all remains to be seen, but it's great to contribute to the debate.

Sp 4: Although we've always had dogs at home, I've only really become concerned about the plight of working animals since I joined the group. It was one of my flatmates who originally begged me to get involved – she's really passionate about wildlife, and lives by her principles. I respect that. We're campaigning to stop experiments on animals in university labs and, hopefully, we can convince the powers that be to rethink their policy on this issue. What campaigning's taught me, actually, is that I'm not cut out for admin – I was elected treasurer, but it wasn't long before I'd completely messed up the accounts. I'll know to steer clear of that sort of thing when it comes to finding a job!

Sp 5: My grandmother helps out in a charity shop, but it's never something I thought I'd do. I mean, I'd expressed interest in helping the children's charity because I'm thinking of going into childcare work after I've graduated, so I have an affinity for the sort of things they do, but the text asking if I'd like to help run the shop came out of the blue. I'm actually quite a shy person and having to talk to and deal with all sorts of people is helping me overcome that. I'm not sure whether to put it on my CV or not – I don't think I'm suited to retail, really, but giving it a try's doing wonders for my self-confidence.

Module 5

Vocabulary development 1

1
1	sustainable	5	lessen	9	enrich
2	owners	6	defence	10	beneficial
3	justify	7	requirements		
4	ecologically	8	disposal		

2
1	downturn	4	insight
2	outlook	5	setback
3	breakthrough	6	build-up

3
1	renewable energy	4	natural habitats
2	toxic fumes	5	ecological footprint
3	limited resources		

4
1	diversity	6	recycle
2	low-impact	7	litter
3	insight	8	pollution
4	conservation	9	global
5	economic	10	climate

Use of English

3 1 C 2 B 3 D 4 A 5 C 6 A 7 D 8 B

Expert language
fiercely territorial

Language development 1

1a 1 h 2 e 3 g 4 b 5 d 6 a 7 f 8 c

1b impossible, outstanding, perfect, remarkable, spectacular

2a Stronger: absolutely, completely, extremely, incredibly, pretty, quite, really, seriously, utterly, very
Weaker: a bit/little, fairly, quite, slightly, somewhat

2b absolutely, completely, utterly

3
1	completely	4	slightly	7	virtually
2	extremely	5	really	8	absolutely
3	totally	6	highly		

4 1 B 2 A 3 C 4 A 5 C 6 A 7 B 8 A

5 Possible answers
1	absolutely/really	8	✓
2	✓	9	highly/incredibly/
3	totally/completely		absolutely
4	✓	10	✓
5	✓	11	✓
6	really/incredibly/very	12	utterly/completely/
7	very/rather/really/a bit		totally

Use of English

4
1	hand	4	into	6	which
2	as	5	Without/	7	when
3	order		Lacking	8	no

Expert language
Particularly upsetting for wildlife campaigners is the fact that …

Listening

1
1 It's an interview, so two speakers.
2 rescuing a bear from drowning

4 1 B 2 C 3 B 4 B 5 D 6 A

Vocabulary development 2

1
1	biometric checks	4	swipe card
2	security guards	5	phone tapping
3	code number	6	Spy satellites

2
1	at	4	in	7	in	10	of
2	in	5	for	8	in	11	on
3	To	6	at	9	on	12	in

3a
| 1 | come, getting | 3 | fall | 5 | catch |
| 2 | hush | 4 | freaked | 6 | take |

3b 1 f, a   2 c   3 g   4 b   5 d   6 e

4
| 1 | firmly, bitterly | 3 | seriously, strongly |
| 2 | vitally, quite | 4 | deeply, vividly |

Reading

4–5   1 A   2 E   3 D   4 C   5 B   6 C   7 D   8 A   9 B   10 E

6
1	hacker hunters	5	rare breed
2	headquarters	6	trustworthy
3	cyber crime	7	family farm
4	shorthand	8	software

7
1. a London-based IT company
2. multi-coloured dots
3. each rose-coloured spot
4. an in-house battalion
5. a 28-year-old former farm boy
6. a one-man hack attack
7. the stock-in-trade of hackers worldwide
8. a hoodie-wearing geek

Language development 2

1
1. want, recommend/will/may/might recommend
2. would get, lived/was living
3. is, will/may/might invest
4. had installed, would have known
5. need, will/can ask
6. hadn't left, wouldn't have been able
7. use, is
8. would feel, carried

2
1	unless	4	whether	7	otherwise
2	as long as	5	Should	8	had
3	provided	6	were it		

3
1. ✓
2. … ~~I had~~ I'd have a smaller car.
3. Should you ~~deciding~~ decide to come …
4. ✓
5. … instead ~~unless~~ if you don't want to.
6. ✓
7. … as long ~~that~~ as you can/~~as long~~ providing that you can …
8. ✓

4
1. If Sam knew how to encrypt the data, our business information wouldn't have been hacked.
2. If I hadn't left my laptop on the train I could get/be getting on with my work.
3. If people weren't generally very/so honest, my phone wouldn't have been returned.

4. If I hadn't lost my credit card, I'd be able to/I could come shopping with you.
5. If there weren't CCTV cameras outside the station, they wouldn't have seen the man that stole my bike.
6. If she didn't know influential people, she wouldn't have got away with it.
7. If I didn't know a computer expert, I wouldn't have been able to sort out the problem.
8. If he was/were aware of how thorough airport security is, he would have allowed enough/more time to catch the flight.

Use of English

4
1	unusual	4	advisable	7	impressive
2	disappears	5	reputable	8	realistic
3	illegal	6	transaction		

Writing

2   A

3
1. the first two
2. First para (2nd note): Main point: More could be done to cut down on energy during school hours. Supporting points: There is no system to allow it to be turned down. Students are too hot. Some parts of the school could be heated less.
   Second para (1st note): Main point: there are too many cars. Supporting points: Engines could be turned off. There could be a bicycle park. Students could share lifts or get a bus.
3. First para: This would only help during winter.
   Second para: Parents are worried about busy roads. Some people live too far away.

4
1. undeniable, flexibility, issue, crucial, restrict, clog, beneficial
2. more could be done; the heating is turned up; parts of the school … could be heated less; engines could be turned off
3. In addition, although, At the very least, However, whilst, Despite this
4. There is something seriously wrong when …; Parts of the school not used …; Even more crucial than this, however …

5   B is better. It is more formal and more persuasive.

6   *Model answer*
There is little doubt that we should be doing everything we can to help our planet survive. And where better to start than in our schools, with the young people who will be living in the environment of the future?

It is undeniable that more could be done to cut down on the amount of energy used during school hours. The heating is turned up far too high and there is no flexibility for it to be switched off or down. There is something seriously wrong when students are in shirtsleeves in mid-winter. In addition, parts of the school not used so often could be heated less, although this is only an issue during winter.

Even more crucial than this, however, is the need to restrict the amount of cars which currently clog the surrounding area. At the very least, engines could be turned off whilst people are waiting, to avoid toxic emissions. If we had a safe bicycle park, more people might cycle to school. However, many parents are worried about the busy roads. And whilst walking is beneficial for the health as well as for the environment, some people live too far away. Despite this, what they could do is to make every effort to share lifts or get a bus.

To sum up, I would argue that pressure needs to be put on students and parents to get to and from school in a more ecologically responsible way. Cutting down on fossil fuels as well as air pollution makes this change the most immediately important.

Audio script 06

Int: My guest today is Adam Warwick, a wildlife biologist, who became a household name in the USA after he rescued a bear from drowning. Adam, welcome.

Adam: Hi.

Int: Tell us what happened.

Adam: Well, I was working as a wildlife biologist on a peninsula in Florida. On one side's the Gulf of Mexico; on the other's a wide bay. Around 5,000 black bears live in Florida, so there's always encounters between bears and the beachfront community there. Someone out fishing had spotted a bear swimming in the ocean about a mile off shore. After that, I kept getting reports of him and hoped that he'd move on. Then one day we got a call. He was in somebody's back yard! My team arrived to find a seven- or eight-year-old and I could tell from his ear tag that he'd once been caught in a trap, so he wasn't going to fall for that again. I decided my only option was to tranquillise him.

Int: You mean, shoot him with a dart containing a sedative – something to send him off to sleep?

Adam: Exactly – so I could approach him safely. We took the shot while the bear had his head in a garbage can. The dart hit him in the hindquarters, but it takes about ten minutes to take effect. He wandered across the road that runs down the peninsula; a few cars stopped, which freaked him out. That's when he headed toward the bay and walked into the water and stopped. You could see he was deciding what to do. As he went a bit deeper, he started stumbling – the drug was kicking in. That bay's about four miles wide. He was eyeing the other side and I could just tell he was going to swim for it.

Int: But he'd never have made it under the influence of the drug.

Adam: No way. So, I took off my shirt – I couldn't just let him drown. He had started swimming out and I dived in to head him off. Forty yards from shore, we met. He was doggy paddling, his pupils dilated – the drug was working. The water was up to my head. I got in front of him and started splashing him. He reared up on his hind legs – he was probably six and a half feet tall. Well, I think he was going to try to climb on me to keep from drowning. Black bears aren't generally in the business of attacking people.

Int: But still, it must've been quite alarming?

Adam: Well, I could sense panic. He lost his balance and went under for a second, so I swam around and grabbed the scruff of his neck, trying to hold his head above water. He thrashed about and threw me off, but I caught him again. Then somebody tried to come up with a boat and I lost control of him. Finally, the boat backed off and I swam with the bear floating on top of me. I eventually got back to where I could touch the bottom and we could get some mechanical equipment to lift him out of the water. Later, he was released – none the worse for his experience.

Int: Whereas you became a sort of national hero?

Adam: Well, afterwards, a couple of TV shows called wanting to interview me and around town people started calling me 'the Bear Man'. I received a lot of bear stuffed animals and fruit baskets – even marriage proposals! I'd like to say I wasn't afraid, but it didn't really enter my mind, so I'm not really a hero. As a professional, when you immobilise a bear, you take responsibility for its well-being – I had no other motivation beyond that. A whole slew of people sent me cheques, some for a hundred dollars. That was kind, but I never cashed them.

Int: But you are a bear fan?

Adam: Sure. They're always up to something and they're super smart. Under their fur, they're like bodybuilders, yet they're not predators – just eating fruit, seeds and insects. It never ceases to amaze me how dextrous they can be: they can weigh up to 600 pounds, yet they're adept at using their claws to eat the tiniest of insects. They have a unique sweet, musky odour, like the saw palmetto plant, because that's also part of their diet. It's not a cologne you'd want to wear, but it's kind of attractive. Since I moved to North Carolina for work, I miss those bears a lot.

Module 6

Vocabulary development 1

1 1 talked Andy out of lending
2 getting the importance of the changes over
3 get by
4 talk it over
5 trying out
6 get through
7 brought up the subject of the pay rise/brought the subject of the pay rise up
8 speak up

2 1 talk 4 speak 7 say
2 saying 5 say 8 speaking
3 speaks 6 talking

3 1 c 2 f 3 b 4 e 5 a 6 d

4 1 means 4 stand 7 effectively
2 achieve 5 express 8 familiar
3 engaged 6 building

Use of English

4 1 D 2 B 3 C 4 A 5 B 6 C 7 A 8 D

> **Expert language**
> **bi**lingualism/**bi**lingual, **mono**lingual

Language development 1

1 1 tidier 4 mosquitoes 7 reliable
2 crashes 5 studied 8 visitors
3 laid 6 cheerfully

2 A ~~desicion~~ decision ~~neccesary~~ necessary
~~liesure~~ leisure ~~deserts~~ desserts
~~garantee~~ guarantee

B ~~Unfortunatly~~ Unfortunately
~~reciept~~ receipt
~~arguement~~ argument
~~definately~~ definitely

C ~~approximmately~~ approximately
~~ocassions~~ occasions
~~embarassing~~ embarrassing

3
1	lose	5	practice	9	whether
2	quite	6	ensure	10	passed
3	affect	7	waste		
4	accept	8	allowed		

4
1	three-hour	6	co-workers
2	✓	7	Indo-European
3	brown-eyed, dark-haired	8	✓
4	ex-girlfriend	9	✓
5	✓	10	15-metre pool

Use of English

4
1	what	4	into	7	more
2	which	5	so	8	on
3	as	6	According		

> **Expert language**
> the US military network that 20 years later **was to evolve** into the internet

Listening

1
1 three
2 Extract One: two language teachers talking about language learning; Extract Two: two academics discussing university courses in other European countries being taught in English; Extract Three: a discussion programme about technology in the workplace

3 1 C 2 A 3 C 4 A 5 B 6 A

> **Expert language**
> 6

Reading

4 1 B 2 D 3 A 4 D

5a 1 e 2 d 3 a 4 c 5 f 6 b

5b
1	ticks the box	4	get under your skin
2	stands up to scrutiny	5	twist in the tail
3	miss the point	6	glued to your seat

> **Expert language**
> incredibly powerful, shockingly delightful

Vocabulary development 2

1
1	on	4	out	7	down
2	in	5	in	8	over
3	in	6	off		

2 1 A 2 B 3 A 4 C 5 A 6 C 7 A 8 B 9 C 10 A

3
1	make a scene	6	fly into a rage
2	drive someone/me mad	7	burst into tears
3	be beside yourself/myself (with worry)	8	pull yourself/myself together
4	keep your/my temper	9	wear thin
5	be thrilled to bits	10	get on your/my nerves

4
1	angry	4	indifferent	7	nervous
2	annoys	5	moving	8	say
3	terrified	6	bored		

5
1	seething	4	snapped	7	welling
2	wound	5	edge	8	scared
3	sick and tired	6	care		

Language development 2

1
1	eating	5	to do	9	becoming
2	to finish	6	to let	10	not to bother
3	drinking	7	try		
4	tasting	8	counting		

2
1 a taxi to bring/take them home
2 her not to drive it
3 them to arrive an hour ago
4 didn't/wouldn't let me go
5 it burning the back of my neck
6 me not to eat them
7 made her do it
8 it lying in the long grass

3
1	to turn off	5	meeting	9	spending
2	to take	6	to be	10	living
3	to do	7	to inform		
4	running	8	leaving		

4
1	I'd better ~~to~~ get back	5	he'll keep ~~to go~~ going
2	I meant ~~buying~~ to buy	6	helping Jo ~~doing~~ (to) do
3	✓	7	✓
4	invited me ~~joining~~ to join	8	Mike ~~do~~ doing the gardening

Use of English

1 sixth sense: knowing something is there without seeing or hearing it

4
1	sensation	5	unaware
2	researchers	6	repeatedly
3	existence	7	sceptical
4	uncomfortable	8	outnumber

> **Expert language**
> 1 carried out
> 2 concentrated on

Writing

1
1 your tutor
2 'discuss two of the points in the notes'; 'explain which point you think is more important'; 'give reasons'

2a
1	health and safety	3	communication
2	language skills		

2b
1 2nd opinion (It's made a huge difference …); agree
2 3rd opinion (People don't bother …); disagree
3 1st opinion (I think they're responsible …); disagree

2c 1 b, c, e 2 d, f 3 a, g

3 *Possible answers*
1 There has been a lot of publicity about how speaking on mobile phones for too long can be bad for you. (b) This is certainly true, **particularly in the case of the very young or old**. For me, this argument is outweighed by the huge benefits that the elderly in particular have gained from using them. (e) **In addition,** it is invaluable for parents checking up on their young people. (c) **On the other hand/However/Despite this**, many accidents are caused by people using their mobiles when they are driving.
2 It is true that people use special text language, but it's not because they cannot write well. (d) **In fact/After All,** it could be argued that this is quite a creative use of language. (f) **Strangely enough/Surprisingly,** some linguists think it has helped young people to express themselves better.

3   I think that people actually get in touch with each other more than they used to, even if they might not actually speak. (a) **The reason for this is that/This is probably because** keeping in contact is so much more convenient than it once was. (g) **For example**, people who are shy find this form of contact much easier.

4   **1** A   **2** B   **3** A   **4** B

5   *Model answer*
    The impact of mobile phones on modern society
    Amongst older people in particular, who did not grow up with them, there are differing opinions about the influence mobile phones have had on our lives and whether the effects are generally positive or negative.
    One of the criticisms frequently made about mobile phones is that people do not engage in conversation as they once did. However, one only has to observe a room of young people to see that people are 'speaking' to each other much more than ever, albeit a different form of speaking. Text speak reigns supreme and because of the convenience of this mode of interaction, people are in contact with each other more rather than less.
    Also on the positive side is the fact that people can reassure themselves as to the well-being of their loved ones. Whether it is a teenage daughter walking home alone late at night or an elderly relative in ill health who lives alone, mobile phones provide an extremely useful way of checking that people are safe and well. True, opinions have been voiced about the dangers of sound waves, but given that texting is far more common, perhaps this should not be taken too seriously.
    I think increased social communication is an excellent reason to make a choice for using mobile phones. However, everything considered, I am convinced that the comfort of being able to check quickly on the health and safety of family and friends is the most important outcome of the mobile phone age. It would be difficult to imagine life without them now.

Audio script 07

Extract One

F: Now Ivan, on the face of it, you seem like the ideal person to run a language learning company.

M: Well, yes. I was born in France but my parents are Swedish, and we came to the UK when I was six. I have a working knowledge of German and Chinese and I'm learning Russian. But more to the point, I'd say that my own experience of learning languages was consistent with the philosophy of teaching that the company had already developed, so there was a real fit there. The whole ethos is to democratise language learning and make it easy and acceptable for everyone – to demystify the whole business.

F: I know what you mean. And it's not like we're all just linguists either; for most of the staff here, a language is just part of a broader skills set. When I first moved to the UK, my parents just threw me into school without a word of English. What's called 'full immersion' – you know, sink or swim! I just had to figure the language out and it was a very isolating experience. I wouldn't recommend it. So I've had that kind of pain, but also the exhilaration of success that you get once you've gone through that.

Extract Two

F: English is fast becoming the lingua franca in some subjects in European universities. And it's not just academics, eager to see their work published in the most respected journals, who insist on it. Students do too. They're prepared to move to another country to study, and universities worldwide that are competing to attract them have to offer courses in the language most of them have learnt. The students become the customers. Universities are no longer institutions but brands. But it can lead to problems, can't it John?

M: Well, if you've got a mixture of native English speakers and non-native speakers, they might hesitate to ask questions or participate in discussions. But there are ways of dealing with this. If you put them in small groups for tutorials, students who don't have English as their first language can be encouraged to speak up. Within three months in a system like that, students make great strides – it's wonderful to see the transformation. Lecture notes are trickier to get down, but technology offers a way around that. We grant permission for students to record lectures on their phones. My faculty's wary of putting lectures online for fear that it would stop students coming to them, but some other parts of the university do.

Extract Three

F: So, Derek, where do you think we are when it comes to the development of workplace technology?

M: What we're noticing in the workplace these days is that barriers are breaking down between networking and communication tools, like phones and tablets and equipment for creating and editing documents. You don't need different tools for communicating and for writing – the separation of these activities into different software applications is a relic of the days when visions of technology were dominated by the telephone and the typewriter.

F: And that's because the needs of workers are changing fast. Mobile access is expected; communication between groups of employees has become far more open, while collaboration around work happens instantly. The sheer volume of information can be overwhelming.

M: As the pressure on workers mounts, the many tools for creating, storing, sharing and collaborating are increasingly starting to converge. It's about integrating different services. And that's how new business software markets often start out, with 'best of breed' suppliers dominating different technology niches, as happened with Microsoft Office, Google and Facebook.

Module 7

Vocabulary development 1

1
1	psychologists	6	uncharacteristic
2	behaviour	7	awareness
3	reaction	8	irrelevant
4	defensive	9	occurrences
5	defiance	10	limitations

2
1	hit home	5	out of house and home	8	home from home
2	at home				
3	homed in	6	at home		
4	come home	7	come home		

3
1	limited	4	childlike	7	principle
2	intense	5	incident	8	lie
3	differ	6	provided		

4
1	take for granted	4	sparks off	8	outbursts
2	downside	5	pointless	9	regards
3	do your own thing	6	stone's throw	10	likelihood
		7	deposit		

Use of English

3   **1** B   **2** D   **3** B   **4** A   **5** C   **6** A   **7** B   **8** D

Expert language
0, 4 and 8

Language development 1

1
1	The one thing	3	The person	6	All
2	The reason	4	What	7	The job
		5	The place	8	The month

2
1 was (to) phone Joe and then drive round to see him
2 was (that) the car in front of me stopped suddenly and I went into it
3 I'd really love to visit one day is Venice
4 we asked them to leave in the end was that it was too much work for us
5 where you'll find the most suitable university course for you is York
6 I'd really love to do is go hang-gliding just once in my life
7 had done is find a job nearer home
8 I've (ever) wanted to do is/has been to work with endangered species

3
1 it's/it was my brother who/that moved there
2 it's squash that I used to play with her
3 it wasn't until 2009 that I left
4 No, it was Philadelphia that we met in
5 it's my parents who/that want to move back here
6 it's only by selling their other house that they'll be able to afford to move

4
1 only when we were nearly home that we realised she wasn't with us
2 a friend of mine who/that suggested we called the police
3 until the end of the year that the council will do anything about the roads
4 the weather that I love most about this country
5 until Wednesday that I was finally able to hand in the work
6 only when/not until I saw her that I realised how bad she was

Use of English

4
1	which	3	little	5	could	7	after
2	In	4	order	6	Having	8	with

Listening

4
1	spare bed	5	place page
2	190/one/a hundred and ninety	6	personal references
3	gift economy	7	user reports
4	honesty	8	flexibility

Vocabulary development 2

1
1	danger	4	stranded	7	self-reliant
2	tricky	5	rough	8	spur
3	nowhere	6	challenge		

2
1	fend	4	blown	7	go
2	stemmed	5	face	8	soak
3	run	6	pack		

3
a6	b2	c4	d1	e7	f3	g8	h5

4
1 B	2 A	3 A	4 C	5 B	6 C	7 B	8 A

Reading

2
1 by car and plane
2 It is a lodge 100 miles from the nearest road. It is family-run. It is popular with celebrities.
3 'because they can be absolutely sure that no paparazzi can get up there'
4 Otter, Piper Super-cub

3-4
1 B	2 F	3 E	4 D	5 A	6 G

Language development 2

1
1	worked	5	wouldn't
2	hadn't eaten	6	didn't keep
3	were going	7	were having
4	would all stop	8	had left

2
1 I could (afford to) go backpacking round the world
2 they/the builders would turn the radio down
3 I had my purse with me
4 I was/were taller
5 I hadn't given up maths
6 I'd seen that documentary
7 he wouldn't leave wet towels everywhere
8 I didn't have a dog because I can't go away for long

3
1	had given	5	had been crying
2	started	6	left
3	didn't criticise	7	saw
4	stopped	8	were

4
1 It feels as if I've been here for years, but it's only been/I've only been here for six months.
2 Suppose I invited your ex-girlfriend, how would you feel about it?
3 I'd rather you didn't ask me to drive all that way!
4 It's time we left - it's after midnight.
5 I'd sooner you'd asked me for directions rather than getting lost.
6 I'd prefer it if we stayed/could stay in a hotel for once.
7 What if we called in and apologised to her?
8 Sometimes you behave as though you were an old man.

Use of English

2
1 wishes (that) he hadn't decided
2 gets the grass cut by
3 (completely) taken aback by
4 as long as they are in
5 the weather improves, there's little
6 requiring parking should get in touch
7 the/a choice, I would far sooner
8 as if/though Sandra is enjoying
9 the less Clare knew
10 ended up spending a great

Writing

1 **1** school and university principals
    2 formal/semi-formal style

2 1, 4

3 **1** c **2** a **3** b

4 Dear Sir/Madam,
I am writing to **make you aware of** our organisation, which I am sure **is likely to be of interest to students at your school or college, many of whom** may well be **interested in taking part in** voluntary work overseas after completing their studies. Every year, volunteers are sent on more than 100 projects across 18 different countries. Our placements are ideal for gap years, short breaks and short work holidays.
There are a wide range of opportunities, the most common of which are teaching and education, healthcare, animals and natural resources, conservation and the environment, community and social development. A typical day's work could involve **assisting** local people to build a well or a school, caring for disadvantaged children or collecting data from the rainforest. For some placements – for example, in the field of medicine or construction – a degree or a particular skill set may be necessary. For others **little more than a high level of commitment is required** and you also need to **demonstrate a capacity for hard work**.
Volunteering will change a student's life. Moreover, it helps the average job-seeker or university applicant to stand out from the crowd. In addition, it can be an invaluable time to recharge batteries, build confidence, confront new challenges and make new friends who will last a lifetime. And of course, what will never be forgotten is the experience of spending **an extended period** in a new culture, perhaps learning a new language at the same time.
Should you need further information, **do not hesitate to contact us** via our website.
Yours faithfully,
Caroline Tulley

5 **1** is likely to be of interest to students; volunteers are sent on more than 100 projects; a degree or a particular skill set may be necessary; little more than a high level of commitment is required; what will never be forgotten
    2 what will never be forgotten; Should you need further information, do not hesitate to contact us
    3 which I am sure is likely to be; the most common of which are teaching and education; make new friends who will last a lifetime
    4 Moreover; In addition

6 See model answer in Exercise 4 above.

Audio script 08

Speaker:

Hi there. I'm Ruby Eversden and on tonight's programme we're looking at an international hospitality network that goes by the name *couchsurfing*. It's an online resource that helps anyone travelling around the world to find free accommodation with local people.

Basically, members offer overnight accommodation to travellers from other countries. This may actually be a spare bed if you've got one, but that's not obligatory; just a sofa or floor space will do, hence the name *couchsurfing*. In return, when you're travelling yourself, there's a network of beds, couches and floors around the world for you to take advantage of.

Couchsurfing's actually been around for more than a decade, and the largest of the various websites has more than nine million members signed up in over 120,000 destinations spread across 190 of the world's nation states.

As you might imagine, the original target user was the backpacker or gap year student, and although 86 percent of couchsurfers are still in the under-35 age bracket, people of all ages are now signed up. Couchsurfing started out as an aspect of what's called 'the gift economy' and like other non-profit and resource-sharing schemes, it's made possible by the internet.

So how do you get involved? Well, first up, you go online and create a profile on the website of your choice. Obviously, you need to make both yourself and your accommodation sound attractive, but don't let your creativity and imagination get the better of you – honesty is the best policy, backed up by lots of realistic photos!

Some websites have social events where hosts in a locality meet up and compare notes. This kind of support network's important. Like, if you live somewhere off the beaten track, you could create what's known as a place page to encourage people to come and visit. Pooling resources for recommendations about eating out, sightseeing, etc. is also a good idea, because one of the big plus points of couchsurfing is that the host can provide tips and introductions in the local area.

By the same token, when it's your turn to go out in search of a couch when you're travelling, careful reading of the member profiles is essential. Another aspect of the scheme is that members have to provide three safeguards. Firstly, personal references are an essential requirement – people who can vouch for the fact that you are who you say you are – that you're a reliable sort of person. Sites often also check your credit card details as a way of confirming your identity. And finally, there are the user reports that people write after staying with members – it's crucial to check these out before agreeing to go and stay with someone.

So, if you do join a scheme, a few points to remember. As a guest, tidiness and consideration are important - always clean up after yourself. A present, however small, always goes down well, but flexibility is the real key to a happy stay. It is somebody else's home, after all, so you need to fit in. And of course, finally, never overstay your welcome. Remember the old adage: It's lovely when guests come to stay – and it's equally lovely to see them go!

Module 8

Vocabulary development 1

1	**1**	started up	**3**	lay off	**5**	take over
	2	took off	**4**	wind down	**6**	turned out

2	**1**	take	**4**	make	**6**	doing,
	2	running	**5**	play, take		making
	3	give				

3	**1**	into	**3**	on	**5**	out
	2	on	**4**	of	**6**	in

4 **1** B **2** C **3** A **4** B **5** A **6** C

5	**1**	entrepreneurs	**6**	sailing
	2	stumbled	**7**	disaster
	3	service	**8**	running
	4	balance	**9**	disillusioned
	5	lucrative	**10**	let

Answer key

Use of English

3 1 D 2 B 3 A 4 A 5 C 6 C 7 D 8 B

> **Expert language**
> **I'd be downloading** later, to ensure I **located** the correct edition

Language development 1

1
1 Under ~~any~~ no circumstances
2 ✓
3 ~~After only~~ Only after borrowing
4 Under no circumstances **do** I ever want to work
5 Not since ~~was I~~ I was a child
6 ✓
7 ✓
8 At no time ~~you must never~~ must you ever touch

2
1 I could never run a company under any circumstances.
2 A business of this kind has rarely taken off so quickly.
3 I was only able to achieve my dreams after borrowing from my family.
4 I never want to work that hard again under any circumstances!
5 I'd never been so afraid of something since I was a child.
6 I'll never see such a fantastic place again.
7 He had hardly taken his coat off when the phone went.
8 You must never touch that switch at any time.

3
1 Under no circumstances must you ever try to …
2 Never would I have given up my day job …
3 Not until they've seen a detailed business plan will investors …
4 At no time should you assume that …
5 Barely was my website up and running when …
6 Rarely have I felt more relieved than when …

4
1 On no account should you have signed …
2 Little did I realise how difficult …
3 Not only will I have to write a business plan, but I'll have to talk …
4 Only after he'd set off for the airport did he remember …
5 No sooner had I arrived at the park with the dog than it started …
6 Rarely do we eat out in places like this.
7 Under no circumstances must you open the door while we're out.
8 Only now are we ready to leave.

5
1 So popular has the film been that we're …
2 Even more impressive than the wildlife is the scenery.
3 Out came the sun, just in time …
4 Lovely it may be, but it's also …
5 Up drove James, just as …
6 Annoyed though he was, he finished the talk.
7 Such was her confidence in her ability that …
8 Outside the hotel was an old man …

Use of English

4
1 supplier
2 unlikely
3 enduringly
4 transactions
5 existence
6 easily
7 application
8 breakthrough

> **Expert language**
> California-based , handwritten, paper-based, data-imprinting

Listening

1 five extracts; running a retail shop

3 1 H 2 C 3 E 4 G 5 D 6 B 7 A 8 H 9 F 10 G

> **Expert language**
> unwilling (to accept defeat)

Reading

4–5 1 A 2 D 3 C 4 B 5 D 6 A

> **Expert language**
> First of all, Additionally, One is that, Another is that, Then there is

Vocabulary development 2

1 1 c 2 f 3 a 4 g 5 h 6 e 7 b 8 d

2
1 be tied up
2 put by
3 scrape by
4 beat (someone) down
5 get ripped off
6 come into money
7 take out
8 help out

3
1 in 4 into 7 beyond
2 on 5 of 8 for
3 by 6 on

4
1 regular 4 costs 7 cause
2 even 5 deal 8 savings
3 earth 6 bargain

5
1 share 4 way 7 handling
2 split 5 extras 8 withdraw
3 rates 6 up front

Language development 2

1
1 about the same 6 easily the biggest
2 slightly less 7 somewhat less
3 considerably more 8 far more likely
4 nothing like as 9 anywhere near as much
5 a great deal more 10 just the same

2
1 too hot for us ~~lying~~ to lie
2 ✓
3 works ~~like~~ as a waitress
4 ~~so~~ such a successful company
5 I'd prefer ~~giving up~~ to give up
6 The ~~little~~ less you know
7 ✓
8 quick enough ~~applying~~ to apply

3
1 far more 6 such a
2 By far 7 to accommodate
3 as 8 less
4 nowhere near 9 easily
5 to rent 10 Slightly

Use of English

2
1 succeeded in getting a place
2 managed to increase its sales in
3 he arrived at the airport did
4 any businesses make a profit
5 talked into asking for an increase
6 could have predicted how the film
7 any club members made the effort
8 has recently been taken over
9 a sharp fall/decrease in the
10 no circumstances may/must/should students make use

Expert language

make a profit (question 4), made the effort (question 7), make use of (question 10)

Writing

1 The second plan answers the question by specifically focusing on contrasting the book and film throughout.
The first plan would only work if the summary made the contrast clear.

2 1 B
   2 A
      (They are both more engaging, attention-catching.)

3 1 that doesn't really come across as well in the film; Perhaps more important was the lack of chemistry; I just didn't find Emma as convincing as in the book; he came over as altogether more likeable; the ending was just as heartbreaking as in the book
   2 However, in my view; After all; Despite this; Oddly, though;
   3 I much preferred his character in the film.
   4 All in all

4 1 overrated
   2 crammed
   3 dodgy
   4 warm to
   5 a touch of humour
   6 heartbreaking
   7 fell (a bit) flat
   8 give (the novel) a go

5 See Coursebook Exercise 2 for a model answer.

Audio script 09

Sp 1: I loved my job in marketing, so wasn't looking to change direction or anything. Then, on a family outing to the seaside, we spotted this little old-fashioned shop, selling sweets by weight out of big jars. My kids loved it and I thought the idea had real potential. Anyway, I found out it's a franchise – you get the stock from a supplier, use the branding for a fee, but the shop's your business. What's more, nobody'd taken out the franchise for our town, so I secured a loan from the bank and went for it. I haven't made my fortune yet and there's a long way to go, but despite the odd elementary mistake, I've broken even in year one.

Sp 2: I've always worked in retail and couldn't imagine doing anything else. I'd always fancied the idea of running my own business though, not because I resent working for a big company, but more because I think I have the skills. So when a distant relation remembered me in her will, it seemed like a golden opportunity. I knew what I wanted to sell – I have good contacts amongst suppliers of costume jewellery – but I also knew that competition is fierce, so I'd need to stand out from the crowd. I'd originally aimed to turn a profit in year one, but I was advised that was unlikely, so reluctantly adjusted my business plan accordingly. I prefer to see it as a temporary setback, really.

Sp 3: I've always been into website design and stuff like that, and my family encouraged me to follow that path at college. I was lucky to get a job with a major retailer, but soon realised that I was in my element working in sales – that the website design was just a means to an end. So I switched direction. I owe a lot to my former colleagues, however. Without their help I'd never have been able to set up on my own. I'm not actually a competitor because I have my own niche market in men's travel accessories. At the moment sales are strong and although the work's every bit as demanding as people tell you, I have no regrets.

Sp 4: I guess I was a bit naive when I decided to set up my own retail business. I mean, I had no family money to fall back on and my friends all thought I'd taken leave of my senses. You see, I was already working in the health food business and a number of colleagues had left to open shops. They seemed to be making a go of it, so why shouldn't I? Well, make no mistake, it's not an easy life. Unless you're willing to commit to it twenty-four seven, it's a real uphill struggle. I'm just about ready to give up, actually – if I can find somebody willing to buy me out. The business is profitable, so that shouldn't be too hard.

Sp 5: When I opened my little shop, selling cupcakes and other craft bakery items I make myself, I never imagined I was treading on anybody's toes. I mean, my prices are much higher than other shops and I thought I'd have a different clientele – people willing to pay for quality. So I was amazed when a shop in the next street started selling stuff that looked just like mine at two for the price of one. I'd heard about supermarket price wars, but cupcakes? I thought it was unfair, really. Anyway, I wasn't out to make a fortune – I just thought I had something special to sell. So, I've moved more into catering for birthday parties now, so I'm less dependent on the shop itself.

Module 9

Vocabulary development 1

1 1 chemistry
   2 invention
   3 astronomical
   4 exploratory
   5 analytical
   6 engineering
   7 atmospheric
   8 geneticist

2 1 rocket
   2 planet
   3 moon
   4 rocket
   5 moons
   6 spaced

3 1 view
   2 sight
   3 glimpse
   4 gazed
   5 peering
   6 glanced

4 1 e 2 d 3 c 4 f 5 a 6 b

5 1 from
   2 on
   3 at
   4 on
   5 In
   6 on
   7 In
   8 On

Use of English

3 1 C 2 B 3 D 4 A 5 C 6 D 7 D 8 B

Expert language

making it easier to detect alien life if it **does** exist

Language development 1

1 1 (that) the world belonged to her
   2 (that) she had/has always believed that nobody should have to clean houses
   3 (that) she was going to build a house to help disabled people
   4 (that) the house had taken her 40 years to complete
   5 (that) she had no idea what would eventually happen to the house
   6 if/whether we would like to go and see the house
   7 if/whether we knew she had been nominated as one of the US' top inventors
   8 (that) she might spend more time doing sculptures

Answer key

2
1. reminded her husband to phone/that he had to phone the bank that day
2. offered to get me a coffee
3. regretted that we hadn't gone/not going/not having gone by train
4. suggested visiting/that we visited the Science Museum the following week
5. accused me of always being late
6. invited us to go and stay with them the following week
7. agreed that the presentation hadn't been very interesting
8. apologised for forgetting/having forgotten about the meeting the previous day/the day before

3
1. for ~~Host~~ losing her phone
2. ✓
3. recommended ~~me to buy~~ buying/that I should buy
4. ✓
5. ✓
6. denied ~~to break~~ breaking the jug
7. insisted ~~to see~~ on seeing the manager
8. explained **to** her

4
1. It was expected that families …
2. It has been promised by some space travel companies that flights …
3. Some rich people are believed to have paid in excess of …
4. It has been claimed (by some scientists) that we may soon …
5. Classes in space tourism are/have been reported to be taking place in …
6. It has been alleged that there is a …
7. Some space tourists are known to have also done …
8. It is claimed (by environmentalists) that space tourism is …

Use of English

4
1. traditionally
2. researchers
3. alterations
4. Undoubtedly
5. distinctive
6. desirable
7. jewellery
8. significant

Listening

1 a radio report; a gadget used by some airline passengers

4
1. tray table
2. light(weight)
3. courtesy card
4. diverted
5. 18,000/eighteen thousand
6. in(-)seat exercises
7. policy statement
8. scanner bag

Vocabulary development 2

1
1. crossed
2. take
3. put
4. speaks
5. make
6. wandering
7. put
8. keep

2 1 e 2 c 3 f 4 a 5 h 6 g 7 b 8 d

3 1 d 2 b 3 f 4 a 5 e 6 c

4a
1. memorise
2. remind
3. recall

4b
1. memory
2. mind
3. mind
4. reminder
5. memory
6. memory/mind

5
1. witted
2. able
3. feet
4. loss
5. uptake
6. dense
7. gifted
8. precocious
9. knowledgeable
10. half

Reading

1 four reviews of *The Organized Mind*

4 1 A 2 C 3 D 4 C

5a
1. to do
2. on
3. of
4. with
5. doing
6. down

5b a 3 b 4 c 1 d 6 e 2 f 5

5c
1. approve of
2. jot down
3. go about
4. expand on
5. aspired to
6. engage with

Language development 2

1
1. with
2. on
3. on
4. for
5. of
6. on
7. from
8. to
9. from
10. by
11. on
12. against
13. on
14. at

2
1. working
2. on giving
3. to shouting
4. me from going
5. to remind
6. me from entering

3
1. at/about not getting
2. for taking
3. of going
4. about winning
5. of/about coming
6. about making
7. about having
8. for finding

4
1. of
2. in
3. in
4. on
5. in
6. at
7. of, on
8. for

Use of English

4
1. capable
2. which
3. as
4. order
5. up
6. making
7. without
8. Although/Though/While/Whilst

Writing

1a **A** note 1   **B** note 3   **C** note 2

1b **A** opinion 3 (disagree)   **B** opinion 1 (agree)   **C** opinion 2 (agree)
Different wording/expressions are used.

2 the first sentence of each paragraph

3
1	Whilst	**6**	whether
2	In fact	**7**	or
3	such as	**8**	In addition
4	not only	**9**	although
5	due to	**10**	Consequently

4
1 Science is generally agreed to be a good …
2 It used to be felt that careers …
3 It has been claimed that science …
4 Science is often assumed by students to be too difficult/is often assumed to be too difficult by students.

5
1	up	**3**	On	**5**	All
2	In	**4**	On	**6**	Overall

6 *Model answer*

In recent years there has been a certain amount of pressure by some governments on schools to encourage students to study science subjects at a higher level. In some countries, the study of science has been made compulsory up until a certain age. It follows then that many of these people will continue their studies at university, eventually going on to become scientists. There are good reasons to believe that this is a positive trend. It is beyond doubt that there are many issues which need scientific input these days if our planet is to survive, due to the ever-increasing demands we make on the world's resources. Future scientists will face huge challenges, whether it is developing new communications systems or contributing towards making the world a better place.

In addition to being highly employable, it has been shown that science graduates are more likely to achieve greater rewards in monetary terms. It is common knowledge that chemistry and physics graduates earn well above the average salary and although that is not the only reason to study these subjects, it is without doubt a strong incentive. Consequently, one would expect science to gain in popularity.

Although being successful and reasonably wealthy is obviously important to some people, it is probably true to say that the prospect of having a career in which one is contributing something worthwhile to society is something that many of us would find even more satisfying.

Audio script 10

Speaker:

We're talking about inventions on today's programme – about gadgets that can transform our daily lives. Sometimes, however, what seems a godsend to some people becomes the bane of other people's lives. Take, for example, the Knee Defender, a gadget that enjoyed short-lived popularity amongst some long-haul airline passengers some years ago.

Most long-haul flights have reclining seats. You press a button and the seat leans back so that you can stretch out and relax. As long as everyone reclines at the same time, this can add to passenger comfort. The Knee Defender, however, was an ingenious gadget, fixed onto the user's tray table rather than the seat itself, that effectively prevented the seat in front from being reclined. It was designed to help those passengers – some with long legs, others wanting to use laptop computers – who wanted to remain upright, and whose personal space was reduced when the seat in front was reclined.

Users reported how effective the pocket-sized gadget was, and underlined how lightweight and simple it was to attach. As a result, sales soared and word spread via social media. But, as you can imagine, not everyone was happy and the potential for a conflict of interests was there from the outset.

Anticipating this, the manufacturers included what they termed a 'courtesy card' inside the packaging; this explained to the passenger in front that the device was fitted and that their seat wouldn't recline. This only fuelled some passengers' anger, however, and arguments often ensued, requiring flight crew to intervene. The last straw came when one flight in the USA had to be diverted after a fight broke out on board over the use of a Knee Defender. There was a call to ban use of the gadgets.

Clearly, amongst long-haul passengers, in economy class at least, the Knee Defender had become a big issue, with 12,500 respondents calling for a ban in an online survey that attracted 18,000. In other words, 70 percent were in favour of a ban.

In response, supporters of the Knee Defender argued that in-seat exercises were recommended by doctors to reduce the risk of deep-vein thrombosis on long-haul flights. Reclined seats, they argued, often prevented passengers from following this advice, and for tall people they made the problem worse.

Opponents of the gadget tended to take a more principled stance, claiming their civil liberties were under attack. If the airlines allowed seats to be reclined, they said, then the right to do so should apply equally to everyone on board. In the absence of any clear legal guidance on the issue, they called for each airline to publish a policy statement about the Knee Defender.

Most large airlines moved to ban the gadget on flights as a result of the controversy. It seems that issues of personal space stir up all sorts of passions when people are confined in a small metal tube for long periods of time. The company then turned its attention to another situation in which airline passengers' nerves become frayed: airport security. The company's scanner bag was designed as somewhere to put all the coins, keys and other stuff that usually lives in your pockets, but which would trigger the alarm. Now, surely, that's an idea nobody could object to!

Module 10

Vocabulary development 1

1
1	ensure	**4**	fitness	**8**	enables
2	invariably	**5**	strength	**9**	commitment
3	dehydration/dehydrating	**6**	resistance	**10**	exceptional
		7	specifically		

2
1	burn	**3**	come	**5**	holds
2	making	**4**	caught		

3
1	under	**4**	in	**7**	In
2	at	**5**	To	**8**	in
3	on	**6**	in		

4
1	d	**3**	a	**5**	h	**7**	b
2	g	**4**	c	**6**	f	**8**	e

Use of English

4 **1** B **2** A **3** C **4** D **5** C **6** D **7** A **8** B

Expert language

whose job it is … as possible; a role which involves … simulator; which are … a glass partition

Language development 1

1
1	both possible	**4**	both possible
2	Because	**5**	so
3	who	**6**	both possible

Answer key

2 1 b   3 c   5 e
   2 a   4 a   6 d/b

3 1 Walking into the room, she saw what had happened.
   2 Having trained really hard, she was disappointed not to be chosen for the team.
   3 People arriving early are more likely to get a place.
   4 Having left the theatre later than we expected, we missed the last train.
   5 Knowing it was going to be really icy on the roads, I refused to let my daughter drive.
   6 Eaten hot, it tastes even more delicious.

4 1 Having invited   5 Worn
   2 Realising   6 Wanting
   3 rescued   7 Having learned/learnt
   4 Convinced   8 Not being able

5 1 Being a member of the club, I get priority booking for home matches.
   2 Given a lot of support, she could be a really good player.
   3 Having run out of the office, I hailed a taxi and jumped in.
   4 Being a bit lazy, I'd never make a world-class tennis player.
   5 Having quickly realised/Quickly realising (that) my team weren't going to win, I decided to leave.
   6 Knowing he wanted to see the game, I bought tickets for both of us.

6 1 My personal trainer phoned me to arrange a session.
   2 I finally got to the football ground, only to discover that my son hadn't been chosen for the team.
   3 To see him play, you'd think he was a professional.
   4 I set off to meet Richard at the cinema, only to realise that I'd got the wrong date.
   5 I travel enough to know that delays are inevitable.
   6 I spent ages writing a proposal to present at the meeting.

Use of English

4 1 on   4 in   7 like
   2 such   5 opposed   8 which
   3 what   6 instead

Expert language
one of the **most** interesting developments; **barely** scratch the surface; **much** greater potential

Listening

1 1 three speakers: the interviewer, Jennie Parks and Paul Grimes
   2 skydiving

3 1 A   2 B   3 A   4 D   5 D   6 C

Expert language
unexpected (question 4), unreliable (question 5)

Reading

4–5 1 A   2 B   3 C   4 B   5 D   6 C   7 A   8 A   9 D   10 B

6 1 b   2 i   3 d   4 a   5 h   6 e   7 g   8 f   9 c

Expert language
scrutinise

Vocabulary development 2

1 1 dramatics   5 creative   9 restoration
   2 amazement   6 friendship   10 optimistic
   3 rewarding   7 incredibly   11 anxious
   4 gardening   8 consuming   12 valuable

2 1 into   4 round   7 around
   2 over   5 away   8 back
   3 through   6 out

3 1 d   2 f   3 a   4 g   5 c   6 h   7 e   8 b

4 1 widely   6 switch   11 paperback
   2 ranging   7 compulsive   12 value
   3 trashy   8 dip   13 swap
   4 works   9 fiction   14 go
   5 caught   10 browse   15 bookworm

Language development 2

1 1 would   6 Would/Will you
   2 won't work   7 will never take/ won't take
   3 will change
   4 Would/Will you   8 She would be
   5 I'll

2 1 could   5 can
   2 didn't have to pay   6 was able
   3 shall   7 weren't able to
   4 could   8 shouldn't

3 1 don't/won't have to do   5 shouldn't be
   2 should have told   6 needn't have made
   3 might be talking   7 can't have left
   4 could have had   8 mustn't be removed

4 1 A   2 C   3 B   4 B   5 A   6 C   7 C   8 B

Use of English

2 1 under a legal obligation to
   2 ought to be reported
   3 widely thought to be on the
   4 is rumoured to be intending
   5 have any objection to
   6 opinion/view, the proposal is unlikely to
   7 wish (that) Sandra wouldn't
   8 it looks/seems as if
   9 won't go fishing unless there
   10 could hardly remember anything/hardly remembered anything

Expert language
airlines, smartphone

Writing

1 4

2 1, 3, 7, 9

4a 1, 4, 5

4b 2, 3, 4, 5

5 A; it is concise and to the point, written in an impersonal style but with a persuasive last sentence.

6 *Model answer*
Lunchtime fitness classes: a proposal
Introduction
In this proposal I shall outline the reasons for setting up a fitness programme for students during the lunch break and make some suggestions.
Reasons for having a fitness programme
Currently, there is nothing organised for students between 12.30 and 2 p.m. Feedback suggests that most students tend to have a light snack and then spend their time chatting or surfing the net. They would prefer to put this time to better use, but feel there

is insufficient time to get into the town centre to use the gym or other facilities there.

Types of fitness activities suggested
1 relaxation/ 'Flexibility' activities, e.g. yoga, Pilates, Tai chi
2 outdoor activities e.g. tennis, football, running

Recommendations

My suggestions would be as follows:

- to begin in the autumn term with two 'taught' activities a week: Pilates and yoga
- to find out as soon as possible the availability of suitable teachers for the classes
- to make the main hall available for these activities
- to ask students to pay £5 each per lesson but be prepared to subsidise the lessons for a period of time should sufficient students not take advantage of the opportunity
- substitute one outdoor activity per week for one of the relaxation classes during the summer term; these could be run by one of the social activities team.

I am convinced that this initiative would be highly beneficial for the well-being of our students and would be a popular addition to our list of social activities in the prospectus.

Audio script 11

Int: My guests today are Jennie Parks, who's been skydiving for many years and has recently taken part in a record-breaking formation jump, and Paul Grimes, who's a skydiving instructor. Jennie, what motivated you to take part in this record attempt?

Jennie: I've been skydiving for 30 years. When I started, hardly any women did the sport. Even now, I've seen an instructors' manual that questions women's aptitude for parachuting. Our world record shows that gender doesn't matter – the previous record was held by a mixed group, but we bettered it with an all-female group. But that's not why I wanted to do it. Your first jump's always the hardest; if you're not worried, then you probably haven't realised what you're doing. But the downside of experience is that you lose some of that nervous excitement – the very thing that made you love skydiving. I guess that's why we seek out new goals – like learning to turn, then to coordinate movements with another skydiver – things that allow us to see how far we can push ourselves – to feel that buzz again.

Int: Hmm .. Now Paul, it can't be easy skydiving in a group. How do you get people up to that level?

Paul: Well, like Jennie says, it's kind of incremental. And incidentally, I don't go along with this notion of a gender divide either. For most people that initial step out of the plane's the barrier they've got to transcend. Though actually, for me, that thrill's never waned. The buzz of the unknown gets replaced by that of the known, the anticipation of that unique sense of freedom you get just free-falling. But sure, I teach my students to turn in the air. All it takes is a little bit of pressure and the wind to move across the body and the body will turn – though it's not quite as straightforward as I make it sound.

Int: So how long before you can start doing formation, like Jennie?

Paul: The average skydiver probably does around 100 jumps a year. You need 50 under your belt before you can jump without an instructor. But in terms of formation jumping, truth is some skydivers fall through the air slowly and some fall faster, and the size and shape of the parachute's going to affect the fall, so it's all in the detailed preparation. I mean, the record Jennie broke is incredible – she was one of 117 skydivers who set a world record for the largest sequential formation. That meant holding one formation for a few seconds, breaking off and then moving to a second formation while freefalling from 18,000 feet. I mean, that requires individual skydiving prowess and great coordination, no doubt about that, but it wouldn't be possible without endless, meticulous attention to detail in the run up to the jump.

Int: Thanks, Paul. Jennie, tell us about the record-breaking jump itself.

Jennie: The previous record was 110 people. We needed seven planes and we had to get the pilots to fly close enough together so that we stood a chance of reaching each other in the sky. We were over Perris drop zone, in California. We'd started practising more than 18 months previously, but with skydivers from 28 different countries, there were logistical problems to overcome, as you can imagine. But once we'd arrived in Perris, we did it in nine days – although we'd all put more time aside in case we needed it – so that was good going. We probably did about 20 build-up jumps in smaller groups, then we joined them together. We then had six attempts at the full skydive before we got it right. I mean, that was the approach – to keep trying till it all fell into place.

Int: What difficulties did you encounter personally?

Jennie: It was important to learn the routine – where to sit inside the plane, where to put your oxygen hose, where to put your radio for coordinating with each other. The person who jumps first is called 'the superfloater'. That's a visual indicator for the others to jump – it's a back-up in case any of the radios fail. The real challenge lies in the heightened senses that are demanded by freefall in order to identify people, colours and where the last grips completing the formation are likely to be. You couldn't physically check 117 grips with your eyes, so you're kind of reading and guessing and sensing.

Int: And it's not just one formation you do, is it?

Jennie: No, we do two. Once the first formation's set and held, the leader signals with a streamer stashed up her sleeve. To make the second formation, 18 different sub-groups consisting of up to three people break off from the main group and then reconnect. Everything has to happen exactly according to the plan we give the judges. So if everyone else has done their part but you grab someone's right leg instead of their left, then the whole attempt goes out the window. You don't want to be the one to mess up and spoil it for the others, so there's extra pressure from that. We've been doing this long enough to know that what you think is a successful record can be discounted for technical reasons. So, afterwards, when the judges told us we'd succeeded, the room exploded with hugging, tears, screaming. It was incredible.

Int: I can imagine. Now, Paul, tell us about the ... *[fade]*

Practice exam

Reading and Use of English

Part 1
1 C   2 B   3 D   4 A   5 B   6 D   7 D   8 A

Part 2
9 much   12 What   15 up
10 made   13 when   16 may/could/
11 order   14 favour   might

Part 3
17 accompanied   21 Undeterred
18 realistic   22 fantasise/fantazise
19 authenticity   23 recruitment
20 responsibility   24 Apparently

Part 4
25 made a great initial impression on
26 lack (any) understanding of how
27 likelihood of your proposal being accepted
28 talked his friend into signing
29 reminded her (that) she had
30 being put off running by his

Part 5
31 B   32 C   33 B   34 A   35 A   36 D

Part 6
37 D   38 A   39 D   40 C

Part 7
41 D   42 G   43 A   44 B   45 F   46 E

Part 8
47 B   48 D   49 A   50 B   51 D   52 B   53 C   54 A
55 D   56 B

Writing

Part 1
1   *Model answer*

Globalisation is part of life in the 21st century, but what has been its greatest effect and has this been positive or negative? The most obvious effect has been in travel. The availability of low-cost flights means we now expect to reach any part of the world easily, cheaply and most importantly, quickly. This benefits both our work and leisure, as companies expand to become multinationals and people travel to far-flung destinations for their holidays. However, this increase in travel has had negative effects including environmental damage. It may be that in future business will be done via the internet and not face to face. The effect of globalisation on leisure might be harder to change, as people might not accept the need to cut down on foreign travel.

However, there is another potential effect of globalisation, which is that individual cultures could disappear. We watch foreign television programmes, share events happening on the other side of the planet, buy products from all over the world – so what about our national identity? Although, on the surface, the argument that it is disappearing appears to be true, the popularity of international sporting events and the enthusiasm with which fans support their national teams suggests this is not the case. People value their own language, history and traditions, and this doesn't seem likely to change in the 21st century even if we are all more closely interlinked.

In my opinion, the greatest effect of globalisation is the way we view the world; travel and technology have made the planet feel very small.

Part 2
2   *Model answer*

The aim of this report is to give information about the college's recent exchange visit to Spain and to suggest improvements for future visits.

Positive aspects of the visit

All students stayed with host families and were looked after very well. The food and accommodation provided were of a high standard and the families were welcoming. There were a number of organised group visits to local places of interest, which were fascinating, and some families arranged extra trips for their students. There were plenty of opportunities to practise Spanish and all the students feel they are more confident in the language even though the visit was only two weeks.

Suggestions for improvement

- The travel arrangements were poor, as travelling so far by train was tiring and uncomfortable. Even if the cost were higher, it would be preferable to travel by plane; it would be quicker and students would not arrive feeling exhausted. In fact, on this trip a whole day was lost while everyone recovered from the journey.
- The visit should be extended. Two weeks was beneficial, but three weeks would allow even greater language improvement.
- Although students were given some initial information about their host family, this was very basic. It would be nice if they were able to contact the family through social media before the visit, as this would remove any nervousness on their first face-to-face meeting.

Conclusion

The exchange visit is a worthwhile initiative that should be continued in future and if implemented, the suggestions above would only improve it.

3   *Model answer*

Hi Sue,

I'm really glad you've got an interview! When I had my first interview I was really nervous, but I didn't need to be – the interviewer was really friendly. He asked me questions about my qualifications and about that part-time job you remember I did in the library during my college course.

I think it's important to be totally honest! Remember to give details when you answer too. For example, the interviewer asked me about things I'd enjoyed about my part-time job and so I gave examples of times I'd been able to help people and said that it was one really positive aspect of the job for me. I think he liked that because the job I was being interviewed for involved contact with the public. So find out exactly what the job is before your interview and make sure you research the company's image.

You must make a good first impression, so don't bring up the salary or the holidays too soon, otherwise the interviewer will think that's all you're interested in! Of course, you can mention them later.

You asked about what clothes to wear. Because of that all-important first impression, look business-like but not overdressed or weird! You should also consider how you will feel in those clothes – there's nothing worse than uncomfortable clothes! Don't wear something new for the first time, in case it itches or something!

Hope that all helps – and good luck! I'm sure you'll be fine.

Best wishes,

Jo

4 *Model answer*
I'm a keen watcher of all types of television programmes and would hate to be without my TV.

One particularly good programme was a drama series called *The Village*. It involved a murder in a small community and how the villagers reacted to it. Two police officers were trying to solve the crime, and they were very complex and interesting people in their own right, which added to the tension of the drama. They were also very sympathetic characters. The location for the series was a beautiful but isolated coastal region, which added great atmosphere and provided a contrast to the horror of the murder. The script was well-written and all the actors performed their roles exceptionally well. The mystery unfolded very slowly over several weeks and it was hard to wait for the next episode! This was television drama at its best.

However, I have to admit that not all television programmes are this good. Some seem to be simply 'fillers' in the television schedule, cheaply produced and with little real importance. One such show is a quiz game called *One Chance*. The contestants are asked easy questions and then have to do a series of physical challenges to win their prize. It is clumsy and, in fact, I would even call it patronising. The contestants are made to look silly when they fail their challenge. In my opinion, this is a waste of time and effort.

In order to retain audiences, it is important for television companies to produce compelling drama series like *The Village*.

Listening

Part 1
1 A 2 C 3 C 4 B 5 A 6 B

Part 2
7	shoulder	11	turn
8	Urban Recovery	12	(core) workout
9	(the) Playpark/Play Park	13	yoga
10	currents	14	backpack/back-pack

Part 3
15 A 16 A 17 D 18 C 19 C 20 B

Part 4
21 D 22 F 23 E 24 H 25 B 26 G 27 F 28 C
29 E 30 H

Audio script 12

Part 1

Extract One

M: My first visit to the Grand Canyon was a bit of a let-down, to tell you the truth. I drove over from Las Vegas, where I was appearing in a show, with the idea of paying homage to one of the great American landscapes. On the way, the car I'd borrowed broke down, so by the time I arrived at the South Rim, the sun was setting. For 15 minutes, I aimlessly photographed the standard views before heading back in the thickening darkness, very much aware that my best intentions had been thwarted.

F: Oh, what a shame! The Grand Canyon, of course, is somehow aloof when you stand on the rim, peering in, even with the benefit of a lovely sunset. To really experience it, to savour the awe, to comprehend the scale and to feel the weight of the prehistoric landscape, you have to hike into it. And what few people realise is that winter's the best time to do this. You won't have the whole National Park to yourself even then, but the bulk of the five million people visiting annually go in summer. More fool them, of course, because the searing heat can make hiking up and down a test of blind endurance!

Extract Two

F: I guess we're all princesses frightened of sleeping on a pea these days – how else do you explain the rising popularity of the mattress toppers, that squidgy extra layer of comfort some people put between their bottom sheet and mattress? I've heard they can be a bit smelly and tend to retain more heat than you'd want. Tom, any views on this?

M: Sounds like you're talking about memory foam, which a lot of these toppers are filled with. But you avoid those issues if you go with natural fillings.

F: Like?

M: Well, woollen bedding is said to promote up to 25 percent more regenerative sleep than synthetic materials – though it's a bit firm for some people's taste. Then there's horsehair, which is thick, firm and has a very good cushioning effect. It's a very durable material and the individual strands are hollow, meaning that moisture passes through quickly, so it's not sweaty. Added to which, the hairs never squash together into a permanent shape, so unlike most other fillings, it doesn't lose its springiness.

F: And for anyone allergic to animal hair?

M: Well, then silk is the only alternative to the synthetic material – but it comes at a price.

Extract Three

F: People say that the internet is killing the market for serious books, but when Mark Zuckerberg of Facebook fame started an online book club, the first title he chose for discussion was a non-fiction book called *The End of Power*, by a Venezuelan writer. Much as I like the book, it's hardly bedtime reading, but after its selection, it sold out overnight. I think it may have been a cynical move by Zuckerberg, actually, a canny PR ploy – I mean, the book is about the power of the internet.

M: I don't know about that, but what it does show is how intellectual fashions can sometimes move in contradictory swings. In recent decades numerous pundits have decried the supposed demise of western intellectual life. Nobody reads newspapers anymore, or so we're told, because we consume soundbites and texts in a distracted world. And while that may be true in some parts of life, it's not the whole tale.

F: Absolutely not. The print circulation of newspapers is shrinking, but as a society we're consuming more media content than ever before. Bookstores may be struggling, but book sales are holding up remarkably well.

M: If you include e-books and self-published titles, it's actually growing. Meanwhile, book clubs are proliferating - with five million Americans signed up to one, according to recent statistics.

F: Sure.

Audio script 13

Part 2

Speaker:
Hi. I'm Matt Selby and I'm going to be talking about the sport known as stand-up paddleboarding. I'm actually a surfer and like a lot of surfers, I used to look down on paddleboarding because it wasn't cool. You stand up on the board and use a paddle to propel yourself. It always seemed a bit tame compared to riding the waves on a surfboard. But recently I gave it a try and I've changed my mind.

In fact, it was injury that forced me to have a go at paddleboarding because it's regarded as a good option for surfers who develop health issues. I've had my fair share of injuries – especially my right knee, which has been playing up for years, though it never stopped me surfing. But a bad shoulder injury last year put paid to my surfing career, and that came as a bitter blow.

I decided to go on a paddleboarding induction course, taking lessons from an outfit called Urban Recovery, who specialise in giving tuition in flat-water city locations, but you can also get lessons from the big-name surf schools like the Extreme Academy in Cornwall, and you can ride waves on a paddleboard once you're proficient at it.

The venue for my lesson was a stretch of water that'd previously been part of a commercial dock, but which is now referred to as the Playpark. Because it's an enclosed stretch of water, where the water level's regulated, conditions are very controlled and this makes it ideal for beginners. In fact, it's actually the absence of currents that makes this type of venue the ideal place to learn the basics of paddleboarding. Other water sports do also use the venue, and you're likely to be sharing the water with people like wakeboarders, but they're beginners too and you're kept well apart.

My tutor taught me some basic techniques. I knew how to use a paddle, so I didn't need any lessons in moving the board forward. Instead, I was shown how to use a reverse motion to turn the board, and I soon got the hang of that. Much harder was kneeling on the board and then eventually having enough confidence to stand. It took a while to look cool and elegant but after a fair bit of wobbling, I got there eventually.

Although it looks sedate once you've mastered the technique, paddleboarding does provide you with a fantastic core workout, so it's certainly worth doing if you want to keep in shape. This is one of the reasons why it's become such a popular sport. There aren't many tricks you can do on a paddleboard and it doesn't really lend itself to competitive events, but I'm told that doing yoga on a paddleboard is what the A-listers and their fans get up to – it's great fun because there's an added challenge in getting the balance right.

The other great thing I've discovered about the sport is that the equipment's easy to transport. If you buy yourself an inflatable board, it fits easily into the boot of a car or indeed inside your suitcase on the plane. Mine folds up into a neat carrying case, indistinguishable from a backpack and just as easy to carry. It's another feature that makes paddleboarding such an accessible and flexible sport.

Audio script 14

Part 3

Int: My guests today are both novelists. Julian Mearsby writes fantasy fiction and Lois Ridge has just finished her fifth novel aimed at teenagers. Before we talk about fiction in general, I notice that according to some recently published research, reading for pleasure at the age of 15 was found to be a strong factor in determining future social mobility. I guess that comes as no surprise to you, Lois?

Lois: Indeed not. But the research goes further, suggesting that it's the most important indicator of the future success of the child, which is the more startling finding for many commentators. And what it highlights is that getting teenagers to read for pleasure isn't just a nostalgic ambition on the part of frustrated parents, harking back to their own adolescence; it's actually a fundamental social issue, as some of us have maintained for years. The research findings need unpicking, however, because a distinction's drawn between different motivations for reading – whether it's done for its own sake or is the result of being cajoled by carrots and sticks – but that doesn't detract at all from the validity of its conclusions.

Int: Julian, you wanted to come in there.

Julian: What the research actually suggests is that those who read for pleasure demonstrate an intrinsic desire to engage with stories, and therefore knowledge. Reading for pleasure reveals a predisposition not just to literature, but to the sort of lifelong learning that explains increased social mobility. This confirms one's intuition. In other words, stories, even fairy stories, aren't just entertainment – they help us understand who we are. They teach us empathy, respect for other cultures, other ideas. They help us articulate concepts that can't otherwise be expressed. Stories help us communicate; they bring us together; they teach us different ways to see the world. Their value may be intangible, but it's still real.

Int: So what conclusion do you draw from all this – that we must encourage our children to read for pleasure?

Julian: That's easy to say and harder to achieve, particularly in the culture in which many young people grow up in Britain today. They have plenty of other leisure activities to choose from. They can, of course, read on a screen, but we read in different ways when reading different formats. Analysis so far of the impact of digital literature is that it can play an important role in building core literacy skills, but there is an ongoing debate about whether it conveys the same benefits as reading a physical book. Initial research in the United States would appear to suggest that it doesn't.

Int: And isn't there also a difference, Lois, between boys and girls in terms of reading for pleasure?

Lois: In Britain, girls read more and have more positive attitudes to reading than boys. This isn't, however, a universal phenomenon. In India, by contrast, it's the other way round, though that may have more to do with questions of gender and access in that society. In Britain, it's about gender and attitude. The reluctance of boys to read for pleasure seems more social than biological. A recent study found that for many boys, reading for pleasure just wasn't something they wanted to be seen doing.

Int: Let's turn now to the plight of novelists in Britain today. Is there really a crisis in storytelling, Lois?

Lois: Well, film and TV scriptwriters and the creators of other on-screen products continue the tradition of storytelling too, of course, but if we're talking about novelists, then yes, there is a problem. And part of it is that, thanks to the media, the public has a distorted view of what the average author's life is like. Not everyone can expect the kind of success earned by the likes of JK Rowling. Indeed, the average full-time author's earnings have dropped by 29 percent since 2005. I'm one of the lucky few who still earns a better-than-average salary just from writing. But that hasn't always been the case.

Int: And now a question for both of you. The 18th-century writer, Samuel Johnson, once said, 'No man but a blockhead ever wrote, except for money.' Was he right?

Julian: If he was, then there are a lot of blockheads in the writing business, and I'd count myself amongst them! Most authors are driven to write – would probably write whether or not they were ever published or paid, just for the joy of it. This is their strength and their downfall. With the exception of a canny few who treat art as a business, writers are often reluctant to think of their work as just another product. We don't insist on our fair share of the profits because we don't like to think of our books as units, to be bought and sold.

Lois: And yet, to the publishing industry, that's exactly what they are: the product of thousands of hours of work – of editing, copy-editing, design, marketing, proofreading and promotion. It takes a lot of people to help create and publish a book. And although the creator – the writer – is surely the most important of these, the average author's earnings no longer reflect that, and writers shouldn't just accept that lying down.

Int: Well, there we have to leave it … *[fade]*

Audio script 15

Part 4

Sp 1: Some students do this sort of work for ulterior motives: it looks good on their CVs or there are opportunities for making friends and networking. I have no problem with that, but I had more altruistic motives. I mean, the number of wild hedgehogs is falling dramatically and something should be done about it. For me, this was another way of helping an organisation that relies totally on voluntary contributions. It was a bit of a blow to discover I had to pay rent for my room, though. They could've told me that beforehand. Anyway, the regular voluntary staff at the rescue centre need summer holidays like everybody else, so overall, I was happy to step in.

Sp 2: Members of my family have been helping out on local wildlife projects for as long as anyone can remember, but I thought it was time to ring the changes. Building conservation is quite a specialised area and I was keen to master some of the techniques. Unfortunately, despite all the hype on the website, the charity was really only looking for casual labour. They had full-time staff doing the interesting stuff and, sadly, volunteers didn't get much of a look-in. I mean, I can't fault the package – the hostel was adequate, and with three meals a day provided, I wasn't out of pocket at all – but I think they should've done more to stretch us intellectually as well as physically.

Sp 3: The trouble with the water-quality project wasn't so much the training – we had two days at the beginning that went into every last detail of the relevant health-and-safety legislation – I mean, thorough isn't the word! No, it was more that, after that, you were pretty much on your own; scary stuff for a bunch of undergraduates looking to enjoy the summer break without adding to their student loan burden! As it turned out, we used our initiative and did OK. And with hindsight, I can see I picked up some useful fieldwork skills that won't go amiss on my CV. Cooking over a campfire was a first for me though, as was sleeping in a tent, but I lived to tell the tale.

Sp 4: I knew that volunteering on the turtle project in Central America would be a life-changing experience. You know, I'd get to do hands-on fieldwork that could feed into my own research back at college – I might even get to use the actual statistics. Anyway, I have no argument with the project – it more than fulfilled all my expectations, but I came away wondering if such important work should be entrusted to volunteers. I mean, for some of the students there, it was just one long holiday – with free board and lodging next to the beach. Despite all the training and support available, you couldn't ask them to do any serious work – they just weren't up for the challenge.

Sp 5: I had very low expectations of life in the rainforest. I knew the hostel would be basic and the food pretty unpalatable, so I was ready for all that. But I did think we'd be given more advice about what to do if we got sick. Like, the friend I went out with cut his leg quite badly, but there was no book where you could record what had happened, what treatment he'd been given. On projects back home, they're pretty strict about stuff like that. We'd been recommended this project as one where you could really get in with the resident botanists, which could lead to interesting volunteering opportunities in the future – and they were very welcoming.

Pearson Education Limited
Edinburgh Gate
Harlow
Essex CM20 2JE
England
and Associated Companies throughout the world.

www.pearsonelt.com

© Pearson Education Limited 2015

The right of Jan Bell and Nick Kenny to be identified as authors of this
Work has been asserted by them in accordance with the Copyright,
Designs and Patents Act 1988.

First published 2005
Third edition published 2015
Second impression 2016
ISBN: 978-1-4479-8060-5
Set in Amasis and Mundo Sans
Printed in Slovakia by Neografia

Acknowledgements
*We are grateful to the following for permission to reproduce copyright
material:*
(Key: b-bottom; c-centre; l-left; r-right; t-top)

123RF.com: Denis Tabler 81tr, Filip Fuxa 30tc, Hongqi Zhang 10c, Luis
Santos 81bl, Oleg Doroshenko 12, sauletas 27br, Sergey Novikov 23;
Alamy Images: Adrian Sherratt 68, Archive Photos 26cl, Blend Images
21bl, DP RM 81tl, dpa picture alliance 10t, Heritage Image Partnership Ltd
24, Holger Burmeister 116, JTB MEDIA CREATION, Inc. 100c, Juice Images
21bc, 104, justin barton 11, Tetra Images 21br; **Corbis:** Bettmann 26tl,
Colin Monteath / Hedgehog House 27bl, Gail Mooney 26tc, Underwood
& Underwood 26tr; **Fotolia.com:** Monkey Business 9, 139b; **FotoLibra:**
Jeff Greenberg 100b; **Getty Images:** Andrew Goodman 88b, Carl Court
AFP 40, Dan Regan 59, Hulton Archive 93, JEWEL SAMAD / AFP 88t,
Jupiterimages 60, NCP / Star Max / GC Images) 88tc, Peter Macdiarmid 28;
Pearson Education Ltd: Ann Cromack. Ikat Design 22; **PhotoDisc:** Doug
Menuez 27tr; **Photolibrary.com:** Andres Rodriguez 108c; **Rex Features:**
111; **Shutterstock.com:** Adriano Castelli 26c, bestimagesevercom 45,
Catalin Petolea 115, Christopher Kolaczan 27c, CreativeNature.nl. 27tl,
Darren Baker 14b, Elaine Nash 30tl, Felix Mizioznikov 46c, gorillaimages
38, Jason Stitt 46cl, John Kropewnicki 36tl, Juan Carlos Zamora 35, KPG_
Payless 139c, Lex-art 71, lightpoet 39, Martin Novak 140c, Mikhail Pogosov
36tr, Minerva Studio 15t, Monkey Business Images 76, racorn 46cr, Richard
Carey 78, Stefan Schurr 108t, StockLite 91, tarasov 63, Tyler Olson 140b,
Vittorio Bruno 30tr, YanLev 107; **Sozaijiten:** 81br; **The Kobal Collection:**
Saul Zaentz Company 50

All other images © Pearson Education

Every effort has been made to trace the copyright holders and we
apologise in advance for any unintentional omissions. We would be
pleased to insert the appropriate acknowledgement in any subsequent
edition of this publication.